Studies in Etymology

Studies in Etymology

Charles W. Dunmore

Associate Professor of Classics
New York University

Focus Books
Focus Information Group, Inc.
Newburyport MA 01950

Distributed in Great Britain and Europe by
Gerald Duckworth and Company Ltd
The Old Piano Factory
London N1 6PB England

ISBN 0-941051-29-3

The term Xerox is the trademark of Xerox, Inc.

Cover: Vase painting depicting instruction in music and grammar at an Attic school. [State Museums, Berlin]

10 9 8 7

Preface

The purpose of this book is to serve as an introduction to the study of the etymology of the English language—that part of the language, that is, that has been derived from Latin and ancient Greek.

This introduction is by no means complete, as the achievement of an all-encompassing text on English etymology is far beyond the scope of any book of this size. Still, the principles of word formation are formulated, and, following the Introduction, which places the English language in its proper historical and linguistic context, the fascinating study of etymology commences. Students using this book should own a good college-level dictionary of English, one that gives the etymology of entry words.

I should like to acknowledge my debt to Rita M. Fleischer, Administrative Director for Foreign Languages at The Graduate School of the City University of New York, for her helpful suggestions, her painstaking reading of these pages in rough typescript, her help in the onerous task of proofreading, and, especially, for the better book that this has become because of her help and advice.

C.W.D.
New York, August 1992

Table of Contents

Foreword

English belongs to the Indo-European family of languages, so named because individual tongues of this great family are spoken across an area extending from the Atlantic coast of Europe in the West to India in the East, with some linguistic islands in between where non-Indo-European languages are spoken. Finnish and Hungarian, for example, belong to the linguistic family known as Finno-Ugric, and Basque, spoken in northern Spain, is unrelated to any other known language. Indo-European (abbreviated IE), also called Indo-Germanic or Indo-Teutonic, especially by German philologists, is but one of many language families spread across the globe. Other linguistic families include Semitic, named for Shem, the eldest son of Noah, of which Arabic, Ethiopic, and Hebrew are the most widely-spoken today, and the related group, Hamitic, named for Ham, Noah's second son, represented today mainly by the Berber, Cushite, and Galla languages of Africa, and, in antiquity, Egyptian, preserved to the present day in the liturgy of the Coptic Church. Sometimes these two groups are known collectively as the Hamito-Semitic or, often, the Afro-Asiatic family of languages. Chinese and Japanese in the Far East, the Bantu languages of Africa (the group to which Swahili belongs), the Polynesian languages of the Pacific, and the Amerind languages of the natives of North America are among other of the myriad non-Indo-European language families of the world.

The original Indo-European language itself, sometimes called Proto-Indo-European, seems to have been spoken at one time by peoples living somewhere in the area between central Europe to the west and the Black Sea to the east. In the light of present knowledge it is impossible to pinpoint the home of these people any more accurately than this. There are no records of this primitive Indo-European language since, by the time that its speakers became literate, they were spread across India and Europe, and the original language had become several different individual and mutually unintelligible Indo-European languages. However, by working "backward," and taking cognizance of the tendency to changes in sound that are governed by regular and rigid linguistic rules within each of the Indo-European language groups, a fairly substantial vocabulary of words in this Proto-Indo-European language, complete with their inflections and meanings, can be reconstructed. Languages that have developed from Proto-Indo-European are called *cognate languages*, and words in these various cognate languages that have developed from a single Indo-European word are called cognate words, or simply cognates, from the Latin adjective *cognatus*, "sprung from the same stock."

About 3000 B.C., or earlier, the Indo-European peoples began to leave their homeland and to migrate, perhaps in search of food, in all directions. The end of these migrations is documented by the archaeological record in Greece and Italy at about 1100-1000 B.C., with the final entry of the ancestors of the Greek-speaking people into Greece, and of the ancestors of the historical Romans, and others, into Italy. By this time the migrations had carried Indo-European people into Iran and even farther, into India, forming the linguistic groups that later spoke Persian and Sanskrit, and people speaking Slavic, Celtic, and Germanic dialects of Indo-European were spread across the face of Europe. Of all these language families, descendants of Proto-Indo-European, it is the Germanic that is of the greatest interest to us, as the Angles and Saxons, the linguistic ancestors of English, spoke dialects of this group.

As long as a language is spoken by living people it is a living language. When it ceases to be spoken and is preserved only in literary texts (if at all), it is called a dead language. Italian is a living language, and Latin is a dead language, despite the fact that it is used in certain rituals of the Catholic Church. Like any other living thing, language changes, but the change is so slow that it cannot be observed by any one generation, and it is only over longer periods that the change becomes evident. One need only to look at a page from one of the works of Shakespeare to see how the English language has changed in the four hundred years from Shakespeare's time to our own. Go back two hundred more years, to the time of Chaucer, and we see that his English, called Middle English, can be read only with some difficulty and with the assistance of notes. The epic of Beowulf, composed about A.D. 1000, in Old English, is in a tongue that is foreign to us and can be understood only by those who have studied this language, just as one studies French, Russian, or Chinese.

It is this tendency of language to change that caused the differentiation of the original Indo-European language into dialects, as various groups broke away and migrated to different areas and lost, for centuries, any contact with each other. By the time that these various groups had become literate, an achievement that took place at widely-spaced times, and left behind them records that we now can read, the individual dialects of Indo-European had become new and, in most respects, different languages. The same phenomenon was repeated much later, when Latin was carried to different areas of Europe, not by migrations, as was the case with Proto-Indo-European, but by Roman soldiers protecting the frontiers of the vast Roman empire and administering its laws. This time the change was from Latin to the various Romance languages, a change which took place during the early Middle Ages.

The reason or reasons why language changes in this way is not known. Physical separation between groups certainly has much to do with it. Witness the regional differences in American English spoken in the United States. Unless the tendency to change had been halted by improved means of travel and, especially, by the invention of radio and television in this century, the local speech of natives of Maine and Georgia, for example, probably would have come to be mutually unintelligible in another two or three hundred years.

THE INDO-EUROPEAN LANGUAGE GROUPS AND THEIR PRINCIPAL MODERN DESCENDANTS

ALBANIAN Albanian

ARMENIAN Armenian

BALTO-SLAVIC

BALTIC	**SLAVIC**	
Lettish (Latvian)	Russian	Slovak
Lithuanian	Ukrainian	Bulgarian
	Polish	Slovene
	Czech	Serbo-Croatian

CELTIC

GOIDELIC (GAELIC)	**BRYTHONIC (BRITANNIC)**
Irish Gaelic	Welsh
Scottish Gaelic	Breton

GERMANIC

NORTH GERMANIC	**WEST GERMANIC**	
Swedish	High German	Frisian
Norwegian	Low German	Flemish
Danish	English	Afrikaans
Icelandic	Dutch	Yiddish

HELLENIC Greek

INDO-IRANIAN

INDIC		**IRANIAN**
Hindi	Assamese	Persian
Bengali	Marathi	Kurdish
Urdu	Sinhalese	Pashto
Gujarati	Sindhi	Baluchi
Punjabi	Romany	Sogdian

ITALIC

French	Roumanian
Spanish	Catalan
Italian	Provençal
Portuguese	Rhaeto-Romanic

Introduction

Part I

The Indo-European Language Groups

The principal Indo-European language groups, with their ancient and modern representatives, are listed here alphabetically.

Balto-Slavic

The two Baltic languages (so named because of the proximity of their speakers to the area of the Baltic Sea) spoken today are Lithuanian, spoken in Lithuania, and Lett (Lettic or Lettish), spoken in Latvia. Prussian, once spoken in the area of East Prussia, is now extinct, having been replaced by German in the eighteenth century, when the kingdom of Prussia became part of the German empire. The Slavic languages are represented today by Russian, Ukrainian, Polish, Czechoslovak (which includes the two languages Czech and Slovak), Bulgarian, Slovene, and Serbo-Croatian.

The earliest documents in a Slavic language are parts of the Bible which were translated by the Greek missionaries Constantine and his brother Methodius in the ninth century into the dialect that is now called Old Church Slavic. The form of the Greek alphabet used by these church brothers and adapted to suit the sounds of the Slavic language is now known as the Cyrillic alphabet, named after Cyril, the name by which Constantine is better known. The languages spoken by the Slavic peoples who were converted to Christianity by missionaries from the Eastern Byzantine Church at Constantinople (modern Istanbul), e.g., Russian, are now written in the Cyrillic alphabet. The languages of those peoples whose conversion was as a result of missionaries sent from Rome, e.g., Polish, are now written in the Latin alphabet. Old Church Slavic has

1

survived down to the present day in the liturgical language of the Eastern Orthodox Church (in just the same way that Latin has survived in the rituals of the Roman Catholic Church).

Celtic

The Celts, or Kelts, in ancient times were spread over a large territory and inhabited Gaul (France), much of Spain, northern Italy, the British Isles, and western Germany (the land formerly known as Bohemia, named after the Boii, a Celtic tribe who lived there). One group, the Galatians, moved into Asia Minor, where they occupied the area known as Galatia, near Ankara in Turkey.

It is not known precisely when the Celts crossed the English Channel to Great Britain, but it seems likely that they were there by 1000 B.C. They occupied most of that island until they were driven to the remote districts of western and northern Britain under successive onslaughts, first by the Romans, early in the Christian era, and later, in the fifth century A.D., by the Angles and Saxons. Ireland was settled by Celtic-speaking peoples from mainland Europe somewhat later than Britain, probably by 600 B.C.

The Celtic language, once spoken over such vast territories, now survives as a spoken tongue only in the language called Irish, or Gaelic, in Ireland; in the Gaelic language of the highlands of Scotland and parts of the Hebridean islands; in the Gaelic language of Wales; and in Breton, the Celtic language spoken in the French province of Brittany. Breton is not a survival of the Celtic language formerly spoken in Gaul but is an importation brought to this region in the fifth century A.D. by Celts of England who were driven out by invading Angles and Saxons.

The surviving languages are the remains of two great, early divisions in Celtic. The Gaelic language spoken in Ireland and Scotland is called *Goidelic*[1] or Gaelic Celtic, while Welsh, the language of Wales, along with Breton, the language of Brittany, is called *Brythonic*[2] or Britannic Celtic. Thus, in respect to language, every Celt is either a *Goidel* or a *Brython*. Cornish, the Brythonic language of Cornwall in Southwest England, ceased to be spoken in the eighteenth century, and Manx, the Goidelic language of the Isle of Man, lying in the Irish Sea between England and Northern Ireland, has been almost completely replaced by English in this century, as most of the Celtic spoken in Ireland and Great Britain already had been.

---

[1]Named from the Old Irish word *Goidel*, a Gael, or Celtic inhabitant of Ireland or Scotland.

[2]From Welsh *Brython*, Briton, any Celtic inhabitant of the British Isles.

The earliest surviving documents in Celtic are some brief prose works and a few hymns dating from the eighth century A.D., or earlier. These are written in Old Irish, as the Irish (Goidelic) Gaelic from this early period is called. But the most important remains are the glosses found scattered in numerous manuscripts, mostly concerned with the New Testament and dating from the eighth and ninth centuries. These glosses are explanations, interpretations, and translations of the Latin text inserted in the margins of the manuscripts by Irish scribes and written in Old Irish.

Germanic

Modern Germanic languages include English, German, Dutch, Danish, Swedish, Norwegian, Icelandic, and Flemish, the language of the Flemings spoken in northern Belgium and a small area of northern France. There is a large body of literature extant in the written records of these languages dating from different periods, the earliest from the fourth century A.D. These remains make it possible not only to see the clear division of the Germanic branch of Indo-European into three distinct groups, but from the early remains of these three groups to reconstruct the original form of this language, usually called Proto-Germanic, before its division. That is, this reconstructed Proto-Germanic represents the earliest form of the Germanic language at the point when it had first separated from and become distinct from Proto-Indo-European. There are no written records in this language, and the date at which it had become a language distinct from Indo-European can only be assumed to have been sometime between 2500 and 1500 B.C., sometime after the beginning of the Indo-European migrations.

The three divisions of Proto-Germanic are called East Germanic, West Germanic, and North Germanic. The principal (and sole) literary document in East Germanic survives in fragments of a translation of the Bible into Gothic, the language of the Goths. In the first century A.D. these people were settled in what is now Poland and represented the easternmost of the Germanic peoples. Shortly after this time they began to move to the east, and by the third century had reached the shores of the Black Sea. In the fourth century some of them were converted to Christianity, and as an aid to conversion, the Bible was translated into the Gothic language by a missionary named Ulfilas (or Wulfilas). This is the earliest document in any Germanic language. By the fifth century the Gothic language was in use over much of Europe and North Africa in the great kingdoms of the Goths of the east and west—the Ostrogoths and the Visigoths—as well as in the kingdom of the Vandals, a people who a contemporary historian says spoke the language of the Goths.[3] With the col-

---

[3]Procopius, a Greek historian during the time of the Roman emperor Justinian in the fifth century. Reference to the Vandals speaking the Gothic

lapse of these great kingdoms, however, Gothic gradually ceased to be spoken, and the last literary reference to it as a spoken tongue is found in the sixteenth century.[4]

The most extensive early Germanic literature is found in North Germanic, the language of the Scandinavian peninsula which, before its division into the modern tongues of Swedish, Danish, Norwegian, and Icelandic, is known as Old Norse. Iceland was colonized by peoples from Norway in the late ninth century A.D., and these settlers brought with them a huge body of heroic literature preserved in the dialect of Old Norse that is called Old Icelandic.[5]

West Germanic is represented today by modern German,[6] Dutch, which developed from a form of the language called Low German,[7] and English. High German, reinforced by Martin Luther's translation of the Bible into that tongue in the sixteenth century, has become the literary language of the Germans, while Low German has maintained itself only as a local spoken dialect in the northern parts of Germany. The linguistic ancestors of English are three of the members of the West Germanic group: the languages of the Angles, Saxons, and (to a lesser degree) the Jutes. The development of the English language following the invasions of Britain by these Germanic groups in the fifth century A.D. will be discussed later.

Hellenic

The ancestors of the historical Greeks, who called themselves *Hellenes*, entered the Greek peninsula around 1900 B.C. as part of the Indo-European migrations, bringing with them the Greek language. A secondary wave of Greek-speaking invaders came around 1100 B.C., and the fusion

---

language is found in his *History of the Wars of Justinian* in the section dealing with the war against the Vandals in North Africa.

[4]In a collection of words and phrases spoken by the Goths of the Crimea collected by an envoy (Ogier Ghislain de Busbecq) at the court of the emperor at Constantinople.

[5]This heroic literature, known collectively as the Icelandic Sagas, recounts the lives and deeds of traditional early heroes of the Norse people. Outstanding among these sagas are the *Elder Edda*, a collection of poems probably of the tenth century, and the *Younger Edda*, a prose work of the twelfth.

[6]Also called New High German, abbreviated NHG, to differentiate it from earlier forms of the language, known as MHG and OHG, Middle and Old High German.

[7]The terms "high" and "low," referring to the Germanic language, apply to the high, mountainous regions of southern Germany where the "High" dialect is spoken, as opposed to the flat, low-lying areas of the northern coastal region where Low German, or *Plattdeutsch*, is spoken.

of these two groups with the pre-Hellenic inhabitants of that land produced the Greeks of the historical period: the Athenians, Spartans, and others. In the earliest records four principal dialects of Greek can be recognized: Attic-Ionic, Aeolic, Arcadian, and Doric (the dialect of the invaders of 1100 B.C.). Attic Greek, a sub-division of Attic-Ionic that was spoken in Attica (i.e., Athens), came to be recognized as the literary language of the Greeks at an early period, since almost all of the great literary figures of ancient Greece were Athenian and wrote in the Attic dialect: Aeschylus, Sophocles, Euripides, and Plato, to name but a few. Because of the prestige that these and other writers bestowed upon Attic Greek, this dialect became the basis for a common Greek language, called *koinē* (from the Greek word meaning "common"), which, by the Christian era, was spoken over much of the Mediterranean world. It is the language of the writers of the New Testament, for example, and through its use in Constantinople, the eastern capitol of the Roman empire, it has formed the basis of the language of Byzantine literature.

But the *koinē* was gradually replaced by other languages of the Mediterranean, particularly Latin in the west and Arabic in the east, and today the Greek as spoken in modern Athens remains the sole survivor of this ancient language, although Latin, and through it the Romance languages and, eventually, English have all been greatly enriched by borrowings from the ancient tongue.

Indo-Iranian

The term Indo-Iranian (or Aryan) refers to the languages spoken by the Indo-European peoples whose migrations took them the farthest to the east of any of these groups and who settled in ancient Persia and in northern India. The Indic branch is represented by Sanskrit,[8] the oldest of the recorded Indo-European languages and probably the one that is closest to the parent Indo-European language in structure. The early speakers of Sanskrit had settled in the valley of the Indus River in modern Pakistan certainly before 1500 B.C. and, by that date, or a little later, had committed to writing a large body of sacred literature known as the Vedas.[9] The language of the Vedas is sometimes called Vedic Sanskrit to distinguish it from a later form of the language called Classical Sanskrit dating from the fifth century B.C. and later. The best known literature of Classical Sanskrit consists of two great national epics, the *Mahabharata*

---

[8]The word "Sanskrit"was applied by the ancient Hindu grammarians to this language. It means "perfectly formed."

[9]The Vedas, named from the Sanskrit word *veda*, "knowledge," consist of four groups of poems, sacred hymns, of which the principal one, and probably the oldest, is the *Rigveda*, a collection of somewhat over one thousand poems of about ten lines each.

and the *Ramayana*. The first of these, "The Great Poem of the Bharatas," recounts the adventures of certain descendants of King Bharata, who himself claimed descent from the moon. The latter poem, "The Story of Rama," tells of the miraculous deeds of a royal prince of India named Rama.

Both Vedic and Classical Sanskrit were written in an alphabet called, in Sanskrit, *Devanagari*, "Writing of the Gods." It has come down unchanged from the earliest times to the present and is the alphabet used in Hindi, one of the modern linguistic descendants of Sanskrit in use in India today. Other modern Indic dialects include Urdu, the official literary language of Pakistan, and Bengali, the language of Bengal in northeast India. The most widely disseminated of the Indic languages is that of the Gypsies, sometimes called Romany. These people are wandering tribes having their origin in northwest India, who, from about the fifth century A.D., carried their language to the west, through Persia and across Europe and, eventually, to America.

Dravidian is the name given both to a race and to a family of languages, of which Tamil is the principal representative, spoken today in southern India. The languages of this family are non-Indo-European, and the original speakers of Dravidian are thought to have been in India when the Indo-Europeans arrived there.

The Iranian branch of Indo-Iranian is represented in antiquity by the language of the ancient Persians spoken in the land now called Iran. The earliest monuments are in the language called Old Persian. These consist of cuneiform inscriptions, mostly on stone, which record the accomplishments of some of the ancient kings of Persia, notably Darius I and his son, Xerxes, rulers during the great wars fought between the Persians and the Greek states during the early part of the fifth century B.C.[10] The principal one of these inscriptions is a long text in three languages: Old Persian, Akkadian (a Semitic language of ancient Babylonia), and Elamite, a language not completely understood today. The text records the rise to power and the achievements of Darius I, and in addition to its linguistic value is an important historical document.[11]

---

[10]Cuneiform, from the Latin, meaning "wedge-shaped," is the name given to the form of writing which employs wedge-shaped marks incised into clay tablets or stone.

[11]This monument, found at the modern site of Behistun, is engraved on a stone cliff alongside the old caravan route between Baghdad and Teheran. It shows King Darius I standing over the fallen body of a pretender to the throne, with the supporters of the rebellion standing roped together. It is all executed in greater-than-life size, and the lowest portion of it is some two hundred feet above the road below. For a complete account of this and other inscriptions in Old Persian, see Roland G. Kent, *Old Persian*, American Oriental Society, New Haven, Conn., 1950.

A dialect of Old Persian called Avestan is represented in the Avesta, the book of sacred writings of the Zoroastrian religion. Only a small portion of the original work survives, and it is thought to date to the time of the prophet Zoroaster (Zarathustra), who lived probably around 600 B.C., although his dates are in dispute.

The modern descendants of Old Persian include Modern Persian, the national language of Iran, Kurdish, the language of the Kurds, and the Afghan language, spoken in Afghanistan. All of these languages are written in the Arabic script and contain a large number of Arabic loan words.

Italic

The ancestors of the historical Romans entered the peninsula of Italy about 1000 B.C. as part of the final phase of the original Indo-European migrations, which had commenced some two thousand years earlier. In the light of available evidence it is not possible to determine just where these peoples had been living prior to their crossing of the Alps and their entry into northern Italy. The Italic dialect later known as Latin was but one of several that these newcomers brought with them. But due to the later, dominant position of those who settled in the plain of Latium in northern Italy, their language, Latin, gradually replaced the others as the Romans asserted their political mastery over the entire Italian peninsula. All that remains of other dialects is scanty documents, mostly inscriptions, the two principal dialects being those of the peoples known as Oscans and Umbrians.[12]

With the expansion of the Roman empire, which reached its greatest size under the emperor Trajan in the early part of the second century A.D., soldiers, administrators, merchants, and travelers carried the Latin language to all parts of this vast domain. So thoroughly were the inhabitants of these areas "Romanized," that for political expediency and for ease in commercial transactions, Latin gradually replaced the languages of the natives of these areas.[13]

---

[12]There is, however, a wealth of written material in Etruscan, found principally in the area of Florence. Etruscan is a non-Indo-European language with no known affinities, ancient or modern, and thus far has resisted translation, despite the fact that it was written in the Greek alphabet.

[13]Not altogether, however, as in many areas of the empire local languages refused to yield to Latin. Greek continued to be the principal language of that land, for example, and the native languages of Asia Minor and North Africa continued to be spoken until many of them gave way to Arabic as these lands were conquered by Islam. Basque, a non-Indo-European language spoken by the inhabitants of the western Pyrenees in northern Spain, was never replaced by Latin and continues to be the speech of this area.

The Latin that was carried through the empire, however, was not the classical literary language of Rome, but the spoken language of the soldiers, merchants, and others. This language, called "Vulgar Latin" (from the Latin *vulgus*, meaning "the common people"), was different in many ways from the literary tongue, and now the trends to linguistic change were accelerated. As was noted earlier, all living things change, and Vulgar Latin, the living language, was no exception, and there came a time when the literary language of earlier days, Classical Latin, was kept alive only artificially in written literature (and as the language of the Church), while the spoken tongue continued its unhampered change. The change progressed until the Latin spoken in distant areas became mutually unintelligible. This is the point at which we can say that vulgar tongues have ceased to be Latin, that the Romance languages have begun their existence. No definite date can be assigned to this linguistic event, and it occurred at different times in different places. But it can be said that, in all likelihood, Latin was a "dead" language—that is, it was no longer the native, spoken tongue of any people—by A.D. 700, probably earlier.

Classical Latin continued to be taught in the schools of Europe, and during the Renaissance was the literary vehicle for scientific treatises and the like, a Universal Language which could be understood by all men of learning. In 1628, for example, William Harvey, a fellow of the Royal College of Physicians in London, published his great work on the circulation of the blood. The treatise was written in Latin and called *Exercitatio Anatomica de Motu Cordis et Sanguinis* (An Anatomical Treatise on the Movement of the Heart and Blood).

The principal Romance languages are: French, Spanish, Portuguese, Italian, and Roumanian. Languages of lesser importance—that is, spoken by relatively few people—include Rhaeto-Romanic, spoken in the Engadin, a valley of the Inn River in eastern Switzerland, Catalan and Galician spoken in Spain, and Walloon, a dialect spoken in southeastern Belgium and adjacent parts of France. Of the Romance languages, it is French that has had the greatest influence on the vocabulary of English. This was due first to the fact that, following the Battle of Hastings in 1066, Norman French kings sat on the throne of England. The language of the Court was French, and words from this language began to enter English. But of even more consequence was the heavy borrowing from French during and following the early Renaissance, from the seventeenth century on. These French influences on English will be discussed in full later.

In 1907 an archaeological expedition in northwest Turkey revealed the capital city of the Hittites, a people known to us mainly from references to them in the Old Testament, and whose empire stretched over a large area of western Turkey in the latter centuries of the second millennium B.C. Clay tablets in cuneiform writing found here show that the language of the Hittites was a form of Indo-European. The precise relationship between Hittite and other Indo-European tongues is not clear, and some scholars think that this language was related to Proto-Indo-European, and suggest that there may have been an earlier language which could be called Indo-Hittite, from which both Indo-European and Hittite were derived.

Early in this century archaeological expeditions in Turkestan uncovered a wealth of linguistic records, among which are some written in what appears to be an Indo-European language and which, from internal evidence in these documents, is called Tocharian. These documents date from the eighth and seventh centuries B.C. and are not fully understood. The presence of Indo-European-speaking people as far east as China at this period has not been satisfactorily explained.

There are two other modern languages belonging to the Indo-European family: Armenian, spoken in the region between the Black and Caspian Seas, and Albanian, spoken in Albania, northwest of Greece.

Part II

The Development of the English Language

The Roman Conquest of Britain

It is not known who the earliest inhabitants of Britain were or what their language was, and little is known of the land and of its inhabitants until the Roman conquest of the island. Around 1000 B.C. two groups of peoples from mainland Europe entered the British Isles bringing with them the languages of the two divisions of the Celtic tongue: first, the Gaelic (Goidelic) Celts, and, a little later, the Brittanic (Brythonic) Celts. It is the modern descendants of the tongues spoken by these two groups that are still spoken in parts of Scotland, Ireland, and Wales today.

In the summer of 55 B.C. Julius Caesar invaded Britain. His first attempt ended in failure but he came back the following year in greater force. After remaining in southeast Britain for a short while, he returned to Gaul, where he had been campaigning since 58 B.C. His reasons for invading the island are not known, and after his departure in 54 B.C. he made no further attempts in that direction. The next time that the British

Celts and the Romans were to meet under arms was a hundred years later. This time the Romans came to stay.[14]

In A.D. 43 the Roman emperor Claudius, impelled perhaps by the desire to have a military conquest added to his own glory, sent a force of some forty thousand men to invade Britain. After about three years of hard fighting with the Celts, who resisted with all their force, most of the southern and central regions of the island were under Roman control. Britain was declared a Roman province, and a governor was sent to maintain order, reinforced by garrisons of Roman soldiers. In A.D. 61 an uprising led by Boadicea, the widow of a Celtic chieftain, almost succeeded in driving the Romans from the island. But this revolt ended in failure, and Roman domination was extended ultimately to the north, to the boundaries of what is now Scotland. Early in the second century the emperor Hadrian built the great stone barrier, now known as Hadrian's Wall, across the island, extending from what is now the city of Carlisle on the Irish Sea to Newcastle on the North Sea, a distance of about seventy miles. A generation later, Hadrian's successor, Antoninus Pius, erected a second barrier farther to the north where Scotland narrows to about thirty-five miles between the Firth of Forth on the east to the mouth of the Clyde river on the west. Both of these great barriers survive visually, although in varying degrees of preservation. After these two great statements of power, no further attempts were made to subjugate the Celts of Scotland. The Celts in Wales, in southwest Britain, proved to be as stubborn fighters as those to the north in Scotland and resisted Roman occupation.

The Romans remained masters of all of Britain, excepting Scotland and Wales, for over three hundred years. Early in the fifth century uprisings and invasions in other parts of the vast Roman Empire necessitated the withdrawal of the troops stationed in Britain. The abandonment of the island by Rome left the Celtic inhabitants unprotected from attack, a situation that was to have far-reaching consequences within but two generations.

It is doubtful if the Latin language of Britain's Roman conquerors was used by the native population to any extent beyond what was necessary for official business between the local people and their Roman magistrates. A handful of words entered the Celtic vocabulary during the period of Roman occupation and was retained in the language.[15]

---

[14]For a firsthand account of Caesar's landings in Britain, see his *Gallic War*, Book 5.

[15]English *mile*, from Latin *milia* (*passuum*), a thousand paces; *wall*, from Latin *vallum*, "rampart," and place-names ending in -*chester* and -*caster* (e.g., Winchester, Lancaster), originally locations of Roman garrisons, from Latin *castra*, "(military) camp," are typical of these loanwords that remain in our language today.

The Germanic Invasions of the Fifth Century

Our principal source for the invasions that brought speakers of Germanic dialects to Britain is the *Historia Ecclesiastica Gentis Anglorum,* "The Ecclesiastical History of the English Nation," written (in Latin) by a British churchman named Bede, later called "The Venerable Bede." His account begins with Caesar's invasion of Britain in 55 B.C. and ends with a listing of the Bishops in the various regions of Britain in A.D. 731, the fifteenth year of the reign of King Ethelbald, a Saxon ruler, the year in which Tatwin was made the ninth archbishop of Canterbury.

In his entry for A.D. 449 he notes that Angles and Saxons came to Britain in three longboats at the invitation of the British king. The reason for this unusual invitation was that, following the withdrawal of the Roman garrisons from Britain, the land began to come under attack in the southwest by the Gaelic tribes of Ireland,[16] and in the north by the savage Picts.[17] The Britons drove the Gaels back to Ireland, but had less success against the Picts. By the year 449 attacks from the north had become so intense that the Britons, unable to defend themselves, invited Germanic peoples from across the English Channel to come to protect them from these attacks. In return, they were granted land in the eastern part of Britain.

These Germanic tribes defeated the Picts, and some of them settled in Britain. Attracted by the fertility of the land and realizing the disinclination of the Britons to go to war, these groups of Angles and Saxons who had made homes for themselves in this new land invited more settlers from their homeland[18] to Britain, and these newcomers were also given grants of land in return for their protection. Bede notes that these "protectors" belonged to three of the most powerful of the Germanic nations: the Angles, the Saxons, and the Jutes.[19]

It soon became apparent that these Germanic tribes, now arriving in great numbers, were in Britain as conquerors, not protectors. The sketchy history that Bede outlines gives only an indication of the savage battles

---

[16]Whom Bede calls the *Scoti,* the Latin word that has given its name to Scotland.

[17]The Picts, named from the Latin adjective *pictus,* "painted," apparently dyed their bodies. Little is known of these people. They were probably a non-Celtic race who had settled in the north of Britain and in the southern part of Scotland.

[18]These peoples belonged to the West Germanic nations and came from the lowlands of the Netherlands.

[19]The Jutes came from the area of Denmark known as Jutland.

fought between the British Celts and the Germanic invaders.[20] The foreigners ultimately gained the upper hand, and their leaders began to carve out small kingdoms for themselves, the seven most powerful of which, known as the Anglo-Saxon Heptarchy, eventually held most of England in their control. Inevitably, one of these kings emerged as sole ruler of Britain. This was King Alfred (ca. 848-900), known as Alfred the Great, who claimed all of England as his realm. Alfred's great task, to which he devoted a full thirty years, until his death, was resisting the onslaughts of the Danes, for these Scandinavian people had arrived in Britain a hundred years before as sea-raiders and had settled there in great numbers, intent on conquering the island for themselves. These people, known better as the Vikings, will be discussed below.

Old English

The Angles and Saxons, who had been invited to Britain in the fifth century to protect the British Celts from the warlike Picts in the north, had conquered the island.[21] But unlike the Romans, who had come as administrators of a province and whose soldiers were there only to maintain law and order, the Germanic invaders had come to make new homes for themselves and to establish their own kingdoms in the new land. The language of the Roman conquerors, Latin, had never been accepted as the vehicle of everyday speech by the native Celts, and with the departure of the Roman garrisons, no more than a few traces of their language remained in the island. Now it was different. So thoroughly was the influence of the Angles and Saxons felt in every part of Britain, that, by the time of King Alfred, in the ninth century, the language of Britain was English, sometimes called Anglo-Saxon.[22] To differentiate this early form of English from its later developments, it is called Old English, usually abbreviated OE.

---

[20]Bede's main concern was with the affairs of the Church, and he gives only passing references to the wars being fought in the land. It should be observed that, in the opinion of many, King Arthur, the hero of romantic legend, was an historical leader of the British who, in the early sixth century, led them in battle against the Germanic tribes. The oldest legends concerning Arthur are found in the *Historia Britonum*, "A History of the Britons," written in the late eighth century by a Welsh historian named Nennius, who says Arthur led the armies of the British against the Saxon invaders in twelve great battles, finally defeating them. Bede makes no mention of King Arthur.

[21]The Jutes, who are mentioned by Bede as having taken part in these invasions, seem to have played little part in the wars between the Britons and the Germanic tribes.

[22]The exact meaning of the term *Anglo-Saxon* is in some doubt. It may refer to the Saxons living in Britain, as opposed to those who remained in their own homeland in northwestern Europe.

Old English was, of course, a Germanic language.[23] It had a few loan-words in it from Latin, words that had been borrowed by the Germanic tribes in Europe when they had come into contact with the Romans centuries before, as well as some Latin words that had entered the Celtic language of Britain during the period of three hundred years when the Romans occupied the island. And there were a few words from Celtic that entered this Germanic tongue. But it is a fact that when an entire people changes its native language for another, very little of the original vocabulary remains in the new tongue. Thus, the Celtic element in Old English is minimal.[24]

Two hundred years before King Alfred's time, that is, in the early part of the seventh century, England became Christianized. The language of the Church had always been, as in a limited sense it still is—or, rather, was, until recently—Latin. From this period a number of ecclesiastical terms from Latin enter Old English, many of them ultimately derived from Greek, the language of the apostles, terms which had entered the Latin language during the period of the early growth of the Church. By the first and second centuries A.D. there was a large element of Greek in the Latin vocabulary, and it was only natural that Latin writers should borrow the Greek terms in ecclesiastical matters.[25]

The word "English" is from the Old English *Englisc*, from *Engle*, the Old English name for the Angles, the term used for the Northumbrian and Mercian peoples who had settled in practically all of England north of the Thames River. The dialect(s) of the Angles was the first to be used for English literature, and, thus, *Englisc* came to be the term used for the language even when literature was written in other dialects. Although King Alfred spoke and wrote in the West Saxon dialect, spoken in practically all of England south of the Thames, his language is called *Englisc*.

There are three main stages recognized in the development of the English language: Old English, Middle English, and Modern, or New, English. The main differences in the successive stages of the language are those characterized by a gradual loss of the inflected endings of nouns, pronouns, adjectives, and verbs, as well as by changes in spelling. Old

---

[23]Or, rather, probably different but closely-related dialects of the West Germanic peoples. Four dialects of OE are usually recognized: West Saxon, Mercian, Northumbrian, and Kentish.

[24]When the people of Cornwall, in Southwest England, ceased to speak Brythonic Celtic and began speaking English during the nineteenth century, very little of the original Celtic vocabulary remained in the new language.

[25]The etymology of ecclesiastical terms will be discussed later in this book. For now, a few samples will suffice: priest (OE *preost*, Latin *presbyter*, Greek *presbyteros*); bishop (OE *biscop*, Latin *episcopus*, Greek *episcopos*); monk (OE *munuc*, Latin *monachus*, Greek *monachos*); devil (OE *deoful*, Latin *diabolus*, Greek *diabolos*); apostle (OE *apostol*, Latin *apostolus*, Greek *apostolos*).

English was a fully inflected language, just as modern German is today, with two numbers: singular and plural; three genders: masculine, feminine, and neuter; and four cases: nominative, genitive, dative, and accusative (the nominative and accusative usually being identical).

An inflected language is one in which words assume different endings to indicate their function in a sentence or to indicate person and number in the verb. Modern English has almost completely lost these inflectional endings, their function being replaced by the use of prepositions with nouns; for verbs, we do without them almost altogether. We can say, for example, "The king is tall," "This is the crown of the king," "I gave the crown to the king." In an inflected language like Old English (or Latin or modern German), the form of the word for "king" would change by the addition of inflectional endings to indicate the fact that the word is used in the nominative case as the subject of the sentence (The king is tall), or the word is used in the genitive case to show possession (This is the crown of the king), or is used in the dative case to indicate the indirect object of the verb (I gave the crown to the king). Similarly, the Old English verb was fully inflected. That is, the form of the verb was altered by the addition of inflectional endings to indicate whether the subject of the verb was singular or plural, or whether the subject was in the first person (I, we), the second person (you), or the third person (he, she, it, they). In modern English it is usually only the third person singular that has retained an inflection (the letter -s).

I see	I run	I sing
you (singular) see	you (singular) run	you (singular) sing
he/she *sees*	he/she *runs*	he/she *sings*
we see	we run	we sing
you (plural) see	you (plural) run	you (plural) sing
they see	they run	they sing

For the noun, modern English inflects only the genitive case and the plural forms: "The king is tall," "I see the king's crown," "There were many kings there."

Following is a paradigm (an example showing a word in all its inflectional forms) of the Old English masculine noun *cyning*, "king":

	Singular	Plural
Nominative	*cyning*	*cyningas*
Genitive	*cyninges*	*cyninga*
Dative	*cyninge*	*cyningum*
Accusative	*cyning*	*cyningas*

It is impossible to assign definite dates to the three stages of the development of English, and it is customary to refer to the period at which Middle and Modern English can be said to be fully developed and assign a date correspondingly. Thus, the Old English period is said to have lasted to about 1100 A.D., and the Middle English period to about 1500.

The earliest examples of Old English that we possess are from the late seventh century. These exist only in fragmentary texts. Complete texts of Old English begin with the *Anglo-Saxon Chronicle*. This monumental work is a compilation of the important events, past and present, in English history. It was begun by King Alfred and incorporated the past history of the English given in Bede's *Ecclesiastical History* (which Alfred is said to have translated from Latin into Old English), with additions from other sources down to Alfred's time. At his death it was continued by other hands down to the final entries, those for A.D. 1154.[26]

By the middle of the eighth century A.D. use of the Celtic language had ceased in practically all of Britain except for Wales, Cornwall, the Isle of Man, and parts of Scotland. Everywhere else the language was the language of the Germanic conquerors of the land, Old English. A substantial literature was in existence, and, except for the Latin terms in use in the Church, foreign influences on the language were all but nonexistent. The only wars fought were those between rival kings within Britain, each struggling to claim supremacy over the whole land, until Alfred was declared King of England in A.D. 871. But beginning almost a hundred years before Alfred's time a new threat to England appeared in the person of invaders from across the North Sea.

The Scandinavian Invasions

Beginning in the latter part of the eighth century and lasting for almost three hundred years, England was subjected to invasion by waves of Scandinavian peoples from Norway and Denmark. The first recorded appearance of these peoples in England was in 789, when, according to the *Anglo-Saxon Chronicle*, three pirate ships from Denmark landed on the coast of Dorset in the south, seized some plunder and sailed away. The raids became more frequent and of greater intensity, affecting the towns and monasteries of the coastal areas. In 850, however, a great fleet of Danish ships arrived, and in the following year the city of London was captured by these invaders. The early years of King Alfred's rule were spent in fierce battles with the Danes, culminating in the Treaty of Wed-

---

[26]What is called the *Anglo-Saxon Chronicle* is actually four distinct chronicles composed in successive stages and at different places. However, all together they present us with a continuous history of England to A.D. 1154.

more in 878, under the terms of which the Danes were allowed to remain in a great area of eastern England, subject to their own law.[27]

The treaty did not last for long, however, and fresh fighting broke out. In 994 the kings of Denmark and Norway joined together in a huge raid and were persuaded to leave only upon the payment of a great sum of money by the English king. This provided only a temporary truce, and in 1014 Svein (or Sveyn), king of Denmark, succeeded in driving Ethelred, the British king, from the throne. Svein was succeeded by his son, Cnut, and England was ruled by Danish kings until 1042, when, upon the death of King Harathacnut, Edward,[28] the son of Ethelred, assumed the throne. Wars between Denmark and Norway precluded any attempts to reconquer England, and this was the end of Danish rule.

Although the throne was restored to English kings, Scandinavian influence upon England remained strong. Large areas of the island had been ceded to the foreigners in an attempt to buy peace, and they had settled in large numbers throughout the greater part of the north and east of England. The result of this was that there came into being great numbers of communities of Scandinavian people who were now permanent residents of England, communities whose populations were steadily increased by newcomers from abroad for a period of over two hundred years. The language, or languages, of these people was either Norse or Danish. Both of these languages were members of the North Germanic branch of Indo-European, and both of them were related to the Anglo-Saxon tongues, which were members of the West Germanic branch.

During and following the Scandinavian invasions, although the invaders eventually adopted the English language, large numbers of Scandinavian words passed into it and remained in it. Due to the similarities at that time between Norse and Danish, it is impossible to tell from which of these languages any given word entered Old English. In an often-quoted passage from the preface to his *Eneydos*,[29] William Caxton (ca. 1422-1492), the first English printer, complains of the changing condition of the English language and tells an anecdote concerning the Scandinavian word *egg* replacing the native English *ey*. Caxton's language is Middle English. The text is that cited in the Bibliography.

> And certaynly our langage now vsed varyeth ferre from that whiche was vsed and spoken whan I was borne / For we englysshe men / ben borne vnder the domynacion of the mone, whiche is neuer stedfaste / but euer wauerynge /

---

[27]Called Danelaw. These Scandinavian peoples were, of course, the Vikings. The word *viking* is from the Norse, and in that language meant simply "sea-rover" or "pirate."

[28]"The Confessor."

[29]Caxton's translation of Virgil's *Aeneid* from the French *Eneydes*.

wexynge one season / and waneth & dyscreaseth another season / And that comyn englysshe that is spoken in one shyre varyeth from a nother. In so moche that in my dayes happened that certayn marchauntes were in a shippe in taymse, for to haue sayled ouer the see into zelande / and for lacke of wynde, thei taryed atte forlond, and wente to lande for to refreshe them; And one of theym named sheffelde, a mercer, cam in-to an hows and axed for mete; and specyally he axyd after eggys; And the goode wyf answerde, that she coude speke no frenshe. And the marchaunt was angry, for he also coulde speke no frenshe, but wolde haue hadde egges / and she vnderstode hym not / And thenne at laste a nother sayd that he wolde haue eyren / then the good wyf sayd that she vnderstod hym wel / Loo, what sholde a man in thyse dayes now wryte, egges or eyren / certaynly it is harde to playse euery man / by cause of dyuersite & chaunge of langage.

Due to the similarities between Old English and the Scandinavian dialects spoken by the newcomers in England,[30] it is difficult to say to what extent English was influenced by the Scandinavian tongues, or, and of more importance, what ultimate influence might have been felt had not another great foreign invasion occurred. This took place in the eleventh century and had a profound effect upon the development of English. This was the conquest of England by William, Duke of Normandy.

The Norman Conquest

If there had been no Norman invasion, the English language today would probably be similar to one of the dialects of modern Dutch; that is, Old English, a West Germanic language, would in all likelihood have developed along the lines of other West Germanic tongues, whose modern descendants are Dutch, Flemish (spoken in parts of Belgium), and Frisian (spoken in the Dutch province of Friesland). But there was a Norman invasion, and the Normans came to stay.

The word Norman is an altered form of Northman and refers to the people from the North, the Scandinavian people whom we call the Vikings. The Viking Age may be said to have begun with the first

---

[30]As an example of the similarity between Old English and Old Norse, see the pair of modern English words shirt and skirt. The former is from OE *scyrte*, while the latter is from ON *skyrta*. Both meant "shirt," and both were related to OE *sceort*, "short." Thus, the words shirt and skirt both mean a "short" article of wearing apparel; the one, from OE, worn on the upper body, and the other, from ON, worn on the lower.

recorded appearance of a Scandinavian pirate fleet off the southern coast of England. This was in A.D. 789. From that point on, the movements of these "Vikings" can be traced with considerable accuracy as far as their attacks on England, Ireland, and Scotland are concerned. While some of these pirate fleets were making attacks upon the British Isles, however, others were striking the northwest coastal areas of France. Lack of historical sources available to us obscures our knowledge of their activities in this region. But what is certain is that before long they had seized a substantial area of France and had settled down on it as permanent residents. The first indication that their occupation was recognized by the French king is a treaty that was struck in 911 between King Charles ("The Simple") of France and Rollo (or Rolf), the Scandinavian chief, under the terms of which a considerable area of land was granted to the foreigners.[31]

The Normans, for the Scandinavians in France should now be called this, were quick to adapt to their new situation, and, as their kinsmen had done in England, adopted the language of their new homeland and, within a few generations, became speakers of French.[32] Rollo died in 929 and was succeeded by his son, William, thus beginning a hereditary dynasty of Dukes of Normandy. The seventh Duke was William, the illegitimate son of Robert ("The Devil").

In England, the Anglo-Saxon King Ethelred II had married Emma, the daughter of Richard, Duke of Normandy, and uncle of William ("The Bastard"). In 1014 Ethelred was driven from the throne by Svein, King of Denmark, and, with his wife and family, took refuge in Normandy. The son of Ethelred and Emma was Edward, and, when Svein's son and successor, Cnut, died without an heir, Edward was recognized as the rightful king, and was crowned King of England in 1043.[33]

At some time before his death, Edward seems to have given assurances to William that he, William, should be recognized as Edward's successor to the throne of England. However, when Edward died in 1066, on his deathbed he indicated that Harold, Earl of West Saxony, was to succeed him. Accordingly, Harold was elected king and was crowned. William challenged the crown, claiming it as Edward's acknowledged successor. Harold, of course, repudiated William's claim,

---

[31]For a discussion of the Scandinavians in France, see *The History of the Norman Conquest of England*, Edward A. Freeman, 5 volumes, Oxford University Press, 1876. For modern views of this, see *William the Conqueror*, David C. Douglas, London 1964, and *The Norman Empire*, John Le Patourel, Oxford University Press, 1976, and bibliography cited there.

[32]The French of this period is called Old French, or Norman French, to distinguish it from the modern language.

[33]This is Edward the Confessor, so called because of his reputation for piety.

and William led a force across the English Channel in the fall of 1066, and on October 14, Harold was defeated at the battle of Hastings, losing his life in the fighting. William, Duke of Normandy, was crowned King of England at Westminster on Christmas Day, 1066.

William I, Duke of Normandy and King of England, could speak no English. He had come at the head of an army of faithful followers, mercenaries, and adventurers from all over Europe, but mostly from Normandy and other regions of France, none of whom could speak English. The new king quickly appointed his Norman French friends and relatives to high positions, and began a systematic program of confiscation of land to parcel out to his followers as rewards for their service. The result of this was the creation, almost overnight, of a new, French-speaking aristocracy of landholders. The same policy was transferred to the Church. In 1070 the Archbishop of Canterbury was deposed and replaced with a Norman French prelate, Lanfranc, and at the time of William's death in 1087, there remained only one English-speaking bishop. Thus, French became the language of the rulers and of the aristocracy, and English was relegated to the position of the language of a subject race.

The English of this period is called Middle English and is characterized by a gradual loss of the inflected endings of Old English and by a gradual introduction of French words into the vocabulary. Had Norman French kings continued to rule England, doubtless the English language would have ultimately given way completely to French just as Celtic had given way to Old English following the Anglo-Saxon invasions of England. But the main bond linking the English kings to France—that is, their rule over Normandy as well as England—was severed in 1204, when Normandy was lost by King John to Philip, King of France. From this point on, the English kings no longer had dual allegiance to England and France. Furthermore, English had always remained the language of the common people, and by the fourteenth century English had replaced French in the schools, the courts of law, and in government, reversing the situation begun under and following William's rule. But the new English was radically changed from Old English, as noted above, having lost most of the inflections and having gained a vast vocabulary of French words.

Modern English

The period of Modern English is said to have commenced around the year 1500, at the beginning of the Renaissance. Words from French continued to enrich the English vocabulary just as they had done following the Norman Conquest of 1066. Norman French, as noted above, had only recently emerged as a language distinct from the Latin spoken in Gaul. The use of Latin had never died out as a "language of learning," and it had been maintained as the language of the Church long after it had become "dead" as a spoken tongue. During the Anglo-Norman period, as the period of Norman rule of England is called, Latin words had been borrowed into the vocabulary of English, as well as French words. Beginning with the Renaissance, however, borrowings from Latin were carried out in wholesale numbers, and, with the revival of the knowledge of ancient Greek, words from that language as well began to enter the vocabulary.

The introduction of the art of printing into England in 1476 by William Caxton had a profound effect upon the English vocabulary. The combination of the revival of learning and the availability of printed books hastened the translation of Latin and Greek authors from antiquity, and it was now that words from these ancient tongues began to enter our language in greater numbers than ever before. This process has continued down to the present day, and, when new words are needed for the expression of new ideas and discoveries, they are either borrowed from the ancient languages or coined from words in these languages. While it has been Latin that has especially enriched our vocabulary in everyday, non-technical words, it has been Greek that has provided us with most of the words in our present-day scientific vocabulary. In the following Lessons in this book, we shall learn a selected vocabulary of both Latin and Greek words, prefixes, and suffixes, and see how these forms have been utilized in the creation of the modern English vocabulary.

Bibliography

The following works have been consulted in the preparation of this book.

Baugh, A.C. and Cable, T. *A History of the English Language*. Third edition, Prentice-Hall, Inc. New Jersey, 1978.

Bede. *A History of the English Church and People*, tr. Leo Sherley-Price. Penguin Books. England, 1955.

Burriss, E.E. and Casson, L. *Latin and Greek in Current Use*. Prentice-Hall, Inc. New York, 1949.

Culley, W.T. and Furnivall, F.J., editors, *Caxton's Eneydos*. 1490. Englished from the French *Liure Des Eneydes*, 1483. Published for The Early English Text Society by the Oxford University Press. London, 1962.

Freeman, E.A. *The History of the Norman Conquest of England*, 5 volumes. Oxford University Press. England, 1876.

Garrison, F.H. *An Introduction to the History of Medicine*, fourth edition. W.B. Saunders Company. Philadelphia, 1929.

Hammond, N.G.L. and Scullard, H.H., editors. *The Oxford Classical Dictionary*, second edition. Oxford University Press. England, 1970.

Le Patourel, J. *The Norman Empire*. Oxford University Press. New York, 1976.

Lewis, C.T. and Short, C. *Harper's Latin Dictionary*. The American Book Company. New York, 1907.

Liddell, H.G. and Scott, R.A. *A Greek-English Lexicon*. Oxford University Press. England, 1953.

Skeat, Rev. W.W. *An Etymological Dictionary of the English Language*. Oxford University Press. New York, 1985.

The Compact Edition of the Oxford English Dictionary. Oxford University Press. New York, 1971.

Thomas, C.L., editor. *Taber's Cyclopedic Medical Dictionary*, ed. 16. F.A. Davis Company. Philadelphia, 1989.

Webster's Ninth New Collegiate Dictionary. Merriam-Webster Inc. Springfield, Massachusetts, 1986.

Wright, J. and E.M. *Old English Grammar*, second edition. Oxford University Press. England, 1914.

Lesson 1

Quot homines, tot sententiae.

As many people, that many opinions. [Terence, *Phormio*]

Prefatory Remarks

ETYMOLOGY is the study of the derivation of words, including an account of their origin and subsequent linguistic history. In studying the etymology of English words that have been derived from Latin and Greek—the purpose of this course—the Latin or Greek source of each word is determined, including prefixes and/or suffixes, and the linguistic changes, if any, that have affected each of these words down to its present form are observed. Note is taken of the changes in the meaning of these words, if such changes have taken place.

The vocabulary of modern English consists of a large number of words whose origin can be traced to Latin or Greek, plus some that have been borrowed from other languages, all added to a substratum of vocabulary that has been inherited from the language, or dialects, of the Anglo-Saxon invaders of Great Britain in the fifth century A.D. These inherited words are called *native words* and are to be distinguished from *borrowed words*, those that have entered our vocabulary from other sources, such as Latin and Greek.

The earliest written documents of the Anglo-Saxon invaders date to the seventh century, and we call the language of these early documents Anglo-Saxon (abbreviated AS) or, more commonly, Old English (abbreviated OE). Changes in the spelling of individual words, undoubtedly reflecting changes in their pronunciation, can be observed in these documents through the centuries, and when the changes have become so profound as to represent sounds substantially different from those found earlier, the language is given a new name: Middle English (abbreviated ME). An arbitrary date of the beginning of the twelfth century, i.e., A.D. 1100, is usually accepted as the starting point for Middle English. Our language, English, is customarily dated from the sixteenth century. Thus, a word that is called Old English is one that is attested in written records from the seventh century A.D. to about 1100; Middle English words are attested in documents from the twelfth century to about 1500, and Modern English words date from the sixteenth century to the present.

The Anglo-Saxon invaders of Great Britain came from the northwestern part of Europe and spoke dialects of the Germanic family of languages, modern descendants of which include German, Dutch, Danish, Swedish, Norwegian, and Icelandic. Etymologies for a few native English words will illustrate the linguistic changes that affected these words from the Old English period to the present. Related forms in Swedish and German are given for comparison.

Old English	Middle English	English	Swedish	German
foeder	*fader*	**father**	*fader*	*Vater*
moder	*moder*	**mother**	*moder*	*Mutter*
sweostor	*suster*	**sister**	*syster*	*Schwester*
brodhor	*brother*	**brother**	*broder*	*Bruder*
sunu	*sone*	**son**	*son*	*Sohn*
dohtor	*doghter*	**daughter**	*dotter*	*Tochter*
hus	*hous*	**house**	*hus*	*Haus*
leoht	*light*	**light**	*lätt*	*leicht*
riht	*right*	**right**	*rätt*	*recht*
hand	*hand*	**hand**	*hand*	*Hand*

Spellings of individual words vary in the ancient manuscripts, and different English dictionaries may give different or alternate spellings for the Old English and Middle English forms.

Words in different languages that are descended from the same parent language like English *sister*, German *Schwester*, and Swedish *syster*, for example, are called *cognates*. In this instance, the parent language is one that we call Proto-Germanic. There are no written documents in this language, and the forms of individual words in it must be reconstructed, working backwards from the earliest written examples of Germanic cognates. Since both Latin and Greek are descended from a common parent language, called Indo-European (abbreviated IE), many cognates can be found in these two languages: Latin *mater, pater*: Greek *mētēr, patēr*, "mother," "father," for example. The Romance languages are rich in cognates, as they are all descended from the same parent, Latin.

Latin Words in English

The great majority of words in the vocabulary of present-day English consists of those that have been borrowed from Latin and, to a lesser extent, ancient Greek. The reason for this enormous borrowing is simply that these words represent objects and ideas for which there was no exact native equivalent. For example, while the early inhabitants of Great Britain brewed beer from grain (OE *beor*, ME *bere*), wine was unknown to them. When the Romans occupied Britain in the first century A.D. and brought *vinum* with them, the word was borrowed along with the beverage: Old English and Middle English *win*, English **wine**.

French Words in English

The influence of the French language was of particular importance in the development of the English vocabulary, and borrowings from this language became increasingly frequent following the period of the Norman invasion of A.D. 1066. The French language, like English, can be divided into three periods: Old French (OF), from the ninth to the fourteenth century A.D., Middle French (MF), from the fourteenth to the sixteenth century, and French (F), from the sixteenth century to the present.

Of special importance is the dialect of Old French spoken in the region of Normandy. This was the language of William "The Conqueror" and his followers, and is called Norman French (NF). England was ruled by Norman kings for two centuries, and Norman French left its mark upon the English language.

During and following the Renaissance, words were borrowed in great numbers from Middle French, and a substantial part of our vocabulary can be traced through Norman French and Middle French back to Old French.

Old French was the language that resulted from the normal changes that Latin suffered through the centuries, and most French words, whether they come from the Old- or Middle-French period, can be traced to a Latin original.

The Renaissance

The period of the greatest borrowing from Latin began with the English Renaissance, after A.D. 1500, when new ideas required new words in which to express them. While Latin had been kept alive in the liturgy of the Church and as a vehicle for scholarly writing, study of the Roman writers of prose and poetry had long been abandoned. Now, with the rebirth of interest in the ancient writers, words were borrowed freely from the language of Vergil, Cicero, and others, either in their original Latin form or with slight changes in spelling, a process that has continued up to the present day.

Often, words were formed from Latin with the same meaning as those already in the native vocabulary, and today we see the old and the new existing side by side, often with slightly different meanings.

Native English Word	Latin Borrowing
brotherhood	fraternity
fatherhood	paternity
motherhood	maternity
sisterhood	sorority
friendly	amicable
holy	sacred
horseman	equestrian
freedom	liberty

The Latin Language

Latin, like French and English, can be divided into different periods, depending upon the date of the language, as determined by the date of written documents. The Latin of each period has been given a name. Texts written before the first century B.C. are said to be in Old Latin (OL). Classical Latin (L), the language of Cicero and other great literary figures, is the name given to the language up to the third century A.D. Documents written from the third to the seventh century are said to be in Late Latin (LL), and the Latin of the medieval period, from the seventh to the fifteenth century, is called Medieval Latin (ML).

In addition to the designations above, the term Vulgar Latin (VL, from L *vulgus*, "the common people") is used to refer to Latin words that are assumed to have been in common use in the spoken tongue but which are not attested in literature. This assumption is based upon cognate words in the Romance languages for which no obvious source can be found in Latin, or upon Medieval or Late Latin words which it is thought should be found in Latin documents but are not.

Often, especially in scientific writing, a Latin word will be given a new and entirely different meaning. Such words are called New Latin (NL). An example of this can be seen in the use of the word *bacillus*. The Latin word meant a small staff, a rod; this name was given to the newly-discovered rod-shaped microorganism. Also, any written documents in Latin that can be dated after the fifteenth century are said to be in New Latin. The monumental work of William Harvey on the circulation of the blood, *Exercitatio anatomica de motu cordis et sanguinis* (An Anatomical Treatise on the Movement of the Heart and Blood), published in 1628, was written in New Latin. Other treatises written in New Latin include

Copernicus' *De revolutionibus orbium coelestium* (Concerning the Revolutions of the Heavenly Bodies), and Linnaeus' *Genera Plantarum* (Genera of Plants) and *Classes Plantarum* (Classes of Plants).

Latin Nouns and Adjectives in English

A noun is the name of a person, place, thing, state, condition, quality, idea, or action; *George, Newark, hand, sleep, health, honesty, revolution, war,* are all nouns, names of something. When Latin nouns are borrowed into English, they appear in one of three ways.

1. In their original Latin form, the form in which they are listed in the dictionary. This is called the *dictionary form*. Many Latin nouns have a characteristic ending of *-us, -a,* or *-um,* usually indicating that the object named was thought of as being either masculine (*-us*), feminine (*-a*), or neuter (*-um*)—that is, neither.

Latin Noun	Meaning	English Word
alumnus	foster son	**alumnus**
alumna	foster daughter	**alumna**
ovum	egg	**ovum**

2. With the characteristic ending dropped.

Latin Noun	Meaning	English Word
digitus	finger	**digit**
matrona	married woman	**matron**
eventum	occurrence	**event**

3. With the characteristic ending changed to silent -e.

Latin Noun	Meaning	English Word
modus	manner	**mode**
causa	reason	**cause**
fatum	prediction	**fate**

An adjective is a word that describes or limits a noun: a *green* book, a *short* journey, a *tall* man, a *pleasant* woman. For many adjectives, the dictionary form of the word ends in *-us,* although this ending is changed to either *-a* or *-um* if the noun that the adjective describes is of the feminine or neuter gender. Most Latin adjectives of this type are found in English either with the *-us* dropped or changed to silent -e.

Latin Adjective	Meaning	English Word
antiquus	ancient	**antique**
aridus	dry	**arid**
firmus	stable	**firm**
privatus	personal	**private**

Suffixes and Stems

Many Latin nouns and adjectives are found as English words with a suffix added to the stem of the Latin word. A *suffix* is a form that has no meaning by itself but which is added to the stem of a word in order to change its meaning in some way. The *stem* (sometimes called the base) of most Latin nouns ending in *-us*, *-a*, or *-um* and most adjectives ending in *-us* is found by dropping these endings; what is left of the word is the stem. Suffixes form either nouns or adjectives. One commonly-found suffix in Latin is *-alis* (*-aris* following a stem that ends in *-l*). This suffix forms English adjectives ending in **-al** (**-ar**).

Latin Word	Stem	Meaning	English Adjective
angulus	**angul-**	angle	**angular**
filius	**fili-**	son	**filial**
ovum	**ov-**	egg	**oval**
stella	**stell-**	star	**stellar**
vita	**vit-**	life	**vital**

Adjectives can be defined in many ways. Since they often indicate a characteristic of someone or something, in this book the definition "characteristic of" will be used. **Filial** devotion is that which is characteristic of a son; an **oval** shape is one that is characteristic of an egg, and **vital** signs are those that are characteristic of life.

Other Nouns and Adjectives

There is a large group of nouns and a smaller group of adjectives that, with a few exceptions, does not have the characteristic *-us*, or *-a*, or *-um* ending but, rather, displays a variety of endings. In order to find the stem of words of this type, another form must be given in addition to the dictionary form of the word. It is traditional for dictionaries of both Latin and of English to give the form of the Latin word that indicates possession, called the genitive case, following the dictionary form of the word. This form, the genitive case, always ends in *-is*, and the stem of these Latin words is usually found by dropping these two letters, although in some nouns and adjectives the *-i-* is retained before certain suffixes, often before English **-al (-ar)**.

Latin Word	Stem	Meaning	English Adjective
cor, cordis	**cord (i)-**	heart	**cordial**
corpus, corporis	**corpor-**	body	**corporal**
mens, mentis	**ment-**	mind	**mental**
tempus, temporis	**tempor-**	time	**temporal**
vox, vocis	**voc-**	voice	**vocal**

It can be seen from the list above that the dictionary form of some of these words has been borrowed as an English word. We can speak of the **corpus** of Ernest Hemingway, meaning the whole body of his works, the complete works of this author, and we use the English term, borrowed from Latin, **vox populi,** "the voice of the people." In this expression the form *populi* is the Latin genitive case of the noun *populus,* "the people," meaning "of the people."

More Adjectival Suffixes

In addition to the Latin adjectival suffix *-alis* (*-aris*), forming English adjectives in **-al (-ar)**, many other adjectival suffixes were in common use. Five of these follow.

Latin Suffix	English Form(s)
-anus	**-an, -ane**
-arius	**-ary**
-ilis	**-il, -ile**
-inus	**-ine**
-osus	**-ose, -ous**

The adjectives formed by these suffixes are to be defined in the same way as those in **-al (-ar)**. However, the suffix **-ose** often has the meaning "full of": **verbose** (Latin *verbum,* "word"): "full of words, wordy."

Stems that end in the letter *-c* often add an *-i* before the suffix **-ous**: *judex, judicis,* "judge": **judicious,** "characteristic of a judge."

Latin Word	Stem	Meaning	English Adjective
urbs, urbis	**urb-**	city	**urban**
mundus	**mund-**	world	**mundane**
tempus, temporis	**tempor-**	time	**temporary**
civis, civis	**civ-**	citizen	**civil**
senex, senis	**sen-**	old, old man	**senile**
ursus	**urs-**	bear	**ursine**
verbum	**verb-**	word	**verbose**
copia	**copi-**	abundance	**copious**

Noun-Forming Suffixes

There are suffixes that form nouns. One of the most common of these in Latin is *-itas* (*-eta*s after a stem ending in *-i*). This suffix was spelled *-ité* in Middle French and, when borrowed into Middle English, ultimately became **-ity** (**-ety**). This suffix formed abstract nouns from Latin adjectives. *Abstract noun*s indicate a state, condition, quality, idea, or action. The abstractions indicated by such nouns have neither body nor substance. Common English abstract nouns include *sickness, health, love, envy, hate, honesty, crime*, and so forth. Honesty has no substance; it cannot be seen, touched, or measured in any way, although we can often observe its effects. The same can be said for love, envy, hate, and the rest of these abstractions. We can see the effect of sickness upon a person, but we cannot see, touch, or measure in any way sickness itself.

The opposite of an abstract noun is a *concrete noun*. These nouns name something that has substance and which can be seen, touched, and measured in some way: *house, cat, typewriter*, and so forth. One Latin suffix forming concrete nouns is *-arium*, forming English nouns in **-arium** or **-ary,** meaning "a place for (something)."

In the following list of Latin words, in subsequent lists, and in the vocabularies and in the Index of Stems of this book, nouns will be identified by the abbreviation *n.*, and adjectives by *adj*. Abstract nouns can be defined by the words "state, condition, or quality (of whatever the stem of the word means)," and adjectives can be defined as "characteristic of" or "pertaining to."

Note that when the genitive case is the same as the dictionary form, the genitive case will not be given in the vocabularies; the stem is found by dropping the final *-is* from the dictionary form.

Latin Word	Stem	Meaning	English Noun
brevis adj.	**brev (i)-**	short	**brevity, breviary**
gravis adj.	**grav-**	heavy	**gravity**
levis adj.	**lev-**	light	**levity**
sanus adj.	**san-**	sound, healthy	**sanity**
avis n.	**av(i)-**	bird	**aviary**
aqua n.	**aqu-**	water	**aquarium**

A word can have more than one suffix: **mentality.** Note how English words have been formed on the model of Latin words. Mentality is from Latin *mentalis,* from *mens, mentis,* "mind," plus the English suffix -**ity.** The word "*mentalitas*" never existed in Latin.

When a suffix is added to a word that ends in a vowel or -**y,** the final vowel or the -**y** drops off: **urbane + -ity = urbanity; sanity + -arium = sanitarium.**

Note that English abstract nouns can often be defined by using the native English suffix -**ness: brevity,** "shortness"; **levity,** "lightness"; **gravity,** "heaviness."

Vocabulary

A. Learn the following Latin words, the stem of each, and its meaning. Here, and in all subsequent vocabularies and in the Index of Stems, Latin nouns will be identified by the abbreviation *n.* following their entry, and adjectives by *adj.*

Latin Word	Stem	Meaning
avis n.	av(i)-	bird
brevis adj.	brev(i)-	short
civis n.	civ-	citizen
cor, cordis n.	cord(i)-	heart
corpus, corporis n.	corpor-	body
fatuus adj.	fatu-	foolish
gravis adj.	grav-	heavy
levis adj.	lev(i)-	light
mens, mentis n.	ment-	mind
mundus n.	mund-	world
provincia n.	provinci-	province
sanus adj.	san-	sound, healthy
tempus, temporis n.	tempor-	time
urbs, urbis n.	urb-	city
ursus n.	urs-	bear
vacuus adj.	vacu-	empty
verbum n.	verb-	word
vox, vocis n.	voc-	voice
vulgus n.	vulg-	the crowd, ordinary people

B. Learn the English form of the suffixes presented in this Lesson, the specialized meanings that any may have, and whether each forms a noun or an adjective.

Notes

Here, and in subsequent Lessons, the Notes are intended to explain both the etymology and the current meaning of selected English words that are derived from Latin words in the vocabulary of the Lesson under discussion.

The Latin noun *provincia* was applied to conquered territory that had been acquired by Rome, usually in war. By the end of the first century A.D. Roman provinces could be found all over the map of the western world: Britain, Sicily, Africa, Spain, Numidia, Asia, Macedonia, to name but a few. The Latin word was also applied to the administration of these territories, and often meant any duty, function, or sphere of influence of a magistrate.

We can see both of these meanings in English derivatives. In Roman times, the adjective *provincialis* was applied to anything that pertained to or came from a province. Thus, today we can speak of a **provincial** attitude as one typical of a **provincial,** a person living far from the big city, one who lacks the polish and refinement of the urban dweller: un-sophisticated. One's **province** today is his or her special area of compe-tence or function. We can say that it is the **province** of the pathologist to determine the cause of a person's death.

Gaul, Latin *Gallia*, modern France, became a Roman province in the first century B.C. after Julius Caesar had campaigned there for nearly ten years. He is said to have referred to it as "his" province, or "the province," and the name remains in the southern coastal area on the Mediterranean Sea, Provence.

The word *Vulgar* in the term Vulgar Latin (VL), the language of the common people, is derived from the noun *vulgus*, "the crowd, ordinary people." Words labeled VL are not attested in Latin literature but are assumed to have existed in the speech of the people during the Classical period due to their presence in later Latin literature and/or from cog-nates in the Romance languages. The first great literary statement in Vulgar Latin was the translation of the Bible into the Latin of the com-mon people. It was called *vulgata edita*, the edition for the people, and was the work of a Roman churchman named Eusebius Sophronius Hieronymus, better known to us as Saint Jerome, in the fourth century A.D. Today, the word **vulgar** refers to anything that is ostentatious or offensive.

The names of the constellations Ursa Major and Ursa Minor, the Big and the Little Bear, owe their names to Greek mythology. Callisto was a beautiful maiden who traveled in the company of Artemis, virgin goddess of the hunt—Diana in Roman mythology. Once upon a time Zeus, the chief of the gods, saw Callisto and seduced her. When the poor girl became pregnant with Zeus' child, Artemis drove her from her company, and Callisto, living alone in the woods, gave birth to a son, Arcas. At this point, Hera, Zeus' wife, driven by jealousy, metamorphosed Callisto into a she-bear. Fifteen years later, Arcas hunting in the woods came upon his mother. About to hurl his spear at her, he was himself changed into a bear by his father, Zeus, and the two of them, mother and son, were whirled up to the heavens as the twin constellations, the Bears. Hera, still rankling at the injustice done to her, went to Ocean and asked this divinity not to allow these two creatures to bathe in the pure waters of the ocean. And that is why Ursa Major and Ursa Minor never sink below the horizon but revolve ceaselessly in the northern sky. Latin *ursa* is the feminine form of the masculine *ursus*, "bear."

The second-century A.D. Roman poet Decimus Junius Juvenalis, better known as Juvenal, wrote a collection of sixteen satires, attacks on the vices and foolishness that he perceived in his fellow Romans. His Tenth Satire was imitated by the English writer Samuel Johnson in his poem *The Vanity of Human Wishes*. In this poem Juvenal asks himself the question, "Is there anything for which people should pray?" and gives the answer, *mens sana in copore sano*, "A sound mind in a sound body."

Using The Dictionary

When using the English dictionary, you will probably be seeking two different pieces of information about the word that you are looking up. You will want to know the current definition of the word—that is, the way that it is used today—and you will want to know the etymology of the word, the course that it has taken through the centuries from the time that its Latin (or Greek) original can be identified. In dictionaries of English, the etymology of a word is usually enclosed in square brackets either just before the definition or just after it. The first piece of information in the etymology will usually be the language from which the modern word has been taken, followed by the form of the word in that language, if it differs from that of the modern word. After that will come the linguistic history of the word in reverse chronological order, ending with the earliest form (in any language) to which the modern word can be traced. Following are some typical etymologies.

fatuous *adj.* [L *fatuus* + English -ous]. This means that the entry word is an adjective and that it is derived from Latin *fatuus*. Since no meaning is given for the Latin word, it means the same as the English entry word. English **fatuous** looks as though it is derived from a Latin adjective **fatuosus*, but this word is not found in Latin literature of any period, and, thus, the English word is thought of as having been formed from the stem **fatu-** of the Latin word *fatuus*, plus the English suffix -ous. The asterisk before **fatuosus* is a convention meaning that the word "looks" authentic, but that it has not been found in Latin literature of any period.

gravity *n.* [MF *gravité*, fr. L *gravitas*, fr. *gravis*, heavy]. This means that the entry word is a noun and that it is derived from the Middle French word *gravité*, which is derived from Latin *gravitas*, which is from Latin *gravis*, "heavy."

temporal *adj.* [ME, fr. L *temporalis*, fr. *tempor-*, *tempus*, time]. This means that the entry word is an adjective and that it is derived from a Middle English word spelled the same way, which is derived from Latin *temporalis*, which is derived from the stem *tempor-* of the Latin word *tempus*, "time."

urban *adj.* [L *urbanus*, fr. *urbs*, city]. This means that the entry word is an adjective and that it is derived from Latin *urbanus*, which is from Latin *urbs*, "city."

verbose *adj.* [L *verbosus*, fr. *verbum* + *-osus*, **-ose**]. This means that the entry word is an adjective and that it is derived from Latin *verbosus*, which is from Latin *verbum*, and the Latin suffix *-osus*, which gives the English suffix **-ose**.

Often, more than one definition will be given for a word, and, when this is the case, definitions will be numbered 1, 2, 3, and so forth. Usually the numbers indicate the chronological sequence of the definitions, with the earliest given first, and the current definition given last.

Exercises

A. Each of the words in italics in the sentences below has been derived from a Latin word given in the vocabulary to this Lesson, with a suffix given in this Lesson. Analyze each of these italicized words. Word analysis consists of separating the English word into stem and suffix, giving the meaning of each. The current meaning of the English word should then be given, in the sense that it is used in each of these sentences. Be careful to distinguish nouns from adjectives in your definitions. Consult the dictionary where necessary.

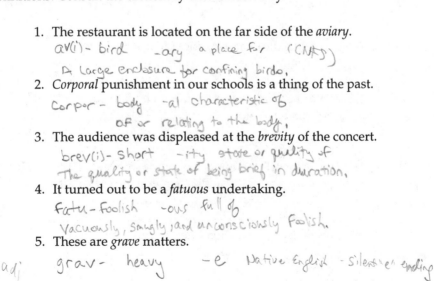

1. The restaurant is located on the far side of the *aviary*.

   av(i)- bird ___ -ary a place for (CNFS)

   A large enclosure for confining birds.

2. *Corporal* punishment in our schools is a thing of the past.

   Corpor- body -al characteristic of

   of or relating to the body.

3. The audience was displeased at the *brevity* of the concert.

   brev(i)- short -ity state or quality of

   The quality or state of being brief in duration.

4. It turned out to be a *fatuous* undertaking.

   Fatu- foolish -ous full of

   Vacuously, smugly, and unconsciously foolish.

5. These are *grave* matters.

   adj grav- heavy -e Native English - silent e ending

   Requiring serious thought; momentous.

AFS

6. The *gravity* of the situation was apparent to all.
grav – heavy   –ty state or quality of
Grave consequence; seriousness or importance.

7. There is no place here for *levity*.   (ABNFS)
lev(i) – light   –ity state or quality of
Lightness of manner or speech, esp. when inappropriate; frivolity.

8. He ignored all *mundane* affairs.   (AFS)
mund – world   –ane characteristic of
Relating to, characteristic of, or concerned with commonplaces; ordinary.

9. It seemed to us that she held a *provincial* attitude toward our
   plans. provinci – province   –al characteristic of
of or characteristic of people from the provinces; not
fashionable.   (AFS)

10. The pathologist said that such matters were not in his *province*.
provinci – province   –e silent s ENG
the range of one's proper duties and functions.

11. "...for the things which are seen are *temporal*; but the things
    which are not seen are eternal." [II Corinthians, 4.18. King
    James Version] tempor – time   –al characteristic of
of, relating to, or limited by time.

12. He pushed his way through the crowd with *ursine*
    indifference. urs – bear   –ine characteristic of

of or characteristic of a bear.

13. She had all the characteristics of an *urban* businesswoman.
urb – city   –an characteristic of
of or located in a city.

14. He had all the characteristics of an *urbane* attorney.
urb – city   –ane characteristic of
Polite, refined, and often elegant in manner.

15. When the judge questioned him, he looked up with a *vacuous*
    expression. vacu – empty   –ous full of

Lacking intelligence; stupid.

16. The chancellor, after giving a *verbose* address to the
    graduating class, read the names of all the candidates.
Verb – word   –ose full of

Using an great many of words; an excessive number of words,

17. The apartment was furnished in *vulgar* taste.
vulg – the crowd   –ar characteristic of

Deficient in taste, delicacy, or refinement.

18. The quotation is from the *Vulgate*.

    vulg – the crowd -ate characteristic of

    The Latin edition of the Bible made by Saint Jerome – end of 4th c.

19. The kite soared with *avian* grace.

    av(i) – bird   -an characteristic of

    of, relating to, or characteristic of birds.

20. The former *sanitarium* upstate has been converted to a
    hospital. *san- sound, healthy   -arium a place for*

    *An institution for the treatment of chronic diseases or for medically
    supervised recuperation.*

21. She greeted him with icy *cordiality*.

    cord(i) heart -al characteristic of   -ity state or quality of

    warm and sincere; friendly

22. Who has the *mentality* to know the best thing for us to do?

    ment- mind   -al characteristic of   -ity state or quality of

    Cast or turn of mind.

23. There are those who live in a *vacuum*, with no concern for
    others. *vacu – empty   -um   neuter L1E*

    A state of being sealed off from external or environmental influences; isolation.

24. The mayor said that these were *temporary* measures.

    tempor – time   -ary characteristic of

    Lasting, used, serving, or enjoyed for a limited time.

25. The workers were extremely *vocal* in their complaints.

    voc – voice   -al characteristic of

    Tending to express oneself often or freely; outspoken.

26. They were married in a *civil* ceremony.

    civ – citizen   -il characteristic of

    A marriage ceremony by a civil official.

27. He is a *civil* engineer.

    *An engineer trained in the design and construction of public works and other large
    facilities.*

28. She is not a *civil* person.

    Sufficiently observing or befitting accepted social usages; not rude.

29. He was arrested for *civil* disobedience.

    *Refusal to obey civil laws in order to induce governmental change, characterized
    by nonviolence.*

30. The land was devastated in a long *civil* war.

    A war between factions or regions of the same country.

31. These people do not know the meaning of the word *civility*.

    civ – citizen -il characteristic of   -ity State or quality of

    Courteous behavior; politeness.

B. The italicized words in the sentences below are from Latin nouns not given in the vocabulary of this Lesson but found in the Index of Stems in the back of this book. Determine the meaning of the stem of each of these words, and define each as it is used in the sentence. Consult the dictionary where necessary.

1. She gave him a *vulpine* look.

   vulp- fox

   Of, resembling, or characteristic of a fox. (foxy).

2. He displayed *taurine* strength.

   taur- bull

   Of, relating to, or resembling a bull.

3. The judge gazed at him with an *aquiline* stare.

   aquil- eagle

   Of or relating to an eagle.

4. She went about her daily affairs with a *bovine* temperament.

   bov- cow

   Of or relating to a cow.

5. The dancers in the ballet moved with *feline* grace.

   fel- cat

   Of or relating to a cat.

6. He waited in the doctor's office with *canine* patience.

   can- dog

   Of or relating to a dog.

7. They fought with *leonine* fury.

   leon- lion

   Of or relating to a lion.

8. He had a *porcine* appearance.

   Porc- pig

   Of or relating to a pig.

9. The room reeked of *piscine* odors.

   pisc- fish

   Of or relating to a fish.

10. The runners displayed *equine* endurance.

    equ- horse

    Of or relating to a horse.

11. The neighborhood was plagued by a pack of *feral* dogs.

    fer- wild

    Existing in a wild or untamed state.

12. They were engaged in *arcane* activity.

    arcan- secret

    Known or understood only by a few.

13. I hesitated to approach this lady, noted for her *acerbity*.

    acerb— harsh, bitter

    Sourness or acidness of taste, character or tone.

14. We learned that she was living a *penurious* existence.

    Penuri— want, need

    Property-stricken; destitute

15. The army's *hibernal* quarters were at the foot of the mountain.

    hibern— of or for winter

    Of or relating to winter.

16. He was showing signs of *senile* forgetfulness.

    sen— old, aged

    of or related to, or characteristic of old age

17. He was a man known for his *probity*.

    prob— honest

    complete and confirmed integrity; uprightness.

18. The accused were freed through the agency of a *venal* judge.

    ven— that which is for sale

    Open to bribery.

19. I used to ridicule my *uxorious* friend.

    uxor— wife

    Excessively submissive or devoted to one's wife.

20. The doctor looked for *vital* signs.

    vit— life

    of, or relating to, or characteristic of life.

Lesson 2

Semper avarus eget.

The greedy person is always in need. [Horace, *Epistles*]

Latin Verbs in English Words

Of all the words that have entered the vocabulary of English from Latin, the majority, by far, has been derived from Latin verbs. The reason for this is twofold: verbs are used to indicate everyday activities—walking, talking, seeing, thinking, working, reading, and so forth; furthermore, the stems of Latin verbs readily combine with suffixes and, especially, prefixes, which will be discussed below, to form numerous English verbs, nouns, and adjectives.

Most Latin verbs have two stems from which English words are formed. These are the stem of the infinitive and that of the perfect participle. The *infinitive* is a form which, in English, means "to (do something)," such as "to walk," "to talk," "to see." There are four classes of Latin verbs, and the infinitive of each of these has its own ending by which it is characterized. The infinitive of one of these classes ends in *-ere*, and the stem of this infinitive is found by dropping these three letters. English verbs are formed from this stem, often by adding a silent -**e**, usually with the addition of a prefix.

Prefixes

A *prefix* is a form that is added to the beginning of a word and which changes the meaning of the word. Six frequently-used prefixes follow, each with the stem of the verb *ducere*, "lead." Since the English form of these prefixes is usually identical with the Latin form, only the English prefixes will be given here. Learn the following prefixes and the meaning of each.

Prefix	Meaning	English Word
con-	together, with; thoroughly	conduc(ive)
de-	down	deduce
in-	in, into	induce
pro-	forward, in front	produce
re-	back, again	reduce
se-	away from	seduce

The *perfect participle* (often called the perfect passive participle) of a Latin verb is an adjective that ends in -*us*, and the stem is found, as in other adjectives in -*us*, by dropping these two letters. In Latin, the perfect participle is used to indicate or refer to past, or completed events; this can be illustrated by the verb whose infinitive is *frangere* and whose perfect participle is *fractus*. The infinitive, *frangere*, means "to break," and the perfect participle, *fractus*, means "broken," as in "a broken window." In all subsequent references to Latin verbs in this book, the verb will be defined by its underlying meaning, without the "to" before it: *frangere, fractus*, "break."

The stem of the perfect participle is often found in English as a verb, noun, or adjective, usually with a prefix added. The stem is also frequently found with a suffix (or suffixes) as well as with a prefix (or prefixes). One very common noun-forming suffix in Latin is -*io*, -*ionis*, forming English abstract nouns in -**ion**; one common adjectival suffix is Latin -*ivus*, forming English adjectives in -**ive**. Examples of these words follow, using *ductus*, the perfect participle of *ducere*, and using the six prefixes introduced above.

conduct	conduction	conductive
deduct	deduction	deductive
induct	induction	inductive
product	production	productive
————	reduction	reductive
————	seduction	seductive

With some verbs, a silent -**e** is added to the stem of the perfect participle to form English words: *vertere, versus*, "turn": **converse, inverse, reverse**.

Latin Verbs in -*ēre*

In addition to Latin verbs whose infinitive ends in -*ere*, there is another class of verbs whose infinitive ends in the same three letters, but with this difference: in the second of these, the first -e- is "long." This means that it was pronounced with a different sound from that used in an infinitive with a "short" -e-. It is traditional in dictionaries of both Latin and English to distinguish between these two infinitives by placing a "long mark," called a *macron* (from the Greek adjective *makron*, "long") over the long vowel of these infinitives: *tenēre*, *tentus*, "hold," *movēre*, *motus*, "move," *sedēre*, *sessus*, "sit," for example. This practice will be followed here. In all other respects, these verbs are treated in the same way as those whose infinitive ends in short -ere.

The Present Participle

There is another form of Latin verbs which has been very productive of English derivatives. This is the *present participle*. For verbs whose infinitive ends in -ere or -ēre, the present participle is formed by adding -ens, -entis, to the stem of the infinitive; this forms English adjectives in **-ent**. In English, present participles are adjectives formed from verbs and which end in **-ing**: talk: the *talking* dog; run: the *running* horse, for example. The stem of the present participle of the Latin verb *vertere*, "turn," is *vertent-*; with the prefixes **in-**, "not," and **ad-**, "toward," the English derivative is **inadvertent**.

Often these present participles, although originally adjectives, are used as nouns: **precedent** (**pre-**, "before," and *cedere*, "go").

Many English words from Latin present participles are spelled **-ant**, where etymologically they should be spelled **-ent**. This is the result of changes that affected these words in Old and Middle French: **tenant**, from Latin *tenēre*, "hold," for example, where we should expect "tenent."

Vowel Weakening

The vowel of the stem of some Latin infinitives and, to a lesser extent, perfect participles changes when a prefix is added to the stem. This change is usually from -a- or -e- to -i-; for verbs in which this vowel weakening, as it is called, occurs, the weakened forms will be preceded by a dash: *frangere*, *-fringere*, *fractus*, "break": **infringe**; *sedēre*, *-sidēre*, *sessus*, "sit": **resident**.

Vowel weakening can also be seen in some adjectives, following a prefix. The prefix *in-*, when used with adjectives, was the negative prefix, meaning "not." The Latin adjective *aptus* meant "fit, suitable, **apt**"; when the negative prefix *in-* was added, the adjective became *ineptus*, "unfit, unsuitable, **inept**." See also the Latin adjectives *amicus*, "friendly, amicable," and *inimicus*, "unfriendly, inimical."

English Nouns in -cy and -ce

In Latin, abstract nouns were often formed by adding the suffix *-ia* to the stem of the present participle; thus, all of these nouns ended in *-ntia*. In the Middle English period, when such words were borrowed into English, the final *-tia* assumed a sibilant, or "s," sound (compare the pronunciation of modern English **militia**), and the spelling usually followed this change in pronunciation. These nouns now end in either **-cy** or **-ce**; it is not possible to predict which ending the English word will have.

Sometimes English nouns were coined in this pattern, as if the appropriate Latin word existed. In such instances, a "Latin" word is given preceded by an asterisk. This indicates that they are hypothetical forms and that the "Latin" word is not found in the literature of any period.

Latin Infinitive	Meaning	Latin Noun	English Noun
currere	**run**	**currentia*	**currency**
tenēre, -tinēre	**hold**	*continentia*	**continence**
sedēre, -sidēre	**sit**	*residentia, praesidentia*	**residence, presidency**

The Latin diphthong *-ae-* usually becomes **-e-** in English words: Latin *aeternitas*: English **eternity**. Thus, the Latin prefix *prae-*, "before, in front of," becomes **pre-** in English derivatives.

Vocabulary

Learn the following verbs, their stems, and the meaning of each. Forms which show vowel weakening after a prefix will be preceded by a dash. Stems of present participles are not given here. These forms are found by adding *-ent-* to the stem of the infinitive. Remember that sometimes this ending has changed to *-ant-* in Middle English.

Latin Verb	Stems	Meaning
cedere, cessus	**ced-, cess-**	go, yield
currere, cursus	**cur(r)-, curs-**	run
ducere, ductus	**duc-, duct-**	lead
frangere, -fringere, fractus	**frang-, -fring-, fract-**	break
ludere, lusus	**lud-, lus-**	play
movēre, motus	**mov-, mot-**	move
tenēre, -tinēre, tentus	**ten-, -tin-, tent-**	hold
sedēre, -sidēre, sessus	**sed-, -sid-, sess-**	sit
tangere, -tingere, tactus	**tang-, -ting-, tact-**	touch
vertere, versus	**vert-, vers-**	turn

Currere loses its second *-r-* except in the present participle: **incur, recur; current.**

Assimilation of Prefixes

Many prefixes that end in a consonant—any letter, that is, other than the vowels **a, e, i, o,** or **u**—*assimilate* to the initial consonant of the following stem. This means that the final consonant of the prefix (if there is one) becomes "similar to" the initial consonant of the stem, or of another prefix, that follows it. This phenomenon is familiar to us from common English adjectives with the negative prefix **in-,** meaning "not": **legal: illegal** (for "inlegal"), **possible: impossible** (for "inpossible"), **regular: irregular** (for "inregular"), and so forth. Not all prefixes assimilate; for those that do, the assimilated forms are given below. The six prefixes given above are included in this list. Since almost all the prefixes have the same form in Latin as in English, the Latin forms will not be given here.

Prefixes

Learn the following English prefixes and the meaning of each. Assimilated forms are given following the dictionary form.

Prefix	Meaning
ab-, abs-, a-	away from
ad-, ab-, ac-, af-, ag-, al-, an-, ap-, ar-, as-, at-	to, toward
con-, co-, col-, com-, cor-	together, with; thoroughly
de-	down, from
ex-, e-, ef-	out of
extra-, extro-	outside, outward
in-, il-, im-, ir-	in, into
in-, il-, im-, ir- (used only with adjectives)	not
intro-	within
ob-, o-, obs-, oc-, of-, op-	against
per-, pel-	through; thoroughly, very
pre-	before
re-	back, again
se-	apart, away
sub-, suc-, suf-, sug-, sup-, sur-, sus-	under
super-	over
trans-, tra-	across, beyond

The Native English Prefix un-

The native English prefix **un-** was used as a prefix in Old English and Middle English to form the negative of adjectives: **like, unlike**; **behaved, unbehaved**. It was also used to form the opposite of verbs: **bend, unbend**; **dress, undress**. From the Middle English period on it was used freely as the negative prefix with Latin stems: **precedented, unprecedented**; **tenable, untenable**.

The Native English Suffixes -ed, -ing, and -ly

The suffix **-ed** is a form that can be traced back through Middle English to Old English. It is used now, as it always was, to form the past tense of certain verbs. Originally found only in some native verbs such as *carry, carried; try, tried; walk, walked*, it is now used with Latin stems to

form the past tense of verbs, as well as adjectives derived from these verbs: an **inverted** picture; a **reversed** direction, for example.

The native suffix -**ing** can also be traced back to Old English. It is found in certain native verbs to form the present participle: *sing, singing; talk, talking,* and it is used with Latin-derived verbs to form both present participles and nouns: she saw the **moving** object; he is taking **reducing** pills; **moving** his arm was painful; **reducing** is difficult.

The native suffix -**ly** sometimes is used to form adjectives indicating certain characteristics: she has *queenly* grace. But its most common use is to form adverbs, both from native verbs and from those derived from Latin stems. An *adverb* is a word that modifies a verb—that is, it describes the action of a verb: she spoke **seductively** to him; he walked **resolutely** to the door; the convict served both terms **concurrently**. In the vocabularies of this book and in the Index of Stems, adverbs will be identified by the abbreviation *adv.* following the entry of the word.

Latin Suffixes -*uus*, -*ium*, and -*ax*, -*acis*

The Latin suffix -*uus* formed adjectives in that language from the stems of infinitives of verbs. These adjectives are not used as English words, but their stems, in -*u*- can be found in English words before certain suffixes, usually -**al**, -**ity**, or -**ous**: **residual, continuity, continuous,** for example.

The Latin suffix -*ium* formed nouns from the stems of infinitives. These nouns now are found as English nouns ending in -**y**: *subsidium*: **subsidy**; compare Latin *studium*: **study**, from *studēre*, "be eager." The original -*i*- of -*ium* remains, however, before another suffix : **subsidiary, insidious**.

The suffix -*ax*, -*acis*, formed adjectives in Latin from stems of infinitives: *tenēre*, "hold": *tenax, tenacis*, "holding fast." This suffix is found in English words only before another suffix, usually -**ity** , forming nouns: **tenacity** , or -**ous** , forming adjectives: **tenacious**. Note that stems ending in -*c* often add an -*i*- before the English suffix -**ous**: *audēre*, "dare," *audax, audacis*, "bold": **audacious**. Since the Latin suffix -*ax*, -*acis*, is invariably followed by either -**ity** or -**ous** in English derivatives, the entire suffixes -**acity** and -**acious** will be considered as one form in this book, although English dictionaries may cite the Latin adjective in -*ax* in the etymology of such words.

The Suffix -ment and the Connecting Vowel

In the Latin language, the suffix -*mentum* was used with the stem of the infinitive to form abstract nouns, many of which became English nouns in -**ment**. Although all of these Latin nouns were abstract, indicating a state or condition or the like, some of the English derivatives have come to be used as concrete nouns: **sediment**, from Latin *sedimentum* (*sedēre*, "sit"), **document**, from Latin *documentum* (*docēre*, "teach"), for example.

In Latin, when a stem ended in a consonant and was followed by a suffix beginning with a consonant, a vowel, called the *connecting vowel*, was usually inserted between the two in order to avoid an awkward combination of consonants. This vowel was usually *-i-* or *-u-*, but other vowels are found in the Latin nouns: *tenementum*: **tenement**; *testamentum*: **testament**.

Often words in **-ment** have been coined in modern times without any Latin example in *-mentum*. These new nouns are usually formed from English verbs, and the suffix **-ment** is added to the end of the verb, whether it ends in a vowel or a consonant:

assess	**assessment**
contain	**containment**
infringe	**infringement**
move	**movement**

The Suffixes -able and -ible

The English suffixes **-able** and **-ible** were derived from Latin suffixes *-abilis* and *-ibilis*. In Latin and in English these suffixes are to be defined as "capable of being (whatever the meaning of the verb is)." For example, **portable**, from the Latin verb meaning "carry," means "capable of being carried," not "capable of carrying." In the same way, **frangible** means "capable of being broken," or, better, "easily broken."

In the Latin language, the suffix *-ibilis*, English **-ible**, was used exclusively with verbs whose infinitive ended in *-ere* or *-ēre*, and *-abilis*, **-able**, was used with certain other verbs. However, this distinction was not always observed in the Late Latin period or, especially, in Old- and Middle French, where **-able** is now found in modern derivatives where **-ible** would be expected. For example, this suffix and the Latin verb *tenēre* should form the adjective "*tenibilis*," English "tenible," but the word is now **tenable**, from Middle French *tenable*.

English Verbs in -ize

Often English verbs in **-ize** are formed from nouns: **hospital: hospitalize; economy: economize; subsidy: subsidize**. This verb-forming suffix comes through Middle English verbs in *-isen* from Middle French, where it was the development of Late Latin verbs in *-izare*, used to form verbs from nouns. This Late Latin suffix was borrowed from Greek verbs in *-izein*, used to form verbs from nouns in that language. It has become overused in English and is now found in such recent formations as **finalize** (1922), **prioritize** (1966), and others.

The English suffix **-ation**, borrowed from Middle English and ultimately from Latin, can be added to verbs in **-ize** to form nouns meaning "a condition resulting from a process or action": **hospitalization**, **subsidization**.

Changed Meaning in English Compound Nouns

Often an English word seems to have a meaning different from the sum of its Latin elements. This is because compound words—that is, words made up from a stem or stems, prefix(es), and/or suffix(es)—formed in the Latin language often, at an early date, assumed specialized meanings seemingly at variance with their etymological meanings. One example of this is the Latin noun *insidiae*. This word is a compound of the stem *-sid-* of the verb *sedēre, -sidēre*, "sit," the prefix *in-*, "in," and the suffix *-iae*, the (feminine) plural of the abstract noun-forming suffix *-ia*. The word *insidiae* was a military term meaning "ambush," literally a "sitting in" a concealed place to await and surprise the enemy. The adjective *insidiosus*, formed from this noun, meant "cunning, deceitful, dangerous," and this is the Latin compound word from which English **insidious** was borrowed. It means "possessing concealed dangers, treacherous." Later formations in English from this adjective are the adverb **insidiously** and the noun **insidiousness**, using the native English suffixes **-ly** and **-ness**. It is difficult to see the original meaning of the stem **-sid-**, "sit," in any of these three English words.

Suffixes

Review the suffixes in Lesson 1. Learn the English form of each of the suffixes below, the meaning of each, and whether each forms a noun or an adjective. Adjectival suffixes are indicated by the abbreviation *adj.*, and those that form nouns by *n*. Unless there is a specialized meaning of a particular suffix, adjectives will be defined as "characterized by," and nouns, if abstract, by "state, quality, action."

Latin Suffix	English Suffix	Meaning
-abilis	**-able** *adj.*	capable of being
-ax, -acis , -osus	**-acious** *adj.*	characterized by
-ax, -acis , -itas	**-acity** *n.*	state, quality
-atio, -ationis	**-ation** *n.*	state, quality, action
-ibilis	**-ible** *adj.*	capable of being
-io, -ionis	**-ion** *n.*	state, quality, action
-ium	**-y** *n.*	state, quality, action
-ivus	**-ive** *adj.*	characterized by
-mentum	**-ment** *n.*	state, quality, action
-orius	**-ory** *adj.*	characterized by
-ura	**-ure** *n.*	state, quality, action
-uus	**-u-**	[found before another suffix]
-ize	**-ize, -iz-**	[forms verbs]

Notes

Here, and in subsequent Lessons, material in the Notes that is enclosed in square brackets is there to explain the derivation of words that look as though they are related to Latin words in the vocabulary of the Lesson under discussion, but which have entirely different etymologies.

As has been noted before, borrowings from French into English were numerous in the period following the Norman Invasion of Britain in A.D. 1066, a process that lasted through the Renaissance and, to a lesser degree, up to the present time. The Latin words in our vocabulary that have come to us through French are usually disguised to a certain degree—often to a great degree.

The stem *ten-* of the Latin verb *tenēre*," hold," is one such example of this. In words compounded with prefixes, the Latin stem *-tin-* became *-tain* in French. This accounts for the spelling of **attain, contain, retain,** and others. The spelling of **continue**, from this same verb, is due to its form in Middle French.

The verb *currere, cursus,* "run," also gives us words thinly disguised by their French spelling: **succor**, from Latin *sub-* and *currere*; **course**, as in **racecourse**, from the perfect participle *cursus*, and its compounds **recourse, concourse,** and others.

[The small, red or black berry, the currant, is not from Latin *currere*, but comes from a Middle English term *rayson of Courante*, "raisin of Corinth," the name given to a particular type of raisin from dried grapes, produced in Corinth, a city of Greece. Later the second part of this name, *Courante*, was applied to currants, while *rayson* (from Latin *racemus*, "cluster of grapes") was kept for the dried fruit, raisins.]

The first example of the use of the word **currency**, the abstract noun formed from the present participle of *currere*, to mean "circulating money" is found in an essay of Benjamin Franklin, in which he wrote, "Money...by being coined is made a currency." The term was later picked up by the Scottish economist Adam Smith, who, in 1776, wrote, "In the province of New York common labourers earn three shillings and sixpence currency."

The English verb **cease** is from the Middle English infinitive *cesen*, from Middle French *cesser*, a verb derived from *cessus*, the perfect participle of the Latin verb *cedere*, "go, yield." The verb **decease** and the adjective **deceased** are from this same Latin verb.

There were a few verbs in Latin that provided a transitive form for an intransitive verb. *Transitive verbs* are those that take a direct object, such as, "I see the man," "The girl likes ice cream"; *intransitive verbs* are those that do not have a direct object of their action, such as, "I am sitting here," "The tree is falling." The Latin verb *sedēre* is an intransitive verb; it means "to be seated." There was a transitive equivalent to this verb, *sedare, sedatus,* which meant "bring (something) to rest, cause (something) to sit." Such verbs as *sedare* are often called "causative" verbs, as they cause something to happen. The English words **sedate, sedative,** and **sedation,** are from the perfect participle *sedatus* of this Latin verb *sedare*.

There are a few such pairs of native English verbs, one of which is intransitive, and the other, transitive: **sit, set; lie, lay; fall, fell.**

Exercises

A. The italicized words in the sentences below have been derived from Latin verbs given in the vocabulary to this Lesson, plus prefixes and/or suffixes from this Lesson and Lesson 1. Analyze each of these words. Word-analysis now consists of separating each word into prefix(es), if any, stem, and suffix(es), if any, and giving the meaning or force of each. Define the word as it is used in the sentence.

1. The newspapers say that we are in a *recession*.

2. The *decedent* was a sixty-two-year-old retired executive.

3. On the advice of their attorneys, the officials of the union demanded *concessions*.

4. This is an *unprecedented* action.

5. Here is an example of early *cursive* writing.

6. At age nineteen she made an *incursion* into the field of politics.

7. It was a *cursory* summary of the events.

8. We went ahead with the plan without the *concurrence* of the official in charge.

9. The mayor and the city council have *concurrent* jurisdiction in this matter.

10. There was only one *deduction* to be made from the evidence at hand.

11. The formal *induction* will take place next week.

12. In his campaign speeches he did not hesitate to *traduce* his opponent.

13. This material is too *frangible* to be of any use.

14. In her early years she was a *fractious* child.

15. This is an *infringement* of our rights under the terms of the lease.

16. The chairman did not tolerate any *infraction* of the rules of order.

17. It was a clear case of *collusion* between the two.

18. His plans for the company proved to be an *illusion*.

19. When questioned on that specific point, she gave an *elusive* reply.

20. The deep hatred that he aroused was a *prelude* to his downfall.

21. There is a *remote* chance of winning tomorrow.

22. What was that *commotion*?

23. If you are ready, let me hear you *emote*.

24. At that time, and with a handsome salary, he lived an *incontinent* life.

25. The lawyer questioned the witness with *pertinacious* hostility.

26. Where are the *pertinent* passages in this letter?

27. During his *tenure* taxes rose to unforeseen heights.

28. The former chairman spent ten years in *detention*.

29. Farming is certainly not a *sedentary* occupation.

30. She was *assiduous* in her attempts to gain the position.

31. The industrial waste buried there was an *insidious* threat to the health of the people.

32. After college, making money became an *obsession*.

33. Will this law *supersede* the previous one?

34. What is your *assessment* of the situation?

35. The walls of the house cracked due to the *subsidence* of the foundation.

36. She began to speak on the matter at hand but soon went off on a *tangent*.

37. The offer is *contingent* upon certain assurances from the other party.

38. Following this severe illness he lost his *tactile* sense.

39. There are certain *intangible* rewards in this.

40. Opposite the factory was a row of *contiguous* houses.

41. I remember him from our college days as an *introvert*.

42. It was an *inadvertent* omission.

43. She clung *perversely* to her position in the face of all arguments.

44. The rapid accumulation of so much wealth began to *subvert* their faith.

45. There was an indecipherable date on the *obverse* of the coin.

46. The program was *subsidized* through a federal grant.

47. This company is a *subsidiary* of that one.

48. In the view of the chairman, this was an *untenable* position to take.

49. She was an *extrovert*.

50. A wide ridge of *sedimentary* rock runs across the entire Great Lakes region.

51. After the refining process, the *residual* oil is a thick, heavy hydrocarbon.

52. This person is a well-known *dissident*.

53. At the end of the book is an *excursus* on the history of the area.

54. She delivered a *discourse* on the habits of these wild creatures.

55. The attorney will take the case on a *contingency* basis.

56. My friend is *averse* to hard work.

B. Each of the words below has been derived from one of the stems of a Latin verb in the vocabulary of this Lesson. For each, form an English word from the other stem of the same verb. Use any prefix(es), suffix(es), or none. Remember that the present participle is formed from the stem of the infinitive of a Latin verb.

Example: reduce: **seductive, induct, reduction**

1. exceed _____   6. recourse _____

2. refraction _____   7. session_____

3. allude _____   8. contact_____

4. abstain_____   9. inversion_____

5. decease _____   10. succor _____

C.   Answer each of the questions below.

1. What is the meaning of the verb *extemporize*?

2. What are *contemporaneous* events?

3. What is an *extemporaneous* performance?

4. What is the meaning of the verb *temporize*?

5. Consult the section in your dictionary on Foreign Words & Phrases, and determine the meaning and the pronunciation of the phrase *tempus fugit*.

D. Answer the following questions.

1. The word *consider* appears to be derived from the Latin verb *sedēre, -sidēre* but is not. Consult the dictionary and determine the etymology of this word.

2. In geometry, a *tangent* is a line that touches the circumference of a circle. It is from the Latin verb *tangere*, "touch." Consult the Index of Stems and determine the verb that has supplied the stem for *secant*. What is a secant?

Lesson 3

Malum nullum est sine aliquo bono.

There is nothing bad that does not have some good. [Pliny, *Natural History*]

Verbs with Infinitives in -*i*

The stem of infinitives ending in -*i* is found by dropping this letter. The perfect participle of these verbs ends in -*us*, and the stem is found by dropping these two letters. The perfect participle of these verbs cannot be predicted and must be learned for each verb.

loqui, locutus	**loqu-, locut-**	talk
sequi, secutus	**sequ-, secut-**	follow

The present participle of some (but not all) infinitives ending in -*i* is found by dropping the -*i* and adding -*ens, -entis*; thus, the stem of the present participle ends in -*ent*: **eloquent, consequent**. Abstract nouns are formed by adding -**ence** (or -**ency**) to the stem: **eloquence, consequence**. Infinitives in -*i* that do not form the present participle in the manner above will be discussed in Lesson 4.

Denominative Verbs. Verbs with Infinitives in -*are*

Denominative (from Latin *nomen, nominis*, "name") *verbs* are verbs whose stem is that of a noun or adjective. The infinitive of these verbs usually ends in -*are*, and the stem is found by dropping these letters. The perfect participle is predictable and is formed by adding -*atus* to the stem of the infinitive. As usual, the stem of the perfect participle is found by dropping the final -*us*.

Denominative verbs were numerous in Latin, and their derivatives are numerous in English. Any noun or adjective could be used in Latin as the stem of one of these verbs, although not all were actually in use.

Latin Word	Meaning	Denominative Verb	English Word
dignus adj.	worthy	*dignare, dignatus*	**indignation**
locus n.	place	*locare, locatus*	**dislocate**
opus, operis n.	work	*operare, operatus*	**inoperable**
unda n.	wave	*undare, undatus*	**inundate**

Occasionally the infinitive of the denominative verb ended in *-ari*: *prex, precis*, "prayer": *precari, precatus*, "pray." An English derivative is **imprecation**, "a prayer against someone, a curse."

There were Latin verbs whose infinitive ended in *-are* and whose perfect participle ended in *-atus* which were not denominative verbs. Two such verbs, *clinare, clinatus*, "lean," and *mutare, mutatus*, "change," will be introduced in part F. of the exercises to Lesson 4.

The present participle of all these verbs is found by adding *-ans, -antis* to the stem of the infinitive; thus, the stem of the present participle ends in *-ant*: *dignare*: **indignant**; *undare*: **redundant**. The first *-d-* in redundant is added to prevent an awkward gap, called *hiatus*, between the final *-e* of the prefix **re-** and the initial *u-* of the stem. We do this same thing in our everyday English when we add an *-n* to the article **a** before a word that begins with a vowel: *a* man, *a* dog, but *an* apple, *an* elephant.

Abstract nouns are formed by adding **-ancy** or **-ance** to the stem of the infinitive: **redundancy, abundance**.

Verbs have been freely formed in English on the model of Latin denominative verbs, even though such verbs never existed in the Latin language. One such example of this is seen in the word **defenestration**, "the act of throwing someone or something out of a window," coined to describe an action that took place in 1618 in Prague, when insurgents threw some state officials out of a window in the room in which they were meeting, an event that preceded the outbreak of the Thirty Years' War. The Latin noun is *fenestra*, "window." The verb was never used in Latin. Another example is **desegregation**, a word first used in 1952. There was a Latin verb *segregare, segregatus*, meaning "to separate from the flock," from the noun *grex, gregis*, "flock, herd," but there never was a verb "*desegregare*."

Often, but not always, Latin adjectives in *-is* retain the *-i-* when forming denominative verbs.

abbreviate, from LL *abbreviatus*, from *abbreviare*, from L *ab-* + *brevis*, "short"

alleviate, from LL *alleviatus*, from *alleviare*, "lighten," from L *ad-* + *levis*, "light"

elevate, from L *elevatus*, from *elevare*, "lift up," from *e-* + *levis*

aggravate, from L *aggravatus*, from *aggravare*, "burden," from *ad-* + *gravis*, "heavy"

Frequentative Verbs

Since perfect participles are adjectives, they, too, can be used to form denominative verbs. When this is done, the resulting verbs are called *frequentative verbs*, as these verbs expressed repeated actions, those frequently performed. There was such a verb, *cessare, cessatus*, formed from the perfect participle of *cedere, cessus*, "go, yield." This new verb meant "to keep yielding, to stop." English derivatives are **cessation**, "a stopping," and **incessant**, "constant, without end."

French Words in English

As has been noted before, the vocabulary of English has benefited greatly from the introduction of many words borrowed from French, some during and following the period of the Norman French occupation of England after the French victory at the Battle of Hastings in A.D. 1066, and others during the period of the Renaissance, beginning in the sixteenth century.

The English spoken from the twelfth to the sixteenth century is called Middle English (abbreviated ME), and the French that was borrowed during this period is known as Old French (OF), Norman French (NF), the language of William of Normandy, "The Conqueror," and his followers, or Middle French (MF), depending upon the period of borrowing. Most of the French words borrowed can be traced to a Latin word, through Medieval Latin (ML) and Late Latin (LL) or, if unattested in literature, to assumed forms in Vulgar Latin (VL), the Latin spoken by the vast populace of the Roman empire. These assumed forms are usually indicated by an asterisk (*). Often the Medieval Latin and Late Latin forms are identical to those of Latin, and these phases of transition can be omitted.

deign: ME *deignen*, MF *deignier*, OF *degnier*, Latin *dignare*, from *dignus*, "worthy"

Note that Middle English verbs, cited in the form of the infinitive, use the native English, that is, Germanic, form, often ending in *-en*, as above, while the Old French and Middle French infinitives are found in typically French forms in *-ier*, from Latin infinitives in *-are* (or *-ere*, and other forms).

The Middle English forms of words differ in the various manuscripts, and not all English dictionaries agree on the spelling of individual words from this period. For example, **voice** is from a Middle English word that is found in the manuscripts variously as *vois, voys, voyce*, and in other spellings. The Middle English word is from an Old French word which is cited as *vois, voiz,* or *voix*, all from Latin *vox, vocis*, "voice."

The Changes from Latin to French

As the Latin spoken by the Roman soldiers and administrators in the conquered territories of the vast Roman empire began to be adopted as the spoken tongue of the natives of those regions, replacing their own languages, the Latin itself began to change imperceptibly at first, until, after a few hundred years, it was no longer recognizable as Latin.

The same linguistic process had been taking place in England, where Old English had begun its own imperceptible change to Middle English, a change that was to continue until the language became modern English. The OE epic of Beowulf, which has come down to us in a manuscript written about A.D. 1000, is in a language foreign to us, and cannot be understood unless it is studied, just as one would study German or any other foreign language. By the time of Geoffrey Chaucer (1342-1400), the language, now called Middle English, can be read only with difficulty and with the aid of notes. All languages change over the centuries; the changes that took place as Latin became French can be noted in rough outline. The order is not chronological, and all of these changes took place gradually.

1. Initial Latin *c-* usually, but not always, became French *ch-*:

   Latin *cantare*, "sing," MF *chanter*, ME *chaunten*: **chant**

   Latin *canalis*, "canal," MF *chanel*, ME *chanel*: **channel**

2. A single consonant standing between two vowels internally (that is, not just before an ending) usually dropped out:

   Latin *focus*, "hearth, fireplace," LL *focalis*, "for the fireplace," OF *fouaille*, ME *fewel*: **fuel**

   Latin *rex, regis*, "king," *regalis*, "characteristic of a king," MF *roial*, ME *roial*: **royal**

3. Latin *-v-*, except when it was the first letter of a word, became French *-f-*:

   Latin *brevis*, "short," MF, ME *bref*: **brief**

   Latin *gravis*, "heavy," MF, ME *gref*: **grief**

4. Latin endings of nouns and adjectives either dropped off or became French -*e*:

> Latin *insignia*, "flags," MF *enseigne*, ME *ensigne*: **ensign**
>
> Latin *invidia*, "jealousy," MF, ME *envie*: **envy**

5. Latin internal vowels underwent complex changes, as can be seen from the examples above.

Doublets

When the Latin adjective *regalis*, "kingly," from *rex, regis*, "king," was borrowed from Middle French into Middle English, the word had undergone some of the changes described above and was now spelled *roial*; the modern spelling is **royal**. It should be obvious that the word **regal** is also from Latin *regalis*. The reason for the two different English words, **royal** and **regal**, is that one was borrowed from Middle French during the medieval period, and the other was borrowed directly from Latin at a later period. Such words in the same language that have entered this language by different routes but from the same source are called *doublets*:

> **grave** and **grief**, both from Latin *gravis*, "heavy"
>
> **legal** and **loyal**, both from Latin *legalis*, from *lex, legis*, "law"

Doublets must come from the *same form* of the Latin original, with the same prefixes and/or suffixes, or without any, as the case may be. **Gravity** and **grief**, for example, are not doublets, as the first word comes from Latin *gravitas*, and the second from *gravis*.

Nouns with Stems in -*u*-

There was a class of nouns in Latin whose dictionary form ended in -*us*, and whose stem is found by dropping only the final -*s*, leaving the stem ending in -*u*. Such nouns as these will be identified in the vocabularies and in the Index of Stems by printing -*u*- following the dictionary form of the word: *manus, -u-*, "hand." This accounts for the -*u*- in the word **manual**, "by hand."

The perfect participle of some verbs was used as one of these *u*-stem nouns. These nouns will be given a separate entry in the vocabularies and in the Index of Stems even if the verb from which they are derived is listed: *vidēre, visus*, "see": *visus, -u-*, "sight." An English derivative is **visual**.

Vocabulary

Learn the following Latin words, their stems, and the meaning of each. Nouns in *-us* whose stem ends in *-u-* are so identified. Denominative verbs are not listed if the words from which they are derived are in the vocabulary.

Latin Word	Stem(s)	Meaning
capsa n.	**caps-**	box
dignus adj.	**dign-**	worthy
grex, gregis n.	**greg(i)-**	herd, flock
invidia n.	**invidi-**	ill will
legere, -ligere, lectus	**leg-, -lig-, lect-**	choose; read
lex, legis n.	**leg-**	law
locus n.	**loc-**	place
loqui, locutus	**loqu-, locut-**	talk
manus, -u- n.	**manu-**	hand
odium n.	**odi-**	hatred
opus, operis n.	**oper-**	work
prex, precis n.	**prec-**	prayer
regere, -rigere, rectus	**reg-, -rig-, rect-**	straighten; rule
rex, regis n.	**reg-**	king
sequi, secutus	**sequ-, secut-**	follow
unda n.	**und-**	wave
vidēre, visus	**vid-, vis-**	see
visus, -u- n.	**visu-**	sight

Prefixes

Learn the following English prefixes and the meaning of each. Some Latin prefixes are found in English words in a changed form due to the influence of French.

Prefix	Meaning
circum-	around
dis-, dif-, di-	apart (*This prefix often forms a word meaning the opposite of the word to which it is prefixed*: **arm, disarm; infect, disinfect; enchant, disenchant.**)
en- (French, from Latin *in-*)	in, into
inter-, intel-	between
pro-	in front
pur- (French, from Latin *pro-*)	in front
sur- (French, from Latin *super-*)	over

Suffixes

Learn the following suffixes and whether each forms a noun or an adjective.

Latin Suffix	English Suffix	Meaning
-itudo, -itudinis	**-itude** *n.*	state, condition
-men, -minis	**-men** *n.*	state, condition, action
-or, -oris	**-or** *n.*	someone *or* something (performing an action)
-ulus	**-ula, -ule** *n.*	little (a Latin diminutive suffix)

Notes

While Latin *vidēre, visus*, "see," has provided the stems of **provide** and **provision**, the verb *visere*, "examine," a denominative verb formed irregularly from *visus*, has given us, through Middle French and Middle English, **revise** and **advise**. **Supervise** and **supervision** were coined in the seventeenth century from Latin *super-* and *visus*.

Latin *visus*, the perfect participle of *vidēre*, became *vis* in Old French, and meant "the face," the part of a person that we see and recognize.

This Old French word was replaced in modern French by *visage*, a word formed from Old French *vis* and the suffix *-age*, from the Latin suffix *-aticum*. Our word **visage**, "the face, the countenance," is borrowed from French. The Old French word *vis* remains in the modern expression *vis-à-vis*, "face-to-face," used in the sense of "in relation to," or "as compared with."

Also from Latin *visus* are **visa**, an endorsement on a passport indicating that the bearer's credentials have been seen, and, from Old French *visier*, from *vis*, "face," the English word **visor**, originally the front piece of a helmet that covered and protected the face of the wearer in combat.

The verb **envision**, "to form a vision of the future," was coined in 1921 by the British biographer Lytton Strachey, as he wrote in his life of Queen Victoria, "His blackest hypochondria had never envisioned quite so miserable a catastrophe." The **en-** in this word is the French equivalent of the Latin prefix *in-*, "in, into."

Visit, **visitor**, and **visitation** are all from Latin *visitare*, *visitatus*, "go and see, visit." **Vista**, "an extensive view," is from Italian *vista*, the feminine of *visto*, the perfect participle of the Italian verb *vedere*, "see," from Latin *vidēre*.

The noun **prudence**, "caution, good judgment," is from the Latin noun *prudentia*, an alternate form of *providentia*, "foresight, foreknowledge," and, thus, is the doublet of **providence**. Related adjectives to these words are **prudent**, "cautious, possessing good judgment," and its doublet, **provident**, "making plans for the future," and **imprudent**, "incautious, lacking good judgment," and its doublet, **improvident**, "failing to make plans for the future."

[While the words *advise* and *advice* are ultimately from the Latin verb *vidēre*, the words *vise* and *vice* are not. The former is from Middle French *vis*, "anything that winds," from Latin *vitis*, "vine," and the latter is from Latin *vitium*, "fault, defect." The "vice" in vice president is from Latin *vicis*, "change, alternation."]

The word **view**, both the verb and the noun, is from Middle English *vewe* from Middle French *veue* from the Old French perfect participle of the verb *veoir*, "see," from Latin *vidēre*. The word **purview**, "authority, competence, responsibility," is from Middle English *purvue* from Middle French from Latin *pro-*, "in front," and *vidēre*. **Survey**, "look over," is from Middle English *surveyen* from Middle French *surveeir* from Latin *super-* and *vidēre*.

The Latin verb *regere*, *rectus*, had two distinct, but related meanings in Latin. The original meaning was "straighten, guide," and a secondary meaning was "rule, govern, control." From the original meaning we have **erect**, **direct**, and **direction**, and from the latter, **regent**, "ruling." Related nouns to this verb were *rex*, *regis*, "king," and *regula*, "a straight stick, a ruler." The first of these two nouns has given us **regal**, while the second has given us **regulation** and **rule**, through Middle English and Middle French *reule*. Another related Latin noun is *regnum*, "kingdom," and from this, through Middle English and Middle French *regne*, we get our word **reign**.

Another Latin verb with two distinct meanings was *legere, lectus*. The original meaning of this verb was "pick, choose." Later, when the Latin-speaking peoples realized the art of writing, this verb was used to mean "read." From the former meaning we have **elect** and **select**, as well as **eligible**, "capable of being chosen," and from the latter, **legible** and **lecture**, originally something that was read.

Exercises

A. Analyze each of the italicized words in the sentences below.

1. Here we can see a *capsule* history of this small country.

2. When the manager was called, the customer became quite *indignant*.

3. Even the dog did not *deign* to bark at him.

4. Although the errors are insignificant in nature, their *aggregate* number is impressive.

5. This is an *egregious* error.

6. It was an *invidious* comment.

7. *Diligence* often brings its own rewards.

8. It was an *eloquent* speech.

9. She is studying *elocution*.

10. The petitioner was granted an *interlocutory* decree.

11. When questioned, the accused resorted to *circumlocution*.

12. I tried to avoid sitting next to my *loquacious* companion.

13. Most of his friends considered it to be an *odious* transaction.

14. Public *odium* fell on the governor for his remarks.

15. After several weeks of living in this manner, a feeling of *ennui* overtook her.

16. Even though he fled the village, *imprecations* followed him.

17. She said that she could not *deprecate* her friends' contributions.

18. This child is *incorrigible*.

19. The attorney approached the judge in an *obsequious* manner.

20. The *undulant* motion of the little boat caused much distress.

21. The flat, grassy plain seemed to *undulate* in the heat of the noonday sun.

22. Far across the *undulating* hills lay the towers of the city.

23. There is too much *redundancy* in this essay.

24. She found herself talking to this man who was a *visionary* idealist.

25. The *providential* arrival of supplies saved us from a long delay.

26. This administration is characterized by *improvidence*.

27. Our meeting must have been an act of *Providence*.

28. *Visualization* of the recent events was a cause of anxiety to her.

29. *Rectitude* was not one of his outstanding qualities.

30. The doctor said that legal matters were not in his *purview*.

31. She said that she could not attend the *obsequies*.

32. We began a strict *regimen* of diet and exercise.

33. The *provisional* government was headed by the former Prime Minister.

B. Each of the following words has been derived from a Latin word that is in this or a previous vocabulary but disguised through French. Consult the dictionary and give the Latin word or words from which each of these is derived, including prefixes and/or suffixes where appropriate.

1. pursue _____ 7. loyal _____

2. annoy _____ 8. lieutenant_____

3. maneuver_____ 9. envy _____

4. dainty_____ 10. surround _____

5. royal _____ 11. survey _____

6. maintain_____ 12. disdain _____

C. Answer each of the following questions. Consult the dictionary where necessary.

1. Use the expression *vis-à-vis* in a sentence. What does it mean and how is it pronounced?

2. What is a *locum tenens*?

3. What is meant by a *locus classicus*?

4. What does a *lector* do?

5. What does a *rector* do?

6. What does a *visor* do?

7. What is the meaning of the term *segue* as used in music? What is its etymology, and how is it pronounced?

8. What is meant by the *sequela* of a disease?

D. Each of the words below has been formed from the perfect participle of a Latin verb in the vocabulary of this Lesson. Form an English word from the infinitive of the same verb, using any prefix, suffix, or none.

1. incorrect _____   3. executive_____

2. collectible _____   4. interlocutor _____

E. Analyze each of the words below.

1. encapsulate_____

2. deregulation_____

3. desegregation_____

4. inoperative _____

5. inundation _____

6. precarious_____

7. inconsequential _____

8. unintelligible _____

F. Each of the words below has been formed from a noun or adjective in the vocabulary of Lesson 1. Give the stem of this word and its meaning. Define the English words.

1. infatuate _____

2. alleviate _____

3. evacuate _____

4. divulge _____

5. aviation _____

6. verbatim _____

G. Each of the words below has been formed from, or on the model of, a Latin denominative verb. Consult the Index of Stems and find the noun or adjective that has supplied the stem of each of these and give its meaning. Define the English words. Consult the dictionary where necessary.

1. defenestration _____

2. eradicate _____

3. defoliation _____

4. elaborate _____

5. reverberate _____

6. scintillate _____

7. eliminate _____

8. equivocate _____

H. What is meant by *subliminal* advertising?

I. Answer each of the following questions.

1. What is meant by a person's *visage*?

2. What is the meaning of the noun *prudence*? What is its doublet?

3. What is the meaning of an *imprudent* choice? What is the doublet of this word?

4. What is meant by an *interregnum*?

Lesson 4

Optimum est pati quod emendare non possis.

It is best to bear what you cannot change. [Seneca, *Epistles*]

Verbs with Infinitives in *-ire* and *-iri*

The final class of verbs to be discussed is that whose infinitive ends in *-ire* or *-iri*. The characteristic of these verbs which distinguishes them from most others is the fact that an *-i* is added to the stem of the infinitive. This *-i* shows up in the present participle, which always ends in *-ient-* (unless affected by French).

> *audire, auditus,* "hear": **audience** (*audient-* + *-ia*)
>
> *oriri, ortus,* "rise": **orient**

As has been noted, in French all present participles were leveled to one ending *-ant*, regardless of the class of Latin verbs from which they were derived. Thus, some English words derived from Latin present participles are spelled differently from what would be expected: *dormire,* "sleep": **dormant** (not "dormient"); *tenēre,* "hold": **tenant** (not "tenent").

I-Stem Infinitives in *-ere* and *-i*

There is a number of verbs whose infinitives end in *-ere* or *-i* that form the present participle in just the way that infinitives ending in *-ire* do, that is, by adding *-iens, -ientis* to the stem.

> *capere, -cipere, captus, -ceptus,* "take": **recipient**
>
> *pati, passus,* "suffer, endure": **patient**

These verbs will be identified in the vocabularies and in the Index of Stems by adding the stem of the present participle to the forms of the verb.

> *capere, -cipere, -cipient-, captus, -ceptus*
>
> *pati, patient-, passus*

Diminutive Nouns

In the previous Lesson, the Latin suffix *-ulus* was introduced. This suffix is one of several in Latin which formed diminutive nouns. The noun thus formed became the name of something thought of as being smaller than the original. Diminutive suffixes, including *-ulus*, are listed below. It should be noted that these suffixes, all ending in *-us* here, the masculine ending, have alternate forms in *-a* and *-um*, indicating that the latter words were thought of as being either feminine or neuter (neither). Only the masculine forms of the suffixes will be listed here, but feminine forms in *-a* and neuter forms in *-um* will be found in the diminutive nouns in Latin and in Medieval Latin and in their English derivatives.

In the listing of the English forms of these suffixes, it will be remembered that the original form of the Latin suffixes can also be used in an English derivative word: **calculus**, from L *calx, calcis*, "stone," + *-ulus*.

Latin Suffix	English Suffix(es)
-culus	**-cle, -cule, -culum**
-ellus	**-el, -ella**
-illus	**-il**
-olus	**-ole**
-ulus	**-ula, -ule**

Sometimes the suffix is added to the dictionary form of the noun instead of to the stem: *corpus, corporis,* "body": *corpusculum,* **corpuscle**.

Often the diminutive noun is not found in Latin literature at any period and has been coined in modern times to suit the purpose. Such formations are called New Latin: *moles, molis,* "mass": NL *molecula,* **molecule**.

Some examples of these diminutive suffixes follow.

mus, muris, "mouse": *musculus,* "little mouse": **muscle**

moles, molis, "mass, bulk": NL *molecula,* **molecule**

morsum, "bite": ML *morsellum,* "little bite": **morsel**

cerebrum, "brain": ML *cerebellum,* **cerebellum**

codex, codicis, "(ancient) book": *codicillus,* "tablet": **codicil**

gladius, "sword": *gladiolus,* "small sword": **gladiolus**

forma, "form, shape": *formula,* "rule, method": **formula**

globus, "sphere": *globulus,* "small sphere": **globule**

Nouns in -*ies*

There are a few Latin nouns that belong to a class whose dictionary form ends in -*ies*. The stem of these words is found by dropping the final -*es*: *species*, "appearance": **special**.

Latin Plurals

Frequently the Latin plural forms of nouns are used as English words. Most nouns in -*us* formed their plurals in Latin by changing the -*us* to -*i*: *alumnus*, "foster son": *alumni*: **alumni**. This -*i* was a "long" vowel, and the length of it should be reflected in the pronunciation of English words that retain the original plural. **Alumni** is pronounced AL-UM' NIGH, with the accent on the second syllable. In the same way, Latin *focus*, English plural **foci**. In English, **c** and **g** are pronounced "soft," that is, like **s** and **j**, before the vowels **e** and **i**; thus, **foci** is pronounced FO' SIGH. Latin *fungus*, "mushroom, **fungus**": English plural **fungi**, pronounced FUN' JEYE, to rhyme with "eye."

Most nouns that end in -*a* in Latin are feminine; thus, while **alumnus** is the word for a male graduate, **alumna** is the word for a female graduate. Most Latin nouns ending in -*a* form their plural by changing -*a* to -*ae*: *alumna*, *alumnae*. In English, the diphthong **ae** is pronounced "ee": **alumnae**: AL-UM' NEE.

In Latin, most nouns that end in -*is* and those whose stem is different from their dictionary form have plurals in -*es*: *index, indicis*, "informer": **index, indices**, pronounced IN' DI- SEEZ; *mos, moris*, "custom": **mores**, pronounced MORE' EEZ.

The plural of all nouns in Latin that are of neuter gender ends in -*a*. Most Latin nouns of neuter gender end in -*um*, although there are some with stems that are different from their dictionary form and which show other endings: *datum*, "something given": **data**; *memorandum*, "worthy of remembering": **memoranda**; *genus, generis*, "race, kind, origin": **genus, genera**. The noun *opus, operis*, "work," was a neuter noun, and, thus, its plural was *opera*. Early in the Latin language, this plural noun became thought of as a feminine singular, and today, **opera** is singular, not plural, and its plural is **operas**.

The plural of nouns in -*ies* is the same form. The word **species** is both singular and plural in both Latin and English.

Vocabulary

Learn the following Latin words, their stems, and the meaning of each. Verbs whose infinitive ends in *-ere* or *-i* and whose present participle ends in *-ient-* will be so indicated. Remember that, in addition to these, verbs in *-ire* or *-iri* form the present participle in this way unless affected by French.

Latin Word	Stem(s)	Meaning
audire, auditus	**aud(i)-, audit-**	hear
capere, -cipere, -cipient-, captus, -ceptus	**-cip-, -cipient-, capt-, -cept-**	take, seize
dormire, dormitus	**dorm-, dormit-**	sleep
genus, generis n.	**gener-**	race, kind, origin
gradi-, gradient-, -gredi-, gressus	**grad-, gradient-, -gred-, gress-**	step, walk
ingenuus adj.	**ingenu-**	frank, candid
nasci, natus	**nasc-, nat-**	be born
oriri, ortus	**or-, ort-**	rise
pati-, patient-, passus	**pat-, patient-, pass-**	suffer, endure
pes, pedis n.	**ped-**	foot
scire, scitus	**sc-**	know
species n.	**speci-**	appearance

Prefix	Meaning
retro-	back, backward

Latin Suffix	English Suffix	Meaning
-orium	**-orium, -ory**	place (for something)

Notes

The original Latin forms of *nasci*, *natus*, "be born," were **gnasci*, **gnatus*; the *g-* appears in the Latin adjectives *praegnans*, *praegnantis*, "pregnant," literally "before birth," and *cognatus* (from *con-* and *gnatus*), "related by blood," literally "born together." The English word **cognate** is used to mean "related by blood," or "related on the mother's side."

Students of language use it to refer to two or more words in different languages, both descended from a common parent-word, as Latin *pater* and Greek *patēr*, as well as Sanskrit *pita*, all derived from an Indo-European word for "father." In the Prefatory Remarks of Lesson 1 there are listed several cognate words in English, Swedish, and German, all descended from words in what is called Proto-Germanic. The English dictionary also lists **agnate**, "related through one's father," from Latin *agnatus*, with the same meaning.

The words **Noel**, "Christmas," and **noel**, "Christmas carol," are borrowed from French and ultimately derived from Latin *natalis*, "concerned with birth," from *natus*, "born." The intervocalic -*t*- dropped out in Old French, as did the ending -*is*, and the remaining two vowels changed to -*oe*-. The adjective **naive**, "unaffected, natural, unsophisticated," also printed **naïve** (the mark over the -**i**- is called a *diaeresis* and indicates that the two vowels **a** and **i** are to be pronounced separately), also borrowed from French, is from Latin *nativus*, with the same loss of the intervocalic -*t*-; it is the doublet of **native**. The Latin noun *nativitas*, "birth," became *naïveté* in Old French and was borrowed into English and is now spelled either with or without the diaeresis but usually with the French acute accent retained on the final -*e*: **naiveté**: "the quality of being naive." It is the doublet of **nativity**.

The **Renaissance**, sometimes spelled **Renascence**, a word borrowed from French and which meant "rebirth," is the name given to the period which saw the revival of the study of the ancient Greeks and Romans, expressed by increased interest in literature and the arts, and marked by the beginnings of modern science. The period of the Renaissance began in Italy in the fourteenth century and moved northward into France and across the channel to England, lasting into the mid-seventeenth century.

The Latin noun *natura*, "birth, property, quality; the world, universe, **nature**," is from the perfect participle *natus* and the noun-forming suffix -*ura*.

The verb *gignere*, *genitus*, "produce, give birth to," is related to *nasci*, *natus*, and both of these verbs are related to the Greek noun *genesis*, "origin." From the perfect participle *genitus* we get **genital** and **genitalia**, a plural word. From the perfect participle of the denominative verb *generare*, *generatus* (from *genus*, *generis*), we get such words as **generator**, **generation**, and **regenerate**.

The adjective *ingenuus* is related to the preceding words. It was a legal term in Rome and meant "freeborn" and pertained to a man (or woman, *ingenua*) whose parents were both freeborn—that is, not slaves—and whose parents before them were both freeborn. Inherent in the meaning of this adjective were all of the qualities that a freeborn Roman had, or should have: honesty, nobility, frankness, and so forth. The word

ingenuous today refers to one who is frank and candid to an extreme measure, often showing childlike simplicity, completely lacking in deceit.

Also related to the above was the noun *ingenium*, which meant one's inborn quality or nature, one's talent or genius. The English word **ingenious** refers to the qualities that a person's *ingenium* should confer on him or her and means "marked by originality and intelligence; clever."

The Swedish botanist, Carl von Linné (1707-1778), better known as Linnaeus, first formulated the principles that are still in use for botanical and biological nomenclature. This system applied a binomial (Latin *bi-*, "two," and *nomen, nominis*, "name") term to plants and animals. Each one is given two names in the form of Latin: the first, capitalized, naming the genus to which it belongs, and the second, not capitalized, a name peculiar to a member of that genus to differentiate it from other members of the same genus. For example, there are many members of the cat family—the wildcat, the lion, the tiger, and so forth—obviously related to one another, and, just as obviously, not related to members of the dog family—the household dog, the wolf, the coyote, and others. The genus of cats is named *Felis*, and, in the binomial system, the wildcat is *Felis catus*, the lion, *Felis leo*, the tiger, *Felis tigris*, and the best known member of this group, the domesticated feline, our common household cat, *Felis domesticus*.

In the four examples above, the first word of the name, *Felis*, is the **genus** or **generic** name, and the second name, *catus, leo, tigris*, or *domesticus*, is the name of the **species.** A species can be defined as a group of animals or plants that shares similar characteristics, although all members of each species are not identical in appearance. That is, all household cats look more or less alike, although they are not identical.

All species of bears belong to the genus *Ursus*. The polar bear is *Ursus maritimus* (Latin *maritimus*, "of the sea," from *mare*, "sea"), the only member of the genus *Ursus* who is at home in the sea; the brown bear is *Ursus arctus* (Greek *arktos*, "the north"), and the grizzly bear is *Ursus horribilis* (Latin *horribilis*, "dreadful," from *horrēre*, "tremble at, dread"). The family dog is *Canis familiaris*, the wolf is *Canis lupus* (Latin *lupus*, "wolf"), and the coyote is *Canis latrans* (Latin *latrare*, "bark"), the "barking dog."

The Latin noun *pes, pedis*, meant "foot," and the denominative verb *expedire, expeditus*, meant "set free, liberate," that is, free an animal's foot from a trap or snare. It came to mean "be profitable *or* advantageous" or "execute promptly," and it is from the last meaning that we get the sense of the English verb **expedite** and the adjective **expeditious**. The noun **expedition** means either "efficient promptness" or "a journey taken for a specific purpose."

The Latin verb which meant the opposite of *expedire* was *impedire*, "entangle the foot, snare, hinder." English derivatives of this verb include **impede** and **impediment**. Latin *impedimenta* (plural of *impedimentum*, "hindrance") meant "baggage," the articles which hindered the army in its advance. We use the word **impedimenta** to refer to things that impede or slow us down, or to any heavy, often unnecessary, equipment.

The **piedmont** region of any land is the area lying at the foot of a mountain (Latin *mons, montis*). It is used particularly for the Piedmont region of Italy (Italian *Piemonte*) in the northwest part of that land, bordering on France and Switzerland, but the term is also applied to areas in this country, particularly to the region lying east of the Appalachian mountains in our South.

The weakened forms of the Latin infinitive and perfect participle of the verb *capere, captus*, "take, seize," *-cipere, -ceptus* are now found in English derivatives borrowed from French as words in -**ceive** and -**cei(p)t**: **receive** and **receipt** (from *recipere, receptus*), **conceive** and **conceit** (from *concipere, conceptus*), **deceive** and **deceit** (from *decipere, deceptus*), **perceive** (from *percipere*) and "**perceit**" (from *perceptus*), an obsolete word last found in English literature in the seventeenth century, replaced by **perception**. Note that, alongside receipt, conceit, and deceit are the later borrowings directly from Latin, **reception**, **conception**, and **deception**.

The Latin imperative of the verb *recipere*, giving the order, "Take!" is *recipe*, the English noun **recipe**. An abbreviated form of Latin *recipe* used in handwritten medical prescriptions was ℞, still retained as a symbol by pharmacists, with the slash through the tail of the R indicating the fact that it was an abbreviation. It is not "RX."

The Latin adjective *princeps, principis*, meant "first in order, foremost," and was formed from the adjective *primus*, "first," and the reduced stem of the verb *capere*, "take, seize." When used as a noun, the word meant "the first, or most outstanding, person." From the time of the early Roman empire it was used as an honorific title for an heir to the throne or, sometimes, for the emperor himself. The word is attested in French literature as early as the twelfth century in the form in which we now know it: **prince**.

Other derivatives of the word include **principal**, from the Latin adjective *principalis*, **principality**, "the jurisdiction of a prince," and **principle**, from Latin *principium*, "beginning, foundation," with the final -**le** added to the stem *princip-* in English on the analogy of other nouns ending in -**ple**, such as **participle**, from Latin *participialis*, from *participium*, "a sharing," from *particeps*, "sharing," from *pars, partis*, "part," and the reduced stem of *capere*, "take, seize." Compare **participant** and **partici-**

pate, from the denominative verb *participare, participatus*, "take part in, share."

From the Latin words *primus*, "first," and *par, paris*, "equal," we have the expression **primus inter pares**, "first among equals."

The adjective **conscious** is derived from the Latin adjective *conscius*, from *con-* + *scire* + *-ous*, and **conscience** is from the present participle of the same verb, *conscient-* + *-ia*. The English adjective **conscionable** is an irregular formation from **conscience** and is found most commonly in its negative form, **unconscionable**, "unreasonable, unfair, unjust, without conscience."

There was a Latin noun, *gradus, -us*, related to the verb *gradi, gressus* and meaning "step, **grade**." The stem of this noun provides the derivation of **gradual**, **graduate**, **graduation**, and also of **retrograde**, "moving backward or opposite to the normal direction," as in retrograde writing, from right to left, the custom in Semitic languages. The opposite of *retrograde* is *orthograde*, from the Greek adjective *orthos*, "straight, regular."

[The words **pass**, **impasse**, **passable**, and **impassable** are not from *passus*, the perfect participle of *pati*, "suffer, endure," but, rather, from the Latin noun *passus*, "step, pace," as in the Latin unit of distance measurement, *milia passuum*, "a thousand paces," or one mile.]

The Latin noun *curriculum*, a diminutive of *currus*, "wagon," and related to the verb *currere, cursus*, "run," meant "race" or "racecourse." It was also used in the sense of the course of one's life, a career. The first use in English of the word **curriculum** to mean a course of study was in the universities of Scotland in the mid-nineteenth century. We use the term **curriculum vitae** (the possessive case of *vita*, "life," meaning "of life") to mean an account of one's career and qualifications. It is customarily presented by a candidate when applying for a position at an institution of higher learning or elsewhere.

Exercises

A. Analyze each of the italicized words in the sentences below.

1. He was a victim of the *incipient* revolution.

2. The idea lay *dormant* in her mind until the time came to put it to use.

3. The house sat close to the road, at the crest of a *gradient*.

4. *Ingress* is forbidden at this time.

5. The document contained twelve lines in *retrograde* writing.

6. Here is a true *Renaissance* man.

7. She felt a *renascent* desire to see her old home.

8. Who could be so *naive* as to believe this?

9. The New Testament tells us of the *Nativity*.

10. She was a charming and *ingenuous* young lady.

11. He told us what had happened in a pleasant and *disingenuous* manner.

12. This wild creature belongs to the same *genus* as the wildcat.

13. To what *species* does this creature belong?

14. The lawyer for the defense delivered a brilliant and *specious* argument.

15. I was told that I could save money by purchasing a *generic* substitute.

16. Separated from the others and unable to *orient* himself, he spent a wretched night.

17. The *abortive* uprising began on Thursday morning.

18. A three-day period of *orientation* will begin on Monday.

19. Please do this in the most *expeditious* way possible.

20. What can I do to *expedite* matters?

21. Those with *prescience* seize the moment for action.

22. It was considered by all to have been an *unconscionable* oversight.

23. He soon regained *consciousness*.

24. The defendant sat there *impassive* throughout the trial.

25. The attorney delivered an *impassioned* speech.

26. Since its *inception*, the regulation has been an annoyance to all.

27. A few months after the great fire, *nascent* flowers could be seen in the fields.

28. I am an *auditor* in this course.

29. The I.R.S.is going to *audit* my tax return.

30. I went for an *audition* yesterday.

B. Analyze each of the following words.

1. auditorium _____

2. audience _____

3. contraception _____

4. ingredient _____

5. naturalization _____

6. dormitory _____

7. impedimenta _____

8. generalize _____

9. incompatible _____

10. patience _____

11. principality _____

12. participation _____

C. Each of the words below is derived from a Latin verb in the vocabulary to this Lesson but has been disguised by the influence of French. For each of these words, give the form (infinitive or perfect participle) of the Latin verb that has supplied the stem.

1. Noel _____   3. deceit _____

2. receive _____   4. naivité _____

D. Each of the words below has been formed from the diminutive of a Latin noun. Consult the Index of Stems and determine the noun that has supplied the stem for each of these words, and its meaning.

1. morsel_____   6. opuscule _____

2. muscle _____   7. umbrella _____

3. gladiolus _____   8. corpuscle _____

4. pupil_____   9. calculus _____

5. libel_____   10. particular_____

E. Answer each of the questions below.

1. What is the meaning of the English term *curriculum vitae*, and how is it pronounced?

2. The two words **principal** and **principle** have the same
   ultimate etymology. What does each mean?

   principal _____

   principle_____

3. Look up the Latin noun *facetiae* in the Index of Stems and
   determine its meaning. What is the meaning of the English
   word *facetious*?

4. What is the meaning of the expression *"primus inter pares"*?

5. The Latin adjective *rudis* meant "unformed, rough, ignorant."
   From the stem *rud-* and the prefix *e-* (for *ex-*, "out of") a
   denominative verb in *-ire* was formed: *erudire, eruditus*,
   which has given us the words **erudite** and **erudition**. What
   is the meaning of the adjective *erudite*?

6. What is meant by the *piedmont* region of any land?

F.   Learn the stems of the verbs below and the meaning of each. Form
an English word from the stem of the infinitive and from the stem of the
perfect participle. Use any prefix(es), suffix(es), or none.

clinare, clinatus, "lean" _____   _____

mutare, mutatus, "change" _____   _____

sumere, sumptus, "take" _____   _____

trudere, trusus, "push" _____   _____

Lesson 5

Ut ager quamvis fertilis sine cultura fructuosus esse non potest, sic sine doctrina animus.

Just as a field, no matter how fertile, cannot bear fruit without cultivation, so the mind cannot develop without instruction. [Cicero, *Tusculan Disputations*]

Inceptive Verbs

Inceptive (often called inchoative, from Latin *inchoatus* or *incoatus*, perfect participle of *inc(h)oare*, "begin") verbs in Latin were those that denoted the beginning of an action. These verbs are characterized by the letters -*sc*- before the ending of the infinitive; they do not appear in the perfect participle. A word element appearing in the middle of a word like this is called an *infix*; thus, -*sc*- is the inceptive, or inchoative, infix. A verb with this infix has already been presented in Lesson 4: *nasci*, "(begin to) be born, come into existence." The perfect participle, *natus*, does not show these two letters.

Most of these verbs do not have a perfect participle, although some that are quite common do. Some of these verbs have a "companion" verb which is not inceptive, and some of them are derived from nouns.

> *adolescere, adultus,* "begin to mature"
>
> *candescere,* "begin to glow," from *candēre,* "glow, shine"
>
> *florescere,* "begin to blossom," from *florēre,* "blossom," from *flos, floris,* "flower"
>
> *valescere,* "begin to gain strength," from *valēre,* "be strong, be healthy"

English Words in -id and -or

The Latin suffix -*idus* was frequently added to the stem of Latin infinitives, especially those in -*ēre*, to form adjectives. These Latin adjectives appear in English as adjectives in -**id**, meaning, "having the quality of" whatever the verb meant. There was often a companion noun in -*or*, to each of these Latin adjectives, giving English nouns in -**or**, meaning "the quality of" whatever the verb meant.

89

candēre, "glow, shine": *candidus*, "shining, **candid**"; *candor*, "sincerity, **candor**"

florēre, "blossom": *floridus*, "blossoming, **florid**"

frigēre, "be cold": *frigidus*, "cold, **frigid**"; *frigor-*, "cold": (*frigorificus*, "cooling, **frigorific**," from *-ficere*, "make")

languēre, "be faint": *languidus*, "faint, weak, **languid**"; *languor*, "faintness, weariness, **languor**"

putrēre, "be rotten": *putridus*, "rotten, **putrid**"

squalēre, "be filthy": *squalidus*, "filthy, **squalid**"; *squalor*, "filth, **squalor**"

stupēre, "be struck senseless": *stupidus*, "senseless, confused, **stupid**"; *stupor*, "insensibility, **stupor**"

tumēre, "be swollen": *tumidus*, "swollen, **tumid**": *tumor*, "swelling, **tumor**"

valēre, "be strong": *validus*, "strong, **valid**"; *valor*, "strength, value, **valor**"

Some few Latin adjectives in *-idus* cannot be traced to verbs: *morbidus*, "diseased, **morbid**," from *morbus*, "disease." **Vapid**, "lacking spirit, dull, lifeless," is from the Latin adjective *vapidus*, which is probably derived from the noun *vapor*, "steam, exhalation, **vapor**," and which originally meant "without life or spirit" and referred to anyone or any creature that had exhaled its last breath. **Acrid** is a recent formation in English from Latin *acer*, *acris*, "sharp-tasting, bitter." There was no Latin "*acridus*," although there was a noun *acrimonia*, "sharpness, bitterness, **acrimony**."

English Verbs in -ish

Sometimes verbs in Middle French, usually those derived from Latin verbs in *-ire*, assumed a stem in *-iss-*, and when such verbs were borrowed into Middle English, this French *-iss-* was usually spelled *-issh-*, and then **-ish** in modern English. This accounts for the spelling of such words as **perish** (ME *perisshen*, from L *perire*, "disappear, be lost," from *per-*, "thoroughly" and *ire*, "go"), **relinquish** (ME *relinquisshen*, from L *relinquere*, "leave behind," from *re-*, "back," and *linquere*, "leave"), and **vanish** (ME *vanisshen*, from VL **exvanire*, from L *ex-*, "out" and *vanus*, "empty"). In this word the Latin prefix has dropped out in Middle English but is assumed to have been there because of the form of the verb *evaniss-* in Middle French.

[**Varnish** is from ML *veronix*, a resin used in the preparation of varnish; the edible root **radish** is from L *radix*, *radicis*, "root," and **rubbish** is from ME *robys*, "trash," of obscure origin.]

English Nouns in -age

Many nouns ending in **-age** come from Old French words which are derived from Latin nouns in *-aticum*, the neuter gender of adjectives in *-aticus*. This ending came to have a variety of meanings in English, some of which can be seen in the following words.

voyage: OF *voyage*, from L *viaticum*, "traveling money," from *viaticus*, "pertaining to a journey," from *via*, "road, way, journey"

village: OF *village*, from L *villaticum*, from *villaticus*, "pertaining to a country house," from *villa*, "country house, farm, **villa**"

damage: OF *damage*, from VL **damnaticum*, from **damnaticus*, "pertaining to loss," from L *damnum*, "loss"

umbrage: OF *umbrage*, from L *umbraticum*, from *umbraticus*, "pertaining to shade," from *umbra*, "shade"

Some words were formed in Old French without any known Latin originals in either *-aticum* or *-aticus*.

carriage: OF *cariage*, from L *carrus*, "wagon"

foliage: OF *feullage*, from L *folium*, "leaf"

[Other words in **-age** include **steerage**, from Old English *stieran*, "steer," **pillage**, from OF *piller*, "plunder," and **garbage**, of uncertain origin. **Sausage** is from Middle English *sausige*, from OF *saussiche*, from Late Latin *salsicia*, from L *salsus*, "salted," from *sal*, "salt." Compare Italian *salsiccia* and French *saucisse*, "sausage," both from LL *salsicia*. The English word **age** is derived from OF *aage*, from VL **aetaticum*, from **aetaticus*, "pertaining to an era," from L *aetas, aetatis*, "age, era."]

Vocabulary

Learn the following Latin words, their stems, and the meaning of each.

Latin Word	Stem(s)	Meaning
calēre, ____	**cal-**	be warm
candēre, ____	**cand-**	glow, shine
caro, carnis n.	**carn-**	flesh
facere, facient-, -ficere, factus, -fectus	**fac-, facient-, -fic-, fact-, -fect-**	make, do
florēre, ____	**flor-**	blossom
folium n.	**foli-**	leaf
ire, itus	**-ient-, it-**	go
-linquere, -lictus	**-linqu-, -lict-**	leave
lucēre, ____	**luc-**	be clear, be light
nocēre, ____	**noc-**	harm
noxius adj.	**noxi-**	harmful
valēre, ____	**val-**	be strong
vanus adj.	**van-**	empty
venire, ventus	**ven-, vent-**	come
via n.	**vi-**	road, way, journey
vorare, voratus	**vor-, vorat-**	eat

Prefix	Meaning
ambi-	around
contra-	against

Latin Suffix	English Suffix	Meaning
-idus	*-id adj.*	having the quality of
-or	*-or n.*	the quality of

Notes

The Latin verb *facere* has produced many derivative words both in Latin and in English. Latin adjectives were formed by adding *-ficus* to the stem of a noun. These adjectives meant "producing (whatever was meant by the noun to which it was added)": *terrificus* (*terror*, "fear, dread"): **terrific**. The meaning of this adjective has changed considerably in modern English, although earlier writers, such as John Milton and Alexander Pope, used the adjective to mean "inspiring fear."

The adjectives **beneficent** and **munificent** are not from the present participle of any verb but have been formed in English as adjectives from the nouns **beneficence** and **munificence**, which are from the Latin nouns *beneficentia* (*bene*, "well") and *munificentia* (*munus, muneris*, "gift; service, duty"); compare English **remunerate**.

The original meaning of *munus, muneris*, was that of a service, duty, or obligation owed to Rome by its citizens who could afford such a burden. These services, called *munera*, included supervision of public roads and bridges, the collection of local taxes, and so forth. Citizens who were exempt from such services, for one reason or another, were *immunis* and enjoyed *immunitas*, freedom from public service. Today we can say that a person is **immune** from arrest or prosecution, or that he or she is **immune** to a disease, or that inoculation and vaccination can produce **immunity** to diphtheria and smallpox. Such a medical procedure as inoculation or vaccination is called **immunization**.

English verbs in -**fy** and -**fied**, the past tense, are derived from Middle French verbs in -*fier* from Latin denominative verbs in -*ficare* which are derived from adjectives in -*ficus*: *magnificus*, "great, highly valued," from *magnus*, "great," *magnificare*, "make much of, value greatly": MF *magnifier*, Middle English *magnifien*: **magnify**. From the perfect participle *magnificatus* of this same verb, we get **magnification**. Similar formations include **beatify, beatification** (*beatus*, "happy, blessed"), **certify, certification** (*certus*, "certain"), and **deify, deification** (*deus*, "god").

From the present stem of *facere* we get the adjective **facile**, "easily done or said," and from the stem of the present participle, **somnifacient** (*somnus*, "sleep"), "inducing sleep," and compounds of -*ficient* such as **efficient** and **efficiency**.

The perfect participle of *facere* has given us such words as **fact, faction**, and **infect, defective, confection**. The passive voice of *facere* was formed in Latin by another verb, *fieri*, "be done," and a form of the subjunctive mood of this verb was *fiat*, "let it be done." The word **fiat** is now used in English as a noun meaning an arbitrary order or decree, as in "It was effected by fiat."

Latin *caro, carnis*, "flesh," has supplied half of the Spanish dish *chile con carne*; the *chile* is from Mexican *chilli*, "hot pepper." **Carnal** thoughts are those that concern the flesh, not the spirit, and the pink flower, the **carnation**, is from Italian *carnagione*, from *carne*, "flesh," so named from the flesh-color of its petals. The word **carnival** is from the Italian *carnevale*, from Old Italian *carnelevare*, meaning "a lifting, or putting away, of flesh," from the Latin denominative verb *levare*, "lift," from *levis*, "light." The Italian *carnevale* was a period of celebration just before Lent, the forty days during which meat was absent from the dining table, from Ash Wednesday to Easter Sunday. The word **carnage** is from French *carnage*, borrowed from Italian *carnaggio*, "slaughter," from Late Latin *carnaticum*, "a tribute of animals given by feudal tenants to their lords," from L *caro, carnis*.

The Latin verb *valēre*, "be strong, be healthy," has given us the pair of adjectives **valid** and **invalid**, as well as the noun **invalid**, pronounced differently from the adjective to differentiate the two words. Just as we wish persons to "fare well" when we take leave of them, the Romans said *vale*, "be well." We find this Latin word at the end of a plaintive lament by the Roman poet Catullus (first century B.C.). His brother had died abroad, and Catullus, in his poem, addresses his brother's remains, telling him that he had traveled through many peoples and across many seas to come to this final resting place, ending with the words, *atque in perpetuum, frater, ave atque vale*: "and forever, brother, hail and farewell."

This verb is found in the same sense of farewell in the words **valedictory**, a farewell address, and **valedictorian**, the one who delivers this address, both from the verb *dicere, dictus*, "speak." *Valēre* had the inceptive form *valescere*, and it is from this verb that we have the words **convalesce** and **convalescent**.

Value is from Medieval French *value*, the feminine form of *valu*, the perfect participle of *valoir*, "be worth," from L *valēre*. **Valor** is from Old French and Medieval Latin *valor*, from the same verb. An *ad valorem* tax is one that is imposed as a percentage of the value of the product. *Valorem* is the accusative, or objective, case of the Latin noun *valor*, "worth, value," following the preposition *ad*, here meaning "for."

The Latin noun *trivium*, from *tria*, the neuter gender of *tres*, the number three, and *via*, "road, way, journey," meant the place where three roads met, or any frequented place, the public square. The adjective *trivialis*, "commonplace," referred to everyday objects of discussion at such a place where people met and talked. The English word **trivia**, although the Latin plural of *trivium*, seems to have been formed in English as a plural noun from the adjective **trivial**, "common, of no consequence."

The Latin noun *ambitio, -ionis*, "a going around," from the prefix *ambi-*, "around," and *itus*, the perfect participle of *ire*, "go," was the word that is represented by the modern expression "canvassing for office," and is the etymology of the word **ambition**. Candidates for public office in Roman times made great efforts to be elected, just as their modern counterparts do, and the solicitation of votes among the populace by various means, including bribery, became so rampant as to cause laws passed forbidding such practices.

A candidate for public office was called a *petitor*, from the verb *petere*, *petitus*, "seek," and his opponent was a *competitor*. Candidates made themselves conspicuous, among other means, by dressing in a dazzling white toga, the outer garment, often adding chalk or some other whitening agent to it. This led to the practice of applying to the *petitor*, the seeker for office, the adjective *candidatus*, "clothed in a white toga," a word derived from the verb *candēre*, "glow, shine"; later, the noun *candidatus*, "candidate for office," replaced *petitor*.

The adjective *candidus*, "shining white," came to mean "unblemished, pure, honest, frank, **candid**"; **candor** is the quality displayed by one who is candid. Early in this century, when electricity came to be used for lighting homes, the new light bulbs were called **incandescent** lights, from Latin *incandescere*, "glow white," an inceptive verb formed from *candēre*, "glow, shine." The Latin noun *candela*, "wax-light, **candle**," is from this verb, as is the noun *candelabrum*, "candlestick, **candelabrum**."

The words **caldron**, **chowder**, **chafe**, and **chauffeur** are all borrowed into English from French and are all ultimately from the Latin verb *calēre*, "be warm." **Caldron** was borrowed from Norman French into Middle English, derived from Late Latin *caldaria*, "warm bath," from Latin *calidus*, "warm." **Chowder** is from French *chaudière*, "kettle," and is derived from the same Late Latin word *caldaria*. The French word came to be applied to the contents of the kettle, a thick soup made by French fishermen, and brought to Newfoundland. The verb **chafe**, "rub, irritate," is from the Middle English verb *chaufen*, "warm," from Middle French *chaufer*, from Vulgar Latin **calfare*, from Latin *calefacere*, "make warm," and originally meant "warm the hands by rubbing them together." **Chauffeur** was borrowed from the French and is from *chauffer*, "heat," ultimately from L *calefacere*, and originally meant "fireman, stoker (of a locomotive or coal-burning ship)." The word came to be applied to a paid automobile driver at the turn of the century and apparently meant the one who "heated up the car."

The suffix **-or** is used in the terminology of medicine to indicate the four classic symptoms of inflammation. These are called "the four *-or* words":

calor, "warmth," from *calēre*, "be warm"

dolor, "pain," from *dolēre*, "be in pain"

rubor, "redness," from *rubēre*, "be red"

tumor, "swelling," from *tumēre*, "be swollen"

The word **calorie**, a unit of heat, was coined in French in 1870 from Latin *calor*. It is used today mainly as a unit to express the heat- or energy-producing value of food when oxidized in the body, and is the amount of heat required to raise one kilogram of water one degree Celsius at a pressure of one atmosphere.

Avoidance of Hiatus

In some few words that have a prefix ending in a vowel and a stem beginning with a vowel, the letter -d- is inserted between these two elements to avoid what is called "hiatus" (Latin *hiatus*, "an opening"), an awkward gap in the sound between prefix and stem. In the word **co-operate**, the hiatus remains, but is accounted for by the use of the dash between prefix and stem. The word **sedition**, from *se-* and *-it-*, the stem of the perfect participle of *ire, itus*, is spelled with the insertion of the -d- in order to avoid the awkward pronunciation of "seition." Other words with this same use of -d- include **redemption**, from *re-* and *-empt-*, from *emere, emptus*, "buy," and **prodigal**, from *pro-* and *-ig-*, the reduced stem of the infinitive of *agere, actus*, "do, drive." These latter two verbs are in the vocabulary of the next Lesson.

Exercises

A. Analyze each of the italicized words in the sentences below.

1. Snow lay on the mountain slopes before them, *candescent* in the afternoon sun.

2. We were surprised by her complete *candor* in relating the events of yesterday.

3. In another *incarnation* he might have been a great leader of the people.

4. "...For if the Gentiles have been made partakers of their spiritual things, their duty is also to minister unto them in *carnal* things." [The Epistle of Paul the Apostle to the Romans 15.27. King James version]

5. He was a large man with shifty, suspicious eyes and a *florid* countenance.

6. This substance is effective as a *defoliant*.

7. The verb "smile" is *intransitive*.

8. After the gloom of the forest, the fields were dazzling in the *ambient* rays of the sun.

9. This restaurant is known both for its good food and its *ambience*.

10. He was jailed for his *seditious* writings.

11. The ship floated low in the water, *derelict*.

12. This *innocuous* remark was the start of long legal proceedings.

13. The mood emanating from the governor's office was that of *ambivalence*.

14. The *efflorescence* of intellectual and artistic genius was never impeded by poverty.

15. Animals usually have the sense to avoid anything *noxious*.

16. We drove slowly through the early-morning *evanescent* mist.

17. The *provenance* of this painting became a point of dispute.

18. She was aided by a *subvention* from this foundation.

19. We were unable to *circumvent* his scheme.

20. The cause of his downfall was wholly *adventitious*.

21. It could never be said that she was a *devious* person.

22. The attorney for the defendant asked for a change in *venue*.

23. He got his job *via* his brother-in-law.

24. After much discussion, we decided that there was no *viable* alternative.

25. Will a traffic signal at this intersection *obviate* the need for a school guard?

26. This action by the dissident legislature was in direct *contravention* of the treaty signed by the president.

27. There was no mention of my friend in the *obit* column of the newspaper.

28. All through his life he pursued these *vain* hopes.

29. She is a *voracious* reader of mystery stories.

30. Her *facile* reply raised some doubts among the members of the committee.

31. He has a *facility* for alienating people.

32. The president was inaccessible, parliament was not convened, and government was by *fiat*.

33. The sandy bottom of the bay was clearly visible through the *pellucid* water.

34. The auditor gave a *lucid* explanation for the missing money.

35. In his *lucid* moments he spoke of recent events.

36. Objects could be seen dimly through the *translucent* curtain.

B. Each of the words below has been borrowed from French at some period but is ultimately derived from a Latin word in the vocabulary of this Lesson. For each of these, give the Latin word, without prefix(es) or suffix(es), and its meaning. Consult the dictionary where necessary.

1. voyage_____

2. issue_____

3. surfeit _____

4. nuisance _____

5. chowder _____

6. vanish _____

7. convey_____

8. perish _____

9. chauffeur _____

10. carnage _____

C. Analyze each of the following words.

1. unambitious _____

2. innocence _____

3. defection _____

4. reconvene _____

5. validation _____

6. eventuality _____

7. efficacious _____

8. elucidate _____

9. contrary _____

10. insufficiency _____

11. impervious _____

12. somnifacient _____

13. munificence _____

14. remuneration _____

15. immunity _____

16. convalescence_____

17. trivial_____

D. Determine the meaning of each of the words below. Consult the Index of Stems where necessary.

1. carnivorous_____   4. frugivorous _____

2. herbivorous _____   5. insectivorous _____

3. piscivorous_____   6. omnivorous _____

E.   Consult the Index of Stems and determine the meaning of the stem of each of the words below.

1. fervid _____   9. prolific _____

2. languid _____   10. soporific _____

3. morbid _____   11. sudorific _____

4. sordid _____   12. mortify _____

5. torpid _____   13. nullify _____

6. turgid _____   14. ossify _____

7. vapid _____   15. petrify _____

8. pacific _____   16. vilify _____

F.   Learn the stems of the verbs below and the meaning of each. Form an English word from the stem of the infinitive and from the stem of the perfect participle. Use any prefix(es), suffix(es), or none.

claudere, -cludere, clausus, -clusus, "shut" _____   _____

haerēre, -herēre, haesus, -hesus, "stick" _____   _____

pellere, pulsus, "strike" _____   _____

spirare, spiratus, "breathe" _____   _____

Lesson 6

Non refert quam multos libros, sed quam bonos habeas.

It does not matter how many books you have, but how good they are. [Seneca, *Epistles*]

Gerundives

Latin verbs had a form called the *gerundive*, an adjective with *-andus*, *-endus*, or *-iendus* added to the stem of the infinitive. These adjectives described something that had to be done, or something which should be done—that is, they denoted necessity or obligation. Many Latin gerundives have been borrowed into English as nouns, most of them with the ending of the neuter singular, in *-um*, or the plural, in *-a*, and now name something or some things which should be done.

memorandum: something which should be remembered (*memorare*, "remember")

memoranda: things which should be remembered

agenda: things which should be done (*agere*, "do")

addendum: something which should be added (*addere*, "add")

addenda: things which should be added

corrigenda: things which should be corrected (*corrigere*, "correct")

propaganda: things which should be spread about (*propagare*, "spread about")

referendum: something which should be brought back (*referre*, "bring back")

quod erat demonstrandum (**Q.E.D.**): that which was to be demonstrated

Some gerundives have passed into English without their characteristic ending, or with the adjectival ending **-ous**.

legend: that which should be read (*legere*, "read")

dividend: that which should be divided (*dividere*, "divide")

subtrahend: that which should be subtracted (*sub-* + *trahere*, "drag")

multiplicand: that which should be multiplied (*multus*, "many" + *plicare*, "fold")

stupendous: causing astonishment (*stupēre*, "be astonished")

tremendous: causing dread (*tremere*, "tremble, fear")

The honorific title **reverend** is from *reverēri*, "respect, honor," from *re-* + *verēri*, "fear."

Latin Nouns in *-ium* From Verbal Stems

Latin nouns ending in *-ium* were formed from the stem of a verb, usually that of the infinitive, but sometimes from the perfect participle. These Latin nouns often appear as English words with the final *-ium* changed to **-y,** but sometimes, when another suffix has been added, all that is left of the *-ium* is *-i-*.

studēre, "be eager": *studium*, "eagerness, **study**": *studiosus*: **studious**

Sometimes the Latin noun in *-ium* is found, but not the verb.

beneficium, "kind deed," from *bene*, "well" and *-fic-*, from *facere*: **beneficial, beneficiary**

solstitium, "stoppage of the sun," from *sol, solis*, "sun," and *-stit-*, from *status*, the perfect participle of *sistere*, "cause to stand": Old French *solstice*, **solstice**

How Prefixes Change the Meaning of Verbs

The Latin language made free use of its total range of prefixes with verbal stems, and the resulting compound verbs, as they are called, often bore little or no resemblance in meaning to the original, unadorned verb. The verb **statuere, statutus**, "stand, place, set up," is a good example of the variety of meanings that a verb can have when prefixes are utilized to form compound verbs.

constituere, constitutus, "set up, establish": **constitute, constitution**

destituere, destitutus, "abandon": **destitute, destitution**

instituere, institutus, "commence, organize, teach": **institute, institution**

restituere, restitutus, "replace, restore": **restitution**

substituere, substitutus, "put in place of": **substitute, substitution**

Or, from *sistere,* (*status*), with the same meaning:

assistere, "stand near": **assist**

consistere, "take a position": **consist**

desistere, "cease": **desist**

insistere, "pursue, urge": **insist**

persistere, "press on, continue": **persist**

resistere, "oppose": **resist**

New Verbs in *-igere, -igare, -igatus*

The infinitive of the verb *agere, actus,* "do, drive," assumed the form *-igere* when a prefix was added to it. The derivative English words from these verbs are usually adjectives in the form of the stem of the Latin present participle: *ex-,* "out," + *agere* = *exigere,* "require, demand": English **exigent,** "requiring attention, needy." Corresponding nouns from these adjectives end in **-ce** or **-cy: exigence, exigency,** "a situation that requires immediate action, emergency."

When another word stem was affixed to *agere,* the new compound verb took the form *-igare, -igatus,* and English derivatives of these verbs are themselves usually verbs ending in **-ate,** with their corresponding nouns ending in **-ation.**

fumus, "smoke," + *agere* = *fumigare, fumigatus:* **fumigate, fumigation**

lis, litis, "dispute," + *agere* = *litigare, litigatus:* **litigate, litigation**

navis, "ship," + *agere* = *navigare, navigatus:* **navigate, navigation**

Vocabulary

Learn the following Latin words, their stems, and the meaning of each.

Latin Word	Stem(s)	Meaning
actus, -u- n.	**actu-**	impulse, drive
agere, -igere, actus	**ag-, -ig-, act-**	do, drive
bene adv.	**ben-, bene-**	well
bonus adj.	**bon-**	good
cavēre, cautus	**cav-, caut-**	be on one's guard
circa adv.	**circa-**	around
dicere, dictus	**dic-, dict-**	speak
dies n.	**di-**	day
diurnus adj.	**diurn-**	by day
emere, -imere, emptus	**-im-, empt-**	buy
fari, fatus	**f-, -fant-, fat-**	speak
ferre, latus	**fer-, lat-**	carry
male adv.	**mal-, male-**	badly
malus adj.	**mal-**	bad, evil
nefarius adj.	**nefari-**	unspeakably evil
otium n.	**oti-**	leisure
salire, -silire, saltus, -sultus	**sal-, -sil-, -sult-**	jump
sistere, status	**sist-, stat-**	cause to stand
stare, status	**sta-, stat-**	stand, be standing
statuere, -stituere, statutus, -stitutus	**statu-, -stitu-, statut-, stitut-**	stand, place
trahere, tractus	**trah-, tract-**	drag, draw

Prefix	Meaning
nec-, neg-	not

Latin Suffix	English Suffix	Meaning
-arius	**-ary** *n.*	person concerned with
-atus	**-ate** *adj.*	characteristic of
-bilis	**-bile, -ble** *adj.*	characteristic of
-bulum	**-ble** *n.*	place for
-icus	**-ic** *adj.*	characteristic of
-ismus	**-ism** *n.*	belief in
-istes	**-ist** *n., adj.*	person concerned with; characteristic of

Notes

Early in the development of the Latin language a phenomenon known as *rhotacism* (named after *rho*, the letter *r* in the Greek alphabet) occurred. It can be explained simply: the letter *s* standing between two vowels became *r*. It cannot be ascertained when or why this process began; it surely must have been a gradual one, and it was completed by the time that the Romans became literate. Examples of rhotacism are common, and it explains why the stem of such Latin nouns as *corpus*, *opus*, and *tempus*, different from their dictionary forms, can be found in the genitive, or possessive, case: *corporis*, *operis*, and *temporis*, forms that had originally been **corposis*, **opesis*, and **temposis*.

Another example of rhotacism is found in the Latin adjective *nefarius*, "unspeakably evil, **nefarious**." The word is from the noun *nefas*, "something contrary to divine law, sin, crime." This noun is from *ne-*, "not," and *fas*, a word related to the verb *fari*, *fatus*, "speak," and meaning "what has been spoken by the gods, divine law." Also related to these words is the noun *festum*, "holy day," and the adjective *festivus*, "joyful." From these Latin words we get **feast**, **festal**, **festive**, and **festival**. French *feston*, borrowed from Italian *festone*, from *festa*, gives us **festoon**. The spelling of French and English *fête* is explained by the fact that, in the transition from Middle French to the modern language, the consonant cluster *-st-* always lost the *-s-*, and the preceding vowel became long in compensation for the lost consonant; the lengthening of the *e* is expressed by the circumflex (^) placed over it. (Other examples of this loss of *-s-* in French include *bête*, "beast," from VL **besta*, from L *bestia*, *tête*, "head," from L *testa*, "clay pot," and *côte*, "edge, shore, coast, " from L *costa*, "rib, side, wall.")

The word **fate** is from L *fatum*, "utterance (of a god), prediction," the neuter gender of the perfect participle *fatus* of the verb *fari*, "speak." This Latin noun referred in particular to the predictions of the Fates, three goddesses who spun, measured, and cut the thread of life for each of us. The names of the three Fates are Greek: Clotho, Atropos, and Lachesis, and the tradition of our destiny being decided by them goes far back in Greek literature through Plato, the tragedians, to Homer, the earliest poet. In Book 7 of the *Odyssey* (lines 195-198), Alcinous, King of the Phaeacians, announces that the stranger (Odysseus) cast up on their shores shall not endure any harm at their hands and will be kept safe until he reaches his home, and only then will he suffer whatever the dread spinners have decided for him with their thread at his birth.

Related to the verb *fari* is the noun *fanum*, "shrine, sacred place." The adjective *profanus* meant "outside of the shrine, common, unholy, **profane**." The adjective *fanaticus* meant "inspired by a god, maddened." Today a **fanatic**, often shortened to "fan," is one who is extremely enthusiastic about anything.

Other derivatives of *fari, fatus*, include **infant** ("not speaking"), **fable** (L *fabula*, "narration, story"), **fatal** (L *fatalis*, "ordained by the Fates, destructive, deadly"), and **infantry** (MF *infanterie*, from Old Italian *infanteria*, from *infante*, "young boy, foot-soldier").

The suffixes **-ism**, "belief, theory, practice," and **-ist**, "one who follows a certain belief, theory, or practice" or "one skilled in a certain action," are derived from French but ultimately, through Latin, from Greek. **Fatalism** is the doctrine that all actions have been ordained and that we can do nothing to change the course of events. The person believing in this doctrine is a **fatalist**.

The suffix **-ist** can also form adjectives. We read about **revisionist** history. This is historical fact that has been "revised" in order to alter, ignore, or conceal events, often those that are unpleasant.

The Latin language had three verbs for the word "stand," where English has but one. We can say "The girl stands the vase on the table," or "The boy stands on his head," or "The economy is standing still." The Latin verb *statuere, statutus*, was transitive—that is, it took a direct object—and meant "place, set (something somewhere)"; the verb *sistere, status*, was also transitive, and meant "cause (something) to stand still, bring (something) to a stop," and *stare, status*, intransitive, meant "stand, be standing, remain standing." It is often difficult to see these shades of meaning in English derivatives of these three verbs. **Statue** and **statute** are from *statuere, statutus*, as are **constitution** and **restitution**; **desist** and **resist** are from *sistere*, while **stance** and **state** are from *stare, status*. The proofreader's mark, **stet**, used as an indication that something that has been marked out of a text is to be restored, is the subjunctive of *stare* and means "let it stand."

The English adjective **stationary**, "fixed, immovable," is from Latin *stationarius*, with the same meaning, from (*stare*) *status* + *-io, -ionis* + *-arius*. In medieval times this adjective came to be used as a noun and the spelling changed to **stationer**; it meant a shopkeeper, usually a bookseller, one who did business from a fixed station, as opposed to an itinerant peddler. The product sold by this shopkeeper was called **stationery**.

[*Statistics*, a branch of mathematics, and its derived word *statistic*, are both from a Greek verb, a cognate of Latin *statuere*.]

The Latin adjective *benignus*, "friendly, kind, well-disposed," from *bene*, "well" and *-gn-*, the stem of *gignere*, "produce," has given us the adjective **benign**, while the adjective **benignant** has been formed in English from **benign** and **-ant**. The Late Latin denominative verb *malignare*, "do harm," is from the Latin adjective *malignus*, "unfriendly, wicked, ill-disposed," and has given us the adjective **malignant** as well as **malign**, both a verb and an adjective.

The Latin verb *cavēre* meant "be on one's guard, avoid, be wary." The imperative of this verb, the form used to give commands, was *cave*, and the expression *cave canem* meant "beware of the dog." We use the subjunctive of this verb, *caveat*, "let (him or her) beware" as a noun meaning a warning against something, and we can say, "Follow these directions, but with this one caveat,…" The expression **caveat emptor** is used in English to mean "Let the buyer beware." From *cautio, cautionis*, derived from the perfect participle of this verb, *cautus*, we get the adjective **cautious**, "on one's guard," and the nouns **caution** and **precaution**, the former also used as a verb.

The Latin noun *otium* meant "leisure, freedom from the call of business." When one was at work there was no leisure time, and, thus, the word for "business" was *negotium*. The denominative verb *negotiari, negotiatus*, "conduct business," is the source of English **negotiate** and **negotiation**.

Exercises

   A. Analyze each of the italicized words in the sentences below.

     1. My brother is an *actuary*.

     2. When we questioned her, her answer was *ambiguous*.

     3. It was obvious that his situation was *exigent*.

     4. Teachers receive high praise and *exiguous* rewards.

     5. The *benefactor* remained unknown.

     6. His *beneficence* was well known.

     7. Before you undertake your trip, here is one *caveat*.

     8. The jury has already handed down an *indictment*.

     9. *Interdiction* has proven to be ineffective in solving the drug problem.

    10. She had made a careful study of *circadian* rhythms.

    11. These are *diurnal* creatures.

    12. The evidence was *circumstantial*.

    13. He bought *redemption* at a high price.

14. The generals urge a *preemptive* attack.

15. The program was *preempted* by the president's speech.

16. Through this entire affair she remained *intransigent*.

17. There were *ineffable* scenes of destruction.

18. It was a *nefarious* act on his part.

19. I had thought that his *indifference* was an affectation.

20. What do you *infer* from this?

21. As he departed he turned and shouted *maledictions*.

22. This is an *otiose* task that you have given me.

23. Are these terms *negotiable*?

24. He proved to be *resilient* in the midst of all of these misfortunes.

25. What are the *salient* features of this plan?

26. After some *desultory* remarks by the chairman, the meeting was called to order.

27. This congressman pays little attention to his *constituency*.

28. This child is *intractable*.

29. The pain in my left shoulder is *intractable*.

30. Attentive to her studies, she paid little heed to the *distractions* of the city.

31. My friend is the *valedictorian*.

32. The jury saw no reason to *indict* him.

33. Her request was a thinly-disguised *peremptory* order.

B. Each of the words below has been derived from a Latin word or words in the vocabulary of this Lesson but is slightly disguised through the influence of French. Give the etymology of each of these words.

1. journey _____

2. redeem _____

3. dismal_____

4. adjourn_____

5. bounty _____

6. maltreat _____

7. portray _____

8. assailant _____

9. distrait_____

10. assault _____

C. Analyze each of the words below.

1. deactivate _____

2. beneficiary _____

3. addictive_____

4. infantile_____

5. preference_____

6. malcontent _____

7. subsistence _____

8. insult _____

9. diary _____

10. dictator _____

11. subtrahend _____

12. referendum _____

13. agenda _____

14. corrigenda _____

15. legendary_____

16. relation_____

D. Answer each of the questions below.

1. What does the abbreviation *cf.* mean? What Latin word does it stand for?

2. What is the difference in meaning between the words *stationary* and *stationery*?

3. Give two doublets of the word *trace*.

4. What is the etymology of *essay*?

5. What is the meaning of *revisionist* history?

6. What is the etymology of *verdict*?

7. What is the meaning of the word *litigious* and what is its etymology?

8. What is the meaning of the Latin expression *caveat emptor*?

9. What Latin words do the initials *Q.E.D.* stand for? What does the expression mean?

10. What is a *fatalist*?

11. Why is the *infantry* so named?

12. What is the etymological difference between a *stable* economy and a horse *stable*?

13. What is meant by a *prodigal* person?

14. The word *ubiquitous* has been formed in English from the stem of the Latin adverb *ubique* and the English suffixes -**it**- (from Latin -*itas*) and -**ous** (from Latin -*osus*). Consult the Index of Stems and determine the meaning of the Latin adverb *ubique*. What does the English adjective *ubiquitous* mean?

15. What does the Latin word *stet* mean, and how is this word used in proofreading?

16. The Latin verb *carēre* (lacking a perfect participle) meant, "be without, lack." One form of this verb, *caret*, is used in proofreading. How is it used, and what does it mean?

E. Consult the Index of Stems and determine the meaning of the stem of each of the words below. Determine the meaning of each of these words. Consult the dictionary where necessary.

1. delirium _____

2. ebullient _____

3. inoculate _____

4. irascible _____

5. jocular _____

6. lapidary _____

7. obfuscate _____

8. profane _____

9. rugose _____

10. serrated _____

11. impeccable _____

F.   Each of the words below has been derived from the perfect participle of a verb in the vocabulary of this Lesson. For each of these, form an English word from the stem of the infinitive of the same verb. Use any prefix(es), suffix(es), or none.

1. reactor _____   3. result _____

2. fatal _____   4. translation _____

G.   Learn the stems of the verbs below and the meaning of each. Form an English word from the stem of the infinitive and from the stem of the perfect participle. Use any prefix(es), suffix(es), or none.

flectere, flexus, "bend" _____   _____

scribere, scriptus, "write" _____   _____

stringere, strictus, "tighten" _____   _____

volvere, volutus, "roll" _____   _____

Lesson 7

Nescire quid antequam natus sis acciderit, id est semper esse puerum.

To be ignorant of what happened before you were born is to remain forever a child. [Cicero, *Orations*].

Vocabulary

Latin Word	Stem(s)	Meaning
cadere, -cidere, casus	**cad-, -cid-, cas-**	fall
caedere, caesus	**-cid-, -cis-**	cut, kill
caput, capitis n.	**capit-**	head
casus, -u- n.	**casu-**	chance
cognoscere, cognitus	**cognosc-, cognit-**	learn, understand
fluere, fluxus	**flu-, flux-**	flow
fundere, fusus	**fund-, fus-**	pour
hospes, hospitis n.	**hospit-**	host, guest
magister n.	**magistr-**	teacher, master
minor, minus adj.	**minor-, minus-**	less, smaller
minuere, minutus	**minu-, minut-**	lessen
os, oris n.	**or-**	mouth
plicare, plicatus or *plicitus*	**plic-, plicat-, plicit-**	fold
specere, -spicere, spectus	**spec-, -spic-, spect-**	look
struere, structus	**stru-, struct-**	build
terra n.	**ter(r)-**	earth
tradere, traditus	**tradit-**	hand over, deliver

Notes

The Latin diphthong *-ae-* is usually reduced to **-e-** in English derivatives: L *aeternitas*, **eternity**; L *haerēre*, "stick," **adhere**. But in the verb *caedere, caesus*, "cut, kill," the diphthong becomes **-i-**. Derivatives of the perfect participle include **incise**, **incision**, and **precise, precision**. Derivatives of the infinitive are mostly words ending in **-cide**, meaning either "the act of killing," as in **suicide** (L *sui*, "of oneself"), **infanticide**,

119

or "a substance used for killing," as in **insecticide**, **pesticide**, and **herbicide**. An exception to this is the verb **decide**, from L *decidere*, "cut off," from *de- + caedere*.

The stem of the infinitive of *cadere, casus*, "fall," has the form *-cid-* following a prefix: **accident**, **incident**, **Occident**, "the place where the sun falls," i.e., the West. While **decide** is from *caedere*, "cut," **coincide** is from *co- + incidere*, "fall upon," from *cadere*, "fall."

The noun **decadence**, "deterioration, decline," and its derivative adjective, **decadent**, are from Late Latin *decadere*, from Latin *de- + cadere*, without the weakening of the vowel of the stem. This verb was borrowed from Old French into Middle English as *decayen*, **decay**.

Cadaver, "corpse," is from Latin *cadaver*, from *cadere*, "fall." **Deciduous** trees are those from which the leaves fall in the autumn, as opposed to the **conifers**, those that bear cones and which remain evergreen.

Some English words ending in **-enza** are from Italian abstract nouns that are derived from Latin nouns ending in *-entia*, from the present participle of verbs with the infinitive ending in *-ere*. The musical term **cadenza**, "a flourish of notes," is from Italian *cadenza*, from Latin *cadentia*, "a falling," from *cadere*, "fall." It is the doublet of **cadence**.

The contagious viral respiratory infection, **influenza**, commonly called "flu," takes its name from Italian *influenza*, from Latin *influentia*, from *fluere*, "flow." In the sixteenth century this name was applied to various epidemic diseases which were afflicting the people of Italy and which were thought of as flowing down from the heavens. Later it was applied specifically to the disease that we know as influenza, which was ravaging western Europe and which, up to then, had been called by the French term *la Grippe*. The words **influenza** and **influence** are doublets.

Latin *caput, capitis*, "head," has many derivatives in English, including some from French, in which the initial Latin *c-* has become *ch-*; **chief**, from Middle English and Middle French *chief*, and its doublet, **chef**, from French *chef de cuisine*, "head of the kitchen." **Chieftain** and its doublet **captain** are from Late Latin *capitaneus*, "headman." **Capital** and **capitol** are not doublets, as they are derived from different Latin words, the former from the adjective *capitalis*, "pertaining to the head," and the latter from *Capitolium*, a temple of Jupiter in Rome. The English word **capitol** is used to mean only the building in which a legislative body sits in a state capital. When applied to the building in Washington in which the U.S. Congress meets, the word has a capital **c**, as it does in the expression *Capitol Hill*, meaning the legislative branch of the U.S. government.

The Latin noun *hospes, hospitis*, meant either "host" or "guest." This double meaning stems from the practice in Roman times of knowing someone in another area with whom one could take lodging and who would act as host. When the friend came to Rome, or wherever his *hospes* lived, the situation would be reversed, and the former host would now be the guest.

The word **hospital** is from Middle English and Middle French from Late Latin *hospitale*, "guest house, place of lodging," the neuter form of the adjective *hospitalis*, "hospitable." The modern French word *hôpital* has the same etymology, with the loss of the -*s*- compensated for by the lengthening of the preceding vowel, -*o*-, indicated by the circumflex accent over that vowel.

English **hospice**, "place of lodging," is from Latin *hospitium*, with the same meaning. **Host** is from Middle English and Middle French *hoste* from L *hospitem*, the accusative, or objective, case of *hospes, hospitis*. Compare the modern French word *hôte*, "host."

Hostel, from Middle English and Old French *hostel*, is from Late Latin *hospitale* and, thus, is the doublet of **hospital**, as is **hotel**, from modern French *hôtel*. The title of the person in charge of a dining room, the headwaiter, **maître d'hôtel**, is from French *maître d'hôtel*, "master of the inn," from Latin *magister*, "teacher, master," a noun from which both English **master** and its doublet, **mister**, are derived.

[The etymology of **hostage** is uncertain. It is derived either from a Late Latin unattested word **hospitaticum*, from Latin *hospes, hospitis*, or from another presumed Late Latin word **obsidaticum*, from L *obses, obsidis*, "hostage," with the initial *h*- added in Middle French by confusion with words derived from Latin *hospes, hospitis*. While the noun (and verb) **host** is ultimately from L *hospes*, "host, guest," the adjective **hostile** is not; it is from L *hostilis*, from *hostis*, "enemy," as is **host**, meaning "a large number."]

The verbs **osculate** and **oscillate** are both from diminutive nouns formed from *os, oris*, "mouth, face." Latin *osculum* meant "little mouth, pretty mouth, kiss," and the denominative verb *osculari, osculatus*, meant "kiss, **osculate**." The Latin noun *oscillum* was used for a little image of a face, in particular, a mask-image of the face of the Roman wine god, Bacchus, which was hung from the trees and which swung back and forth in the breeze. The denominative verb *oscillare, oscillatus*, meant "swing back and forth, **oscillate**."

The denominative Latin verb *orare, oratus*, "speak," was formed from the noun *os, oris*, "mouth," and from this verb we get our words **oration**, **oratory**, and others. From this verb there was formed in Latin a noun *oraculum*, which meant "oracle." An **oracle** was a place to which one could go for answers to questions; it also meant the answers themselves. There were many oracles in the ancient world, the most famous of which was the oracle of Apollo at Delphi, in Greece. Apollo also had an oracle in Italy at Cumae, on the bay of Naples, and this one was presided over by the Sibyl, Apollo's priestess there. The Roman poet Vergil tells us in Book 6 of the *Aeneid* that, when Aeneas and his followers, survivors of the destruction of Troy at the hands of the Greeks, arrived in Cumae, Aeneas appealed to the Sibyl for permission and help to go to the Underworld, known to the Romans as Avernus, to visit the shade of his dead father, Anchises. The Sibyl replied:

> ... *facilis descensus Averno:*
> *noctes atque dies patet atri ianua Ditis;*
> *sed revocare gradum superasque evadere ad auras,*
> *hoc opus, hic labor est.*

"Easy is the descent to Avernus: the door of black Death lies open night and day; but to retrace the steps and to come again to the upper air, that is the task, that is the work."

Nevertheless, she agreed to guide him safely on his journey, and, twelve hundred years later, just as Vergil described the Sibyl leading Aeneas through the realms of the dead, Dante made Vergil his own guide in *Inferno*.

The verb *tradere, traditus*, "hand over, deliver," is a combination of the prefix *trans-, tra-*, "across," and the verb *dare, datus*, "give." This latter verb has a few derivatives in English, including **datum**, "something given (as a basis for reasoning)," usually found in its plural form, **data**, both from the noun *datum*, the neuter gender of *datus*. Related to this verb is the Latin noun *donum*, "gift," and the denominative verb *donare, donatus*, "make a gift," from which we get **donor**, **donate**, and **donation**.

The verb *tradere, traditus*, has given us **tradition** and, through French, its doublet, **treason**, both from L *traditio, traditionis*, "a handing over." Also through French, we have the word **traitor**, from L *traditor*, "betrayer."

[The English word *trade* does not come from L *tradere*; it is a native word, derived from Old English *tredan*, "tread."

Although **confound** is from L *con-* and *fundere*, "pour," **profound** is not from this verb; it is from the adjective *profundus*, "deep," from *pro-* and *fundus*, "bottom, foundation."]

The Latin adjective *praeceps, praecipitis*, was formed from the prefix *prae-*, "before, in front of," and *caput, capitis*, "head," and meant "headfirst, headlong, in haste." From this adjective a denominative verb, *praecipitare, praecipitatus*, was formed, meaning "throw (something) down, rush headlong, drop suddenly." English derivatives of the verb include **precipitous**, **precipitate**, and **precipitation**.

While **imply** and **reply** come from the infinitive *plicare*, "fold," with the spelling due to changes in French, **supply** comes from another verb, *supplēre*, "fill up."

Exercises

A. Analyze each of the italicized words in the sentences below.

1. These are *deciduous* trees.

2. The *cadence* of the tiny waterfall was conducive to sleep.

3. The *incidence* of tuberculosis is rising.

4. This is a fine example of *incisive* writing.

5. Cases of *infanticide* are not uncommon here.

6. Her works were paid small attention except by the *cognoscenti*.

7. He wandered among the people of the country *incognito*.

8. Their teachers failed to take *cognizance* of the abilities of these children.

9. A remarkable *confluence* of ideas resulted in this grand plan.

10. This great city was founded at the *confluence* of these three rivers.

11. The *effluents* from the factory were the cause of this condition.

12. The storekeeper became more *effusive* in his apologies.

13. What this business needs is an *infusion* of money.

14. She was given an *inhospitable* reception.

15. The *magisterial* tone of this letter is annoying.

16. The music is marked *diminuendo* at this point.

17. What is the *minuend*?

18. The movement of the glacial mass was *inexorable*.

19. The chairman gave an *oracular* response to the question.

20. There will always be *oscillations* in the value of these jewels.

21. The *implication* was that he would refuse the nomination if it were offered.

22. What do you *imply*?

23. Acceptance of the nomination was *implicit* in his reply.

24. How would you *construe* these remarks?

25. The *superstructure* was painted a dark green.

26. We must *restructure* our plans.

27. The secretary has provided us with a *conspectus* of the plan.

28. We must be *circumspect* as we move ahead.

29. The mayor is an extremely *perspicacious* person.

30. I remember him as a quiet, *introspective* man.

31. We have no treaty of *extradition* with this country.

32. Her *precipitous* action had disastrous results.

33. There was a *precipitous* path leading from the roadway down to the river.

34. The hostility that arose between these two men *precipitated* a bitter controversy between the opposing parties.

35. There was little *precipitation* last night.

36. In the eyes of the Law, he was a *minor*.

37. The pin was fashioned of red enamel in the form of a tiny rose, with *minuscule* diamond chips on it, glistening like drops of dew.

38. The *minority* leader in the Senate led the opposition to the plan.

B. Each of the words below is derived from a Latin word in the vocabulary of this Lesson, but disguised by the influence of French. Determine the etymology of each of these words.

1. chance_____   5. destroy _____

2. reconnoiter_____   6. despise _____

3. chef _____   7. traitor _____

4. menu_____   8. decay_____

C. Give a doublet for each of the words below.

1. cadenza _____   4. mister _____

2. hostel _____   5. treason_____

3. influenza _____

D. Answer each of the questions below.

1. What is a *connoisseur* and what is the etymology of this word?

2. What is a *minuet* and what is the etymology of this word?

3. What is the meaning of the Latin expression *terra incognita*? How is this expression used today in English?

4. What are the meaning and the etymology of the French term *maître d'hôtel*?

5. What is meant by a *capitol*?

6. What is the *Occident* and why is it so named? What is its opposite and why is it so named?

7. What characterizes an *affluent* person?

8. What is the meaning of the verb *disinter*?

9. What is a *terrarium*?

10. What is the meaning of the noun *extraterrestrial*?

11. The Latin word *infra* meant "below, beneath." What is meant by the expression, "keeping the city's *infrastructure* in repair"?

12. What is the etymological relationship between the words *cadaver* and *accident*?

13. What is the meaning of the word *conifer*? What is its etymology?

E.   The stem or stems of the words below have not been given in the vocabularies of this book. Consult the Index of Stems and determine the meaning of the stem(s) of each of these words. Define each word. Consult the dictionary where necessary.

1. companion _____

2. peninsula _____

3. enervating _____

4. querulous _____

5. supercilious _____

6. ineluctable _____

7. vitiate _____

8. vicissitude _____

9. exhume _____

10. funicular _____

F.   Each of the italicized adjectives below is derived from the present participle of a Latin verb. Consult the Index of Stems and determine the verb from which each of these words is derived and the meaning of the verb. Define each English word.

1. *fervent* protests _____

2. *refulgent* jewelry _____

3. *latent* talents _____

4. *mordant* criticism _____

5. *diffident* speakers _____

G.   Learn the meaning and the stems of each of the verbs below. Form an English word from each stem. Use any prefix(es), suffix(es), or none.

1. *mittere, missus,* "send" _____   _____

2. *petere, petitus,* "seek" _____   _____

3. *rodere, rosus,* "gnaw, eat away" _____   _____

4. *vincere, victus,* "conquer" _____   _____

Lesson 8

Ἐν ἀρχῇ ἦν ὁ λόγος.

In the beginning was the word. [The Gospel according to St. John]

The Greek Alphabet

Upper Case	Lower Case	Name of Letter	English Transliteration
Α	α	alpha	a
Β	β	beta	b
Γ	γ	gamma	g
Δ	δ	delta	d
Ε	ε	epsilon	e
Ζ	ζ	zeta	z
Η	η	eta	ē
Θ	ϑ	theta	th
Ι	ι	iota	i
Κ	κ	kappa	k
Λ	λ	lambda	l
Μ	μ	mu	m
Ν	ν	nu	n
Ξ	ξ	xi	x
Ο	ο	omicron	o
Π	π	pi	p
Ρ	ρ	rho	r
Σ	σ, ς	sigma	s
Τ	τ	tau	t
Υ	υ	upsilon	u, y
Φ	φ	phi	ph
Χ	χ	chi	ch
Ψ	ψ	psi	ps
Ω	ω	omega	ō

Greek Words in English

The alphabet was introduced into the Greek world probably early in the eighth century B.C. It was borrowed from the Phoenicians, a people speaking a Semitic language who lived in Asia Minor, now usually called the Middle East, in an area roughly corresponding to southern Lebanon today. With some adaptations to fit sounds in the Greek language for which there were no equivalents in the Phoenician language, the alphabet, as it was called (Greek *alphabetos*, from the first two letters, alpha and beta), was soon put into use, and the western world became literate.

In the adaptation of certain of the Phoenician symbols for use as vowels in the alphabet, the Greeks began, but did not complete, an interesting idea. They made a distinction in writing between short and long *e* and short and long *o*, but this is where the process stopped, and there was no such differentiation in the other vowels. In this text, long *ē* (eta) and long *ō* (omega) will be indicated with macrons, as was done with long *ē* in certain infinitives in Latin. It should be remembered, however, that these two sets of long and short vowels were different letters in the Greek alphabet. See the alphabet on the first page of this Lesson.

In early inscriptions the letters were carved in what we call capital letters, and our "s," Greek sigma, was represented by the character Σ. Later, when manuscript writing began, the capital letters were modified into a sort of cursive script, and two versions of sigma were used: one form, σ, was used anywhere in a word except at the end; when the sigma did occur as the final letter, it was written ς. The capital letter remained Σ.

It can be seen in the list of Greek letters in this Lesson that there was no character for our letter "h," and no letter for this sound is found in the inscriptions. Later, in manuscript writing, this "h" sound at the beginning of a word was represented by a tiny character resembling an inverted comma; we call it the "rough breathing," and it was placed over an initial vowel when this aspirated sound was needed. It was a weak sound, however, and it frequently disappeared in Greek writing as well as in English derivatives, especially after a prefix or some other word element: Greek *periodos*, "a period of time," from *peri-*, "around" and *hodos*, "road, way, journey," English **period,** but English **harmony** from Greek *harmonia*, "agreement."

When the sound of English "h" followed the consonants *t, p,* or *k* in Greek, a character was devised to indicate each of these sounds: theta (*th*), phi (*ph*), and chi (*ch*); many Greek words had combinations of these letters, and this explains the awkward spelling (and pronunciation) of such words as **diphtheria,** (from *diphthera*, "leather"), so named because of the leather-like membrane that forms around the windpipe in those suffering from this disease, and **autochthonous,** (from Greek *autos*, "self" and *chthōn*, "the earth"), meaning "indigenous, native, found in the place where it originated," such as autochthonous rock.

When a Greek word began with the letter rho (*r*), it always had the rough breathing. It has become traditional in English transliteration of these Greek words to indicate the aspiration *after* the initial *r-*, and this is why English words derived from Greek words beginning with a rho are spelled *rh-*: **rhythm, rhetoric, rhinoceros**, and so forth. Furthermore, if a prefix or another stem preceded a word beginning with rho, or if the rho was in the middle of a word, it was doubled, and the rough breathing followed the second rho: **myrrh, hemorrhage, diarrhea**.

The letter *k* was not used in the alphabet of the Romans in the classical period except for the spelling of two words: *Kalendae*, the Calends, the first of each month, and *Karthago*, Carthage, a city in North Africa. Latin *c* was always pronounced "hard," like English *k*, and, when Greek words containing a kappa (*k*) were borrowed into Latin, they were spelled with a *c*: Greek *Korinthos*, Latin *Corinthus*, Corinth, a city in Greece. Later borrowings from Greek into English retained this tradition, but with a few significant exceptions: Greek *leukos*, "white," **leukocyte**, "white blood cell," Greek *kinētikos*, "relating to motion," **kinetic**, but Greek *kephalikos*, "relating to the head," **cephalic**; *kranion*, "skull," **cranium**.

Greek Diphthongs in English

When the Latin-speaking people of Italy borrowed the alphabet from the Greeks, the Greek diphthong omicron upsilon (ου) was written as simple *u* in Latin letters, as the Latin language, at that time, did not use the diphthong *ou*; then, the simple Greek letter upsilon was written *y* in Latin words in order to differentiate it from the diphthong. English retains this tradition, and, in this book, a single Greek upsilon will be transliterated **y**, the practice in most English dictionaries, while the Greek diphthong omicron upsilon will be transliterated **ou**.

Since it is the tradition in English to spell Greek words as they were spelled in Latin, words with the omicron upsilon diphthong will be given their Latin spelling: Greek *Mousa*, "a goddess, patron of the Arts," Latin *Musa*, English **muse**; *Ouranos*, "the god of the heavens, " Latin and English **Uranus**.

The Greek diphthong *ei* usually became *i* in Latin: Greek *eidōlon*, "image," Latin *idolum*, **idol**. Greek *ai* became *ae* in Latin: Greek *sphaira*, Latin *sphaera*. It has been mentioned in a previous Lesson that the Latin diphthong *ae* usually became *e* in English derivatives: Latin *sphaera*, **sphere**. British derivatives of Greek-derived words with this diphthong usually retain the Latin *ae*: Greek *haimorrhagia*, "violent discharge of blood," Latin *haemorrhagia*, British English *haemorrhage*, American English **hemorrhage**.

The Greek diphthong *oi* usually became *e* in Latin, and English derivatives of such words retain the *e*: Greek *oikos*, "house": **economy** (-**nomy**, "law, rule, arrangement," from *nomos*, "law").

The Greek diphthongs *au* and *eu* were spelled the same way in Latin, and English words derived from Greek words with those diphthongs keep the same spelling, even if the word was not borrowed into Latin: Greek *autos*, "self," English **autistic**; Greek *Euripidēs*, Latin and English **Euripides**.

The Greek letter gamma (*g*) assumed a nasal "n" sound, as in English *sing*, before another gamma and before kappa (*k*) and xi (*x*), and in Latin borrowings the spelling reflected this sound: Greek *aggelos*, Latin *angelus*, "messenger," English **angel**. Since all Greek words that contain this sound, whether borrowed into English from Latin or from the original Greek, are now spelled with this nasal "n," the Greek originals of these words will be given here in the Latin spelling; for example, Greek *lynx*, "a wild feline creature," **lynx**, (not Greek "*lygx*"), Greek *enkryptein*, "hide (something)," **encrypt**. In these two English words, the **y** represents Greek upsilon.

When a Greek word contained the sound of *p* followed by that of *s*, there was a single character, psi (ψ), that represented these two sounds; this letter is found in such words as **pseudonym** (*pseudēs*, "false" and *onyma*, "name") and **psychology** (*psychē*, "the mind" and English -**logy**, "study of," from Greek -*logia*).

Greek Nouns

Greek nouns, like those in Latin, were considered to be either masculine, feminine, or neuter (neither) gender. Many Greek nouns had endings resembling those in Latin:

Masculine	Feminine	Neuter
-*os* (Latin -*us*)	-*ē* or -*a* (Latin -*a*)	-*on* (Latin -*um*)

English derivatives of these nouns are found in one of three ways:

1. With the original Greek ending
2. With the ending changed to the Latin form
3. With the ending dropped or changed to silent -**e**.

Sometimes the final -**e** derived from Greek nouns in -*ē* or -*a* is pronounced: Greek *akmē*, "highest point," English **acme**. The ending -*ia* is frequently changed to English -**y**: Greek *harmonia*, "agreement," English **harmony**.

Commencing here and in the vocabularies of this book, Greek words will be printed in Greek characters, followed by a transliteration into Roman letters. Accent marks found in printed works will not be indicated on the Greek words. The rough breathing ("h") will be shown as an inverted comma over an initial vowel or rho, and over the second of a doubled rho.

Greek Noun	Meaning	English Derivative
κοσμος *kosmos*	the universe	cosmos
ῥομβος *rhombos*	four-sided figure	rhombus
κωνος *kōnos*	fir cone	cone
ὑμνος *hymnos*	festive song	hymn
ακμη *akmē*	highest point	acme
ζωνη *zōnē*	belt	zone
Μουσα *Mousa*	a goddess of the Arts	muse
μυρῥα *myrrha*	aromatic gum	myrrh
ἁρμονια *harmonia*	agreement	harmony
νευρον *neuron*	sinew, tendon	neuron
κρανιον *kranion*	skull	cranium
πεταλον *petalon*	leaf	petal

Greek Adjectives

One class of Greek adjectives, by far the largest, had the endings *-os*, *-ē* (or *-a*), or *-on*, depending upon the gender of the noun that the adjective governed. In this book, adjectives of this class will be given in the vocabularies and in the Index of Stems only in the form of the masculine, ending in *-os*. The stem of these adjectives is found by dropping these two letters.

Greek Adjective	Stem	Meaning	English Word
μικρος *mikros*	**micr-**	small	**microcosm**
φιλος *philos*	**phil-**	loving	**Anglophile**
αριστος *aristos*	**arist-**	best	**aristocracy**
σοφος *sophos*	**soph-**	wise	**philosophy**

The Combining Vowel

Many English words derived from Greek have two or more stems, as can be seen in the examples above. If the first stem ends in a consonant—that is, any letter other than the vowels *a*, *e*, *i*, *o*, or *u*—and the second stem begins with a consonant, a vowel, called the *combining vowel*, is inserted between the two stems. In Greek-derived words this vowel is usually **o**, and it is inserted only for the purpose of pronunciation: **microcosm**, for example, rather than the unpronounceable "micrcosm." Occasionally, however, the combining vowel is found following stems ending in a vowel: **geology** (ge-, "the earth," from Greek *gē*).

Words with More Than One Stem

When Roman writers began to translate Greek words into Latin, in many instances there was no Latin word that was the equivalent of the Greek, and, rather than attempting to coin a Latin word, they simply borrowed the Greek one. Thus, Cicero, the Roman statesman and writer, encountering the Greek word *philosophia* and finding no Latin equivalent, borrowed it. It is, of course, our word **philosophy**. The elements of the word are Greek *philos*, "loving" and *sophia*, "wisdom, knowledge," from the adjective *sophos*, "wise, skilled."

The Greek language, more so than Latin or English, lends itself readily to such multiple-stem formations, and, just as Cicero did, English writers borrowed words and, especially, formed new ones from Greek elements.

Greek *hydrophobia*, "fear of water," from *hydōr*, "water" and *phobos*, "fear," was borrowed into Latin in that same form, and later, into English. On the analogy of such -*phobia* words in Greek and Latin, this element became an English word, **phobia**, "any illogical fear," and new words were freely coined in English to name specific fears: **ailourophobia** (Greek *ailouros*, "cat"), **thanatophobia** (*thanatos*, "death"), **nyctophobia** (*nyx, nyktos*, "night"), **panphobia** (*pan*, "all, everything"), and even **phobophobia**, "fear of fear itself." English formations from Greek *phobos* include words in which the second element is -**phobe**, meaning "a person who has a specific fear, aversion, or dislike," such as **Francophobe**, "one who dislikes the French," **Anglophobe**, "one who dislikes the English," and **xenophobe**, "one who dislikes anything foreign," from *xenos*, "stranger."

In just such a way as English words in -**phobia** and -**phobe** entered our language, other Greek words were used as the second element of new compound words. The element that meant the opposite of -**phobe** was -**phile**: **Anglophile**, "a lover of things English," and **bibliophile**, "a lover of books" (Greek *biblion*, "book"), to give two examples.

From Greek words ending in -*logia*, from *logos*, "word," there are many English words in -**logy** meaning "the study of (whatever is indicated by the first element of the word)": **psychology** (*psychē*, "the mind"), **geology** (*gē*, "the earth").

Word elements such as -**phobia**, -**phobe, -phile**, and -**logy** are called *combining forms*. These and others will be listed following the vocabulary of this Lesson.

The Greek suffix -*istēs* meaning "a person concerned with (whatever is indicated by the preceding element)" gives us the suffix -**ist** and such words as **psychologist** and **geologist**.

Vocabulary

Learn the following Greek words, the stem of each, and its meaning. Here, and in all subsequent vocabularies, nouns will be indicated by the abbreviation *n.*, adjectives by *adj.*, and adverbs by *adv.* Greek words in the vocabularies and in the Index of Stems will be listed alphabetically by their English stem.

Greek Word	Stem	Meaning
αριστος *aristos adj.*	**arist-**	best
βιος *bios n.*	**bi-**	life
χρονος *chronos n.*	**chron-**	time
κοσμος *kosmos n.*	**cosm-**	order; the universe
κρατος *kratos n.*	**crat-**	power, rule
δημος *dēmos n.*	**dem-**	the people
γη *gē n.*	**ge-**	the earth
λογος *logos n.*	**log-**	word
μετρον *metron n.*	**metr-**	measure
μικρος *mikros adj.*	**micr-**	small
φιλος *philos adj.*	**phil-**	loving
φοβος *phobos n.*	**phob-**	fear
ψυχη *psychē n.*	**psych-**	the mind
σκοπος *skopos n.*	**scop-**	observer
σοφος *sophos adj.*	**soph-**	wise
τηλε *tēle adv.*	**tele-**	far away

Combining Forms

Learn the combining forms below and the meaning of each. Determine the meaning of the English words given as examples. Note that in Greek stems ending in -*t*, as in *krat-*, from *kratos*, "power, rule," the combination of this final -*t* and the noun-forming suffix -*ia* often results in English words in -**cy**: Greek *dēmokratia*, from *dēmos*, "the people," **democracy**.

-cracy (*kratos*, "power, rule"), "rule by"	aristocracy
-crat (*kratos*), "believer in the rule by"	democrat
-logist (*logos*, "word"), "one who studies"	biologist
-logy (*logos*), "the study of"	cosmology
-meter (*metron*, "measure"), "instrument for measuring"	micrometer
-metry (*metron*), "the process of measuring"	geometry
-phile (*philos*, "loving"), "one who loves *or* admires"	Francophile
-phobe (*phobos*, *"fear"*), "one who fears *or* dislikes"	Anglophobe
-phobia (*phobos*), "the fear *or* dislike of"	acrophobia
-scope (*skopos*, "observer"), "instrument for observing"	telescope
-scopy (*skopos*), "the process of observing"	microscopy

The form **-meter** was coined in English in the seventeenth century irregularly from Latin *metrum* (Greek *metron*), while the form **-metry** is a regular development in English from Greek nouns in *-metria*, from *metron*.

Suffixes

Suffixes that form nouns will be indicated by the abbreviation *n.*, and those that form adjectives by *adj.*

Greek Suffix	English Form	Meaning
-ια	**-ia, -y** *n.*	process, condition
-ικος	**-ic** *adj.*	characteristic of
-ιστης	**-ist** *n.*	person concerned with

Notes

The fear of water implicit in the word **hydrophobia** (Greek *hydōr*, "water") is caused by painful spasms of the larynx when one suffering from this dread disease attempts to drink. The ancient Greeks and Romans knew of the disease. Celsus, the first century A.D. Roman writer, calls it by its Latin name, *rabies* ("madness"), and tells us that in those who have been bitten by a rabid dog there arises a fear of water, which the Greeks called *hydrophobia*, "in which the sufferer is tormented simultaneously by thirst and dread of water." He goes on to say that there is little hope for those who are in this state and then proposes one last remedy: "Throw the patient unexpectedly into a pool of water when he is not looking. If he cannot swim, allow him to sink and drink the water, and then raise him up; but if he can swim, keep pushing him under so that he becomes filled with water, although unwillingly. In this way both his thirst and his fear of water are removed at the same time." (*De Medicina* 5.27.2).

The Phi Beta Kappa Society was founded in order to give recognition to students in American colleges who have achieved academic distinction. Those who are elected to this Society receive a gold key bearing the initials Φ Β Κ, standing for the motto of the Society, *philosophia biou kybernētēs*, "Philosophy the Guide of Life." The Greek word *kybernētēs* meant "helmsman of a ship," and is related to the Latin *gubernator*, which has the same meaning. The Latin word is the source for English **gubernatorial** and, through French, **governor**. The Greek word *kybernētēs* has given us our word **cybernetics**, "the science of automatic control systems"; the suffix **-ics** in this word means "the science of."

To the early Greeks, the word *philosophia* meant the love of knowledge, or the study and systematic treatment of any subject. The earliest Greek philosophers of whom we have any record were concerned with what we would call physical science—the reasons for natural phenomena such as rain and wind, as well as the physical structure of the universe around them.

It was Socrates (*c.* 470-399 B.C.) who is thought of as directing the mind of man from the world outside to the soul within, and, for this, is known as the father of modern philosophy. It was during Socrates' lifetime that the Sophists appeared in Greece. These were teachers of rhetoric, the art of speaking, and one of the most important elements of their lectures was the art of speaking with equal forcefulness on either side of any argument. The Sophists have left their name in the English words **sophism**, "an argument seemingly valid, but in actuality not," **sophistic**, "believable but specious," and **sophistry**, "the use of sophistic argumentation; deceptive reasoning."

The original meaning of the Greek noun *kosmos* was "orderly arrangement" and meant the opposite of *chaos*, "disorder." Later this term was applied to the universe, from its perfect order. English words from this meaning of the Greek word include **cosmos**, **cosmology**, and **cosmic**. From the meaning "order," a denominative verb was formed meaning "put in order, adorn, embellish," and from the Greek verb an adjective, *kosmētikos*, was coined, meaning "skilled in adornment." From this adjective we get our adjective **cosmetic**, "decorative, ornamental," and the noun **cosmetic**, "anything that adorns or beautifies," usually found in the plural, **cosmetics**, and the recent (1926) coinage, **cosmetologist**.

The adjective **cosmopolitan**, "worldly, having wide-ranging interests," is from the Greek noun *politēs*, "citizen," and, thus, has the literal meaning of "characteristic of a citizen of the universe." The suffix **-an** is from Latin *-anus*.

Exercises

A. Give the English spelling for each of the following. Identify each. Consult the list of Biographical Names in your dictionary if necessary.

1. Ποσειδων _____

2. Οδυσσευς _____

3. Σωκρατης _____

4. Αφροδιτη_____

5. Ευριπιδης _____

6. Σοφοκλης _____

7. Περικλης _____

8. Αθηνα _____

9. Διονυσος_____

10. Αισχυλος _____

B. The stem or stems of the italicized words in the sentences below can be found in the vocabulary of this Lesson. Separate each of these words into its elements (stem or stems and suffix, if there is one) and give the meaning of each element. Define each word as it is used in the sentence.

1. On the hill, overlooking the river, were the homes of the *aristocracy* of the town.

2. My friend is studying *microbiology*.

3. Scientists are searching for the *microbe* that causes this disease.

4. This is not the *democratic* way to do things.

5. I always hated *geometry*.

6. The attorney for the defense was skilled in *sophistic* argumentation.

7. These eyeglasses have *telescopic* lenses.

8. This lady has *psychic* abilities.

9. Someone has taken the *chronometer*!

10. This and other *chronic* disorders yield slowly to treatment.

11. He maintained a *philosophic* view of the troubles that continually assailed him.

12. This community is a *microcosm* of our country.

13. When the subject was introduced at the convention, it started an argument of *cosmic* proportions.

14. This man insists that he is being bombarded with *cosmic* rays.

15. The improvements brought about by the new president were largely *cosmetic*.

16. Who is there who will bring *cosmos* out of this chaos?

C. One of the two stems in each of the words below will be known to you from the vocabulary of this Lesson. Consult the Index of Stems and determine the meaning of the other stem. Define each word.

1. Philadelphia _____

2. philodendron _____

3. plutocrat_____

4. sophomore_____

5. xenophobe _____

D. Consult the Index of Stems and determine the meaning of the Greek word that has supplied the stem for each of the following.

1. zone_____   4. strategy_____

2. Bible_____   5. arctic_____

3. cynic _____   6. Xerox _____

E. Consult the Index of Stems and determine the meaning of the word that has supplied the stem for each of the phobias below.

1. agoraphobia _____   7. necrophobia_____

2. ailourophobia_____   8. ornithophobia _____

3. arachnophobia_____   9. panphobia _____

4. claustrophobia_____   10. ponophobia _____

5. heliophobia_____   11. thanatophobia _____

6. hypnophobia _____   12. zoophobia _____

F. Answer each of the following questions.

1. What is the significance of the name of the disease *hydrophobia*, and what is the Latin name for this disease?

2. The English word *cybernetics* is from the Greek noun *kybernētēs*. What did this Greek word mean, and what is the meaning of the English word?

3. What is the etymology of the word *governor*? Give an English word borrowed directly from the Latin stem of this word.

4. Socrates, the Athenian philosopher of the fifth century B.C., was accused of being a sophist—that is, of practicing what we now call *sophistry*. What is the meaning of this English word?

5. What are the Greek names for the letter Φ B K, and what do the words represented by these letters mean?

6. What does a *cosmologist* study? What does a *cosmetologist* study?

G. Consult the Index of Stems and determine the field with which each of the following specialists is concerned.

1. dendrologist _____   7. ichthyologist _____

2. dermatologist _____   8. ornithologist _____

3. enologist_____   9. petrologist _____

4. ethnologist_____   10. seismologist_____

5. gerontologist _____   11. speleologist _____

6. herpetologist _____   12. trichologist _____

Lesson 9

Κακῆς ἀπ᾽ ἀρχῆς γίγνεται τέλος κακόν.

From a bad beginning comes a bad finish. [Euripides, *Fragment*]

More Greek Nouns

There were Greek nouns other than those with the endings *-os*, *-ē* or *-a*, *-on* discussed in Lesson 8. Two such classes of nouns had endings in *-is* and *-ēs*; the stem of each of these is found by dropping these two letters: Greek *basis*, "pedestal, foundation," English **basis**, **basic**, **base**; Greek *chartēs*, "leaf of papyrus (used for writing)," English **chart**.

As in Latin there was a class of nouns whose stem could be found only by knowing some form other than the dictionary form of the word. For these nouns it has become traditional, as in Latin, to give the case of possession, called the genitive case, along with the entry word. This form in Greek nouns always ends in *-os*, and the stem is found by dropping these two letters. Sometimes the dictionary form itself is used as an English word or as a stem.

Greek Noun	Stem(s)	Meaning	English Word(s)
ανηρ, ανδρος *anēr, andros*	**andr-**	man	**androgynous**
γυνη, γυναικος *gynē, gynaikos*	**gyn-, gynec-**	woman	**misogynist, gynecology**
ἑλιξ, ἑλικος *helix, helikos*	**helic-**	spiral	**helix, helicopter**
φως, φωτος *phōs, phōtos*	**phos-, phot-**	light	**phosphorus, photograph**

More Greek Adjectives

There were Greek adjectives ending in *-ēs*, and, as with nouns, the stem is found by dropping these two letters: *pseudēs*, "false," **pseudonym** (*onyma*, "name"). There was a large group of adjectives ending in *-ys*; the stem is found by dropping the final -s: *polys*, "many," **polygamy** (*gamos*, "marriage").

Finally, there were a few adjectives whose stem can be found only in the possessive case, as with the nouns discussed previously: *melas*, *melanos*, "black," **melanoma** (Greek *-ōma*, "swelling").

Greek Verbs

Greek verbs are cited in most English dictionaries in the form of the present infinitive, just as Latin verbs are. The infinitive of most Greek verbs ends in -ειν (*-ein*), although several other endings are found, such as -αν (*-an*), -ουν (*-oun*), and -εσθαι (*-esthai*). In all of these, the stem is found by dropping the ending.

Greek verbs can have as many as six principal parts, as they are called, from which the various tenses are built, but stems of forms other than those of the infinitive are rarely used in English words. When the stem of some form other than the infinitive is found in an English word, a Greek noun can usually be found to supply this stem. For example, the Greek verb meaning "suffer" was πασχειν (*paschein*); there are no English words from the stem *pasch-*. There is, however, another form of the verb whose infinitive is *pathein*, with the stem *path-*, as in such words as **empathy**, **sympathy**, and **pathetic**. For such English words we can cite a noun, παθος (*pathos*), "suffering," for the stem of these words, as well as for the Greek noun itself, **pathos**.

Sometimes within the Greek language itself, a combining form was created from a verb, with a stem slightly different from that of the verb. For example, from the verb *pherein*, "carry, bear," with the stem **pher-**, a combining form *-phoros* is found, forming adjectives meaning "carrying, bearing," as in *phōsphoros*, "light-bearing." When such is the case, the two stems will be given for the verb in the vocabularies and in the Index of Stems: *pherein*, "carry, bear," **pher-**, **phor-**.

Vocabulary

Greek Word	Stem(s)	Meaning
ανηρ, ανδρος *anēr, andros n.*	andr-	man, a male
ανθρωπος *anthrōpos n.*	anthrop-	human being
αυτος *autos n.*	aut-	self
κρυπτειν *kryptein*	crypt-, cryph-	hide (something)
γαμος *gamos n.*	gam-	marriage
γραμμα, γραμματος *gramma, grammatos n.*	gram-, grammat-	something written; small weight (only with numbers)
γραφειν *graphein*	graph-	write, record
γυνη, γυναικος *gynē, gynaikos n.*	gyn-, gynec-	woman
ἑλιξ, ἑλικος *helix, helikos n.*	helic-	spiral
μονος *monos adj.*	mon-	single, one
ονυμα, ονυματος *onyma, onymatos n.*	onym-, onymat-	name
πας, παντος *pas, pantos adj.*	pan-, pant-	all, every
παθος *pathos n.*	path-	suffering; disease
φερειν *pherein*	pher-, phor-	carry, bear
φωνη *phōnē n.*	phon-	sound, voice
φως, φωτος *phōs, phōtos n.*	phos-, phot-	light
πολυς *polys adj.*	poly-	many
θεος *theos n.*	the-	a god
τοξον *toxon n.*	tox-	bow (in archery); poison

Prefixes

Note that when a prefix ended in a vowel and the following stem began with a vowel or *h*, the final vowel of the prefix usually dropped off. Also, a final consonant of a prefix usually assimilated to an initial consonant of the following stem. Assimilated forms will be given here.

Greek Prefix	English Form(s)	Meanings
α- (αν-)	a- (an- before a vowel)	not, without
αντι-	ant-, anti-	against, opposite
απο-	apo-	away from
δυς-	dys-	bad, disordered
εν-	en-, em-	in, into
επι-	ep-, epi-	on, upon, after
ευ-	eu-	good, well, pleasant
συν-	syn-, sym-, syl-, sys-	with

Suffixes

Greek Suffix	English Suffix	Meaning
-ητικος	-etic *adj.*	characterized by
-ισμος	-ism *n.*	belief in
-ιζειν	-ize (forms verbs from nouns)	
-οειδος	-oid *adj.* and *n.*	having the form *or* appearance of
-τικος	-tic *adj.* and *n.*	characterized by
-ωσις	-osis *n.*	state, process

The suffix *-in* or *-ine* was adapted from *-ina*, the feminine gender of the Latin adjectival suffix *-inus*, and now indicates a chemical compound. It is commonly used with both Latin and Greek stems: **insulin** (Latin *insula*, "island"), **toxin** (Greek *toxon*, "poison"), **chlorine** (Greek *chloros*, "green").

Notes

It will be observed that many English words derived from Greek stems have Latin-derived prefixes and/or suffixes. The Greek adjective *phōsphoros*, "light-bearing," for example, has been borrowed into English as **phosphorus**, with the Latinized ending *-us*. The word **anonymous** shows the English suffix **-ous** derived from Latin *-osus*. Such words, with elements from both Greek and Latin (or from any two or more languages) are called "hybrids" or "hybrid words," from the Latin noun *hybrida*, a name given to an animal produced from two different species, or to a person whose parents were of different races. The term was often applied to the child of a Roman father and a foreign woman, or of a freeman and a slave. Multiple-stem hybrid words are frequently found with one stem derived from Greek, and the other from Latin: **television** (Greek *tēle*, "far away," and Latin *visus*, from *vidēre*, "see"), **automobile** (Greek *autos*, "self," and Latin *mobilis*, "movable"), and **neonatal** (Greek *neos*, "new, recent," and Latin *natalis*, "of birth," from *natus*, perfect participle of *nasci*, "be born").

The Greek noun *toxon* meant "bow," as used in archery, and, in the plural, *toxa*, often meant "arrows." The noun *toxikē* meant "archery," and the adjective *toxikos* meant "skilled in the use of the bow." The noun *pharmakon* meant any drug, remedy, medicine, or poison; thus, the term *toxikon pharmakon* referred to the poison that was smeared on arrowheads in order to disable the enemy in war or an animal in the hunt. It is from this use of the adjective *toxikon* that we get our adjective **toxic**, "poisonous," and the noun **toxicology**, "the science that deals with poisons."

In Medieval Latin, a denominative verb *intoxicare, intoxicatus*, "make senseless with alcoholic liquor," was coined, the source of the English words **intoxicate** and **intoxicant**.

The suffix **-in** or **-ine** is used in words meaning chemical compounds, thus our words **toxin** and **antitoxin** (Greek *anti-*, "against"). The original meaning of the Greek noun *toxon* is retained in the English word **toxophilite**, "a lover of archery," from Greek *philos*, "loving," and the suffix *-itēs*, English **-ite**, "a person concerned with."

Many Greek words have Latin cognates—words in that language derived from the same parent Indo-European word as the Greek words. One such pair of cognates is the Greek and Latin verbs *pherein* and *ferre*, both with the same meaning, "carry, bear." The Greek adjective *phōsphoros* meant "light-bearing," and, as a noun, meant the morning star that heralded the break of day, the planet Venus. The morning star is also called Lucifer, a word derived from Latin and meaning "light-bearing," from *lux, lucis*, "light," and **-fer**, from *ferre*. This Lucifer is thought of as being the rebel archangel who attempted to dethrone God and who was cast down from heaven, an action referred to in the Old Testament in *Isaiah* 14.12: "How art thou fallen from heaven, O Lucifer, son of the morning! how art thou cut down to the ground…" [King James Version].

The Greek form -οειδος, *-oeidos*, given in the list of suffixes, is not really a suffix, but a Greek combining form. The initial omicron (*-o*) represents the combining vowel, and the rest of the form is the noun *eidos*, "form, shape, appearance." It is convenient to treat it as an adjectival suffix, spelled **-oid** in English: **spheroid**, "sphere-shaped." As adjectives can be used as nouns, some words in **-oid** are nouns: **android**, "a robot in human form."

The Greek noun *pathos*, "suffering," is related to the Latin verb *pati*, "suffer." In English derivatives it often has a milder sense, that of feeling or compassion, as in the word **empathy**, "the capacity for understanding the problems of others," or of awareness, as in **telepathy**, "communication by extrasensory means."

The ancient Greek writers used the word *pathos* to mean the unpleasantness associated with any calamity, misfortune, or accident, and Galen, a Greek medical writer of the second century A.D., used the word *pathologia*, **pathology**, to mean the branch of science concerned with the origin and nature of disease.

More recent medical writers have consistently used the stem **path-** to mean "disease," and we find it in such terms as **pathogenesis** (Greek *genesis*, "origin"), "the origin of a disease," and **cardiopathy** (Greek *kardia*, "heart"), "heart disease."

The Greek verb *graphein*, "write, record," and the noun *gramma*, *grammatos*, "something written," have given us the stems **graph-** and **gram-** as used in such words as **cardiograph**, **cardiography**, and **cardiogram**, all from *kardia*, "heart," cognate with Latin *cor*, *cordis*, with the same meaning. In these **cardi-** words and in all similar formations in English, the word ending in **-graph** means the instrument used to make the record, the word ending in **-graphy** means the process of making the record, and the word ending in **-gram** means the actual record itself. Other similar formations include **telegraph**, **telegraphy**, and **telegram**. Note that the noun **telegraph** is now used as a verb, as in "to telegraph someone." **Graphite** is the black carbon used in pencils, and **graphology** is the study of handwriting.

The Greek noun *gramma*, "something written," was used in antiquity also as the word for a very small weight, and, today, the kilogram (Greek *chilioi*, "a thousand") is the unit of weight in the metric system, as is the meter (Greek *metron*, "measure") the unit of distance, and the liter (Greek *litra*, "a pound") the unit of volume. The metric system was adopted by France in a decree of the National Assembly on December 10, 1799, and in 1801 the new system became compulsory in that country, followed by similar action elsewhere.

In the year 1875, there was established in Paris the International Bureau of Weights and Measures, whose function is to provide standards for the kilogram, the meter, and the liter for countries using this system. Until recently, the length of the meter was defined as a fraction of the terrestrial meridian, a hypothetical line passing around the earth and touching the two poles. This length was marked on a metal bar that was stored in a vault near Paris. In 1984, however, the standard for the meter was redefined as the distance that light travels through a vacuum in one-299,792,458th of a second.

Exercises

A. Analyze and define each of the italicized words in the sentences below. Analysis consists of separating a word into its prefix(es), if any, stem(s), and suffix(es), if any, and giving the meaning or force of each. Be careful in your definitions to distinguish between nouns and adjectives. Consult the dictionary where necessary.

1. Have you read this *autobiography*?

2. In her letter she writes of the *autocratic* nature of her supervisor.

3. The students in my class all wear *androgynous* clothing.

4. What is the *gynecologist's* name?

5. She was a well-known *philanthropist*.

6. The chimpanzee is an *anthropoid* ape.

7. An architect in private life, he served as a *cryptographer* in the army.

8. When we asked for an explanation, she gave a *cryptic* reply.

9. As it turned out, *polygamy* was not illegal in that society.

10. Conversation with him was a tedious process, as his remarks were often *epigrammatic*.

11. We found several *helicoid* shells along the shore.

12. Alexander the Great was the *eponymous* founder of this city in 322 B.C.

13. The donor of this gift requested *anonymity*.

14. I cannot find an *antonym* for this word.

15. Her name is *synonymous* with great wealth.

16. Following a brief *eulogy*, we departed.

17. The administrators seem *apathetic* to our problems.

18. The account of these unfortunate adventurers was told with *pathos*.

19. It seemed evident that there was a *psychopath* loose among us.

20. He claimed to have the gift of *telepathy*.

21. The guest speaker was troubled with *aphonia*.

22. The *phonology* of this oriental language is difficult to master.

23. The landscape was a *symphony* of autumn colors.

24. A *euphonious* sound issued from the auditorium.

25. We stood in the stern of the great ship, fascinated by the *phosphorescence* of the vessel's wake.

26. Those with measles often suffer from *photophobia*.

27. It is extremely difficult for the diplomats in this *theocratic* nation.

28. This is a *monotheistic* society.

29. He is a giant in the *pantheon* of corporate executives.

30. Have you visited the *Pantheon*?

31. She abjured tennis and became a confirmed *toxophilite*.

32. There is no *antitoxin* for the venom of this snake.

33. My friend is a *toxicologist*.

34. A *symbiotic* relationship has been formed between the permanent residents and the summer vacationers.

35. The lichen offers an example of *symbiosis* between an alga and a fungus.

36. The doctor prescribed an *antibiotic*.

B. Answer the following questions.

1. What is the *Apocrypha*?

2. What is meant by an *apocryphal* story?

3. What is the common term for a *polygraph*? To what does the *poly-* refer?

4. As a result of the work of James Watson and Francis Crick, it was shown that the structural arrangement of DNA is a *double helix*. What is meant by this?

5. The Greek verb *poiein* meant "make." What is the meaning of the English word *onomatopoeia*? How is this word pronounced? Give some examples of this.

6. What does the word *euphoria* mean?

7. What does an *epidemiologist* do?

8. What is meant by a *pandemic* disease?

9. What is the meaning of the name *Christopher*?

10. The Greek prefix *meta-* meant "after" or "change." Give an example of a *metaphor* in English.

11. What is meant by the *apotheosis* of the Roman emperor Augustus?

12. What does a *graphologist* do?

13. What is an *android*?

14. The Greek suffix *-ōsis* in medical terminology means "an abnormal, non-inflammatory condition." What is meant by the word *toxicosis*?

15. The Greek adjective *akros* meant "outermost, topmost." What is an *acronym*? Give an example of one.

16. What is *acrophobia*?

17. The Greek word for "city" was *polis*. What is an *acropolis*?

C. The meaning of one of the stems of each of the following words should be known to you from the vocabulary of this Lesson. Consult the Index of Stems and determine the meaning of the other stem. Define the word. Consult the dictionary where necessary.

1. pseudonym _____

2. homonym _____

3. paleoanthropology _____

4. misogynist _____

5. orthography _____

6. stenography _____

7. calligraphy _____

8. polychromatic _____

9. helicopter _____

10. autochthonous _____

11. semaphore _____

12. monochrome _____

13. angiogram _____

14. cardiography _____

15. cardiopathy _____

D. Define each of the following words.

1. pathetic _____

2. apathy _____

3. empathy _____

4. antipathy _____

5. sympathy _____

6. pathology _____

7. polyandry _____

8. polygyny _____

9. polytheism _____

10. pantheism _____

11. monogyny _____

12. monogamy _____

13. monogram _____

14. monograph _____

15. monocracy _____

16. dysphoria _____

17. Pan-American _____

18. theologian _____

E. Answer each of the following questions.

1. The Greek adjective *kakos* meant "bad." What is the meaning of the word *cacophony*?

2. The Greek adjective *homoios* meant "like, resembling." What is the basis of the medical practice called *homeopathy*?

3. What is the meaning of each of the words below?

a. encrypt _____

b. decrypt _____

c. cryptogram _____

d. crypt _____

4. What Greek-derived word means the same as the Latin name Lucifer, "light-bearer" (Latin *lux, lucis*, "light" + -**fer**, from *ferre*, "bear")?

F. Consult the Index of Stems and determine the meaning of the Latin-derived component of each of the hybrid words below. Define each of these words. Consult the dictionary when necessary.

1. radiologist_____

2. radiography _____

3. virologist_____

4. audiologist _____

5. audiophile_____

G. Each of the Greek words below has been borrowed into English, either in its original form, or with the ending dropped from the stem or changed to agree with English morphology. Give each of these English words. (These Greek words will not be listed in any of the Indices of this book.)

1. Ασια "a land to the east of Greece" _____

2. Αιγυπτος "a land to the south of Greece." _____

3. αγγελος "messenger" _____

4. αμοιβη "change" _____

5. λυγξ "wild feline creature" _____

Lesson 10

Σκηνὴ πᾶς ὁ βίος.

All life is a stage. [Greek Anthology]

Vocabulary

Greek Word	Stem(s)	Meaning
αρχαιος *archaios adj.*	archa(e)-	old, ancient
αστηρ *astēr n.*	aster-	star
αστρον *astron n.*	astr-	star
δοξα *doxa n.*	dox-	opinion
ενδον *endon adv.*	end-	within
λιθος *lithos n.*	lith-	stone
μορφη *morphē n.*	morph-	form, shape
νεος *neos adj.*	ne-	new, recent
νομος *nomos n.*	nom-	law, rule
οδους, οδοντος *odous, odontos n.*	odont-	tooth
ορθος *orthos adj.*	orth-	straight, correct
παλαιος *palaios adj.*	pale-	ancient
θερμος *thermos adj.*	therm-	hot
τοπος *topos n.*	top-	place

Prefixes

Greek prefixes are often flexible in their meaning, and sometimes it seems impossible to find a specific meaning that will fit the sense of the word of which one is a part.

Greek Prefix	English Prefix	Meaning
ανα-	ana-	up, back
δια-	dia-	through, across
ὑπο-	hypo-	under
μετα-	meta-	after, change
παρα-	para-	alongside, contrary to
περι-	peri-	around

Suffixes

Greek Suffix	English Suffix	Meaning
	-er *n.*	person who
	-ics *n.*	the science of
-ισκος	-isk *n.*	a little

The suffix **-er** is derived from Old English *-ere*, meaning "a person who (does something)," and is found in many English words derived from Latin and Greek: **plumber** (Latin *plumbum*, "lead"), **cycler** (Greek *kyklos*, "circle, wheel"), **mover** (Latin *movēre*, "move").

The suffix **-ics** was originally used in English as the plural of adjectives in **-ic**, from the Greek adjectival suffix *-ikos*, but it came to be thought of as a singular noun meaning "the science of (whatever it was suffixed to)," and was used with both Latin and Greek stems: **linguistics** (Latin *lingua*, "tongue, language"), **economics** (Greek *oikonomikos*, from *oikos*, "house, household" and *nomos*, "law, rule").

Combining Form

-**nomy** (*nomos*, "law, rule")   "a system of laws governing (something)": **astronomy**

Notes

The word **disaster**, "a sudden, great misfortune," was borrowed from the French word *désastre*, which was coined from Latin *dis-*, used in a sense of negation, and *astrum*, "star," borrowed from Greek *astron*. In the earliest examples of the word in English, it had the meaning of "an unfavorable star," and is found with this meaning in Shakespeare's *Hamlet*: "Stars with trains of fire and dews of blood; Disasters in the sun; ..." The French word was probably influenced by the Old Italian *disastro*, "misfortune, bad luck."

The narcotic drug **morphine** was named after Morpheus, in Greek mythology one of the three sons of Hypnos, the God of Sleep. Morpheus sends visions of various kinds to humans in their sleep, and the drug was so named because of the dreams induced by its use. The god took his name from the noun *morphē*, "form, shape," from the varied forms that he could assume in the dreams of mortals.

The *Metamorphoses* is the epic work of the first-century B.C. Roman poet Publius Ovidius Naso, known to us as Ovid. In 11,990 lines, it tells stories from Greek mythology, all concerned with changes in form, beginning with the creation of the universe and ending with the transformation of Julius Caesar into a star after his death, in March of 44 B.C.

Eos (Greek Ηως), Goddess of the Dawn, was one of the three children of the Titans Hyperion and Theia, who themselves were two of the twelve children of the primeval couple, Sky (*Ouranos*) and Earth (*Ge*). The brother and sister of this goddess were the Sun (*Helios*) and the Moon (*Selene*, sometimes called *Phoebe*). Eos gives her name to the Eolithic Age, the dawn of the three aspects of the Stone Age, the period when primitive man first began to use stone implements. The Eolithic Age was followed by the Paleolithic and Neolithic Ages, which were succeeded by the Bronze and then the present, the Iron Age.

Thermopylae ("hot gates," from Greek *thermos* and *pylai*, plural of *pylē*, "gate, entrance") was the entrance into ancient Greece from the north, named for the hot springs nearby. It was here in 480 B.C. that the Greeks had to withstand the gigantic force of the Persian army led by its king, Xerxes, which was invading their land. The Greeks were so vastly outnumbered that, when it became obvious that the Persian advance could not be stopped, the Spartan general, Leonidas, dismissed all of his allies and, with one hundred of his own men, delayed the enemy until he and his loyal soldiers were all slain. This gave the Athenians the opportunity to return to their city to prepare for the inevitable approach of the hostile army. This act of heroism by Leonidas and his small group was celebrated ever after in Greece.

The Greek soldiers who were slain were buried on the battlefield where they fell. Simonides, the Greek poet, wrote three inscriptions that were placed over the site, one of which was written expressly for the Spartans and contains a message from their dead heroes to anyone passing by:

> *Stranger, tell the Spartans that we lie here obedient to their commands.*

Exercises

A. Analyze each of the italicized words in the sentences below.

1. The inscriptions were in an *archaic* form of the language.

2. The *archaeological* evidence for the date of the city's destruction is overwhelming.

3. She was an interesting speaker, although her listeners were often puzzled by her *archaisms*.

4. The first *asteroid* was discovered in 1801 by an Italian monk.

5. He has become a specialist in the field of *archaeoastronomy*.

6. The elegant handwriting of this letter is an *anachronism*.

7. The *synchronous* occurrence of these several events aroused suspicion.

8. *Orthodox* wisdom urges us to vote this governor out of office.

9. *Paradoxically*, we have embraced our old enemy as an ally.

10. Vestiges of hundreds of *Neolithic* dwellings were found in this area.

11. These implements belong to the *Paleolithic* period.

12. It was remarkable that there was no apparent discontent under his *monolithic* rule.

13. The purpose of these *monoliths* is disputed.

14. The gods of the ancient Greeks were *anthropomorphic*.

15. The white, *amorphous* clouds sped across the sky.

16. The central government was shaken by demands for *autonomy* from several districts.

17. I must visit my *periodontist*.

18. *Orthodontia* is recommended for this child.

19. *Thermography* has revealed the precise location of the problem.

20. The patient was suffering from *hypothermia*.

21. Birds floated lazily on the *thermals* rising from the plain.

22. Disorders of this nature often respond favorably to *diathermy*.

23. The *topography* of this region is not known with certainty.

24. There are many Viking *toponyms* here.

25. This medication is to be applied *topically*.

B. Answer each of the following questions.

1. What is a *lithograph*?

2. Language is usually thought of as being constituted of three elements: vocabulary, phonology, and morphology. What is meant by the *morphology* of a language?

3. What is the etymology of the word *disaster*?

4. What is the difference between *astronomy* and *astrology*?

5. What is meant by the term *neologism*?

6. With what is *endodontics* concerned?

7. What does a *paleographer* do?

8. What is meant by *neonatology*?

9. What is a *metamorphosis*?

10. What does an *asterisk* resemble?

11. What is an *endoscope*?

12. What is meant by a *neolith*?

C. The meaning of one of the stems of each of the words below should be known to you from the vocabulary of this Lesson. Consult the Index of Stems and/or the dictionary and determine the meaning of the other stem. Define the word.

1. agronomy _____

2. economics _____

3. Eolithic _____

4. heterodox _____

5. neophyte _____

6. Paleozoic _____

7. taxonomy _____

8. thermolabile _____

9. lithosphere _____

10. astronaut _____

D.   Listed below are five Greek nouns, each of which has yielded but one or two English derivatives. Learn the meaning of each of these Greek words, and define their italicized derivatives in the sentences following.

Greek Word	Stem	Meaning
ἡδονη *hēdonē n.*	**hedon-**	pleasure
ἡμερα *hēmera n.*	**hemer-**	day
μιασμα *miasma n.*	**miasm-**	pollution
μυριας, μυριαδος *myrias, myriados adj.*	**myriad-**	ten thousand
πελαγος *pelagos n.*	**pelag-**	the sea

1. This person is a confirmed *hedonist*.

2. We read of the *ephemeral* empire of Alexander.

3. She managed to escape the *miasma* of her childhood days.

4. We gazed at the *myriad* stars above.

5. These *pelagic* creatures are fascinating.

E. Each of the Greek words below has been borrowed into English, either in its original form, or with the ending dropped from the stem or changed to agree with English morphology. Give each of these English words. (These Greek words will not be listed in any of the Indices of this book.)

1. μαρτυς, μαρτυρος "witness" _____

2. δραμα "an action" _____

3. παραδεισος "enclosed park" (a Persian word) _____

4. ἱστορια "knowledge obtained by inquiry"_____

5. δαιμων "evil spirit" _____

Lesson 11

ΝΙΨΟΝΑΝΟΜΗΜΑΜΗΜΟΝΟΝΟΨΙΝ.
Νίψον ἀνόμημα μὴ μόναν ὄψιν.

Cleanse your sins, not only your face.
[Palindrome engraved on the fountain in front of Hagia Sophia in Istanbul]

Vocabulary

Greek Word	Stem(s)	Meaning
αισθησις *aisthēsis n.*	esthe-	feeling, perception
βαλλειν *ballein*	ball-	throw
βολη *bolē n.*	bol-	a throwing
δρομος *dromos n.*	drom-	a running, race
γνωσις *gnōsis n.*	gno-	knowledge
γνωστος *gnōstos adj.*	gnost-	known
λυειν *lyein*	ly-	loosen, break down
μεσος *mesos adj.*	mes-	middle
παλιν *palin adv.*	palin-, palim-	back, backwards, again
πλασσειν *plassein*	plas-	form, shape
πρωτος *prōtos adj.*	prot-	first
ῥις, ῥινος *rhis, rhinos n.*	rhin-	nose
στασις *stasis n.*	sta-	standing, position
θεσις *thesis n.*	the-	setting, placing
τυπος *typos n.*	typ-	impression, image, model
ζωον *zōon n.*	zo-	animal

Prefixes

Greek Prefix	English Prefix	Meaning
κατα-	cata-	down, according to
εκ-	ec-	out, out of
ὑπερ-	hyper-	over, excessive

Suffixes

Greek Suffix	English Suffix	Meaning
-μα, -ματος	-ma, -mat- *n.*	state, condition, procedure
-σια	-sia *n.*	state, condition, procedure
-σις	-sis *n.*	state, condition, procedure

Notes

The Greek verb *ballein*, "throw," and its related noun *bolē*, "a throwing," had many derivatives both in Greek and in English. The verb *hyperballein*, from *hyper-*, "over, beyond," meant "throw beyond, exceed," and the noun *hyperbolē* meant "excess, exaggeration, **hyperbole**." The noun was also used by the Greek geometer Euclid to name the plane curve, the **hyperbola**.

The verb *paraballein*, from *para-*, "alongside," meant "throw side by side, compare," and its derivative noun *parabolē* meant "comparison," and was later used to mean the geometric curve, the **parabola**. This Greek noun was borrowed into Latin as *parabola*, and in early Christian literature meant "proverb, **parable**," and then it was used for speech of any kind. A denominative verb *parabolare*, "talk," was coined in the Late Latin period, and became so widely used that it replaced the Classical Latin verb *loqui* in the development of the Romance languages. It is the source of the French verb *parler*, "talk," as well as the noun *parole*, "word." The French words are the source for English **parole**, "word of honor," **parlor**, "a room for conversation," **parliament**, "council of state," **parley**, "discussion," and **parlance**, "manner of speech."

The Greek verb *diaballein*, "throw across," came to mean "accuse falsely, slander," and, from this verb, a noun was formed, *diabolos*, "one who slanders, an evil person." In the Septuagint, the Greek translation of the Hebrew Scriptures, this noun is used to translate the Hebrew word for Satan. The Greek word was borrowed as *diabolus* in the Vulgate, the Latin translation of the Scriptures, and is the ultimate source of the

English word **devil**. The Greek noun *diabolos* remains in the English adjective **diabolic**, "devilish."

Other English derivatives of the stem **bol-** include **symbol**, from *symbolon*, "signal, token," and **metabolism**, from *metabole*, "change." The verb *ballein* is the source for **ballistics**, "the science of the motion of projectiles."

The first use of ether to deaden the pain of surgery took place on October 16, 1846, in the Massachusetts General Hospital, Boston, when Dr. John Warren employed it during an operation to remove a tumor from a patient's neck. Dr. Warren had been told of the usefulness of ether by a friend, a dentist, William Morton, who had realized its effectiveness shortly before this. An article in the *Boston Medical and Surgical Journal* by Dr. Henry Bigelow announced the successful use of ether in surgery to the medical world. The words "anesthesia" and "anesthetic" were proposed by a prominent Boston physician, Oliver Wendell Holmes, father of the United States Supreme Court justice. Holmes coined the words from the Greek negative prefix *an-* and the noun *aisthesis*, "feeling," which is from the verb *aisthanesthai*, "feel, perceive." The negative form of the noun, "*anaisthesia*, the state of no feeling, **anesthesia**," did not exist in the Greek language. As with many other words with the Greek diphthong alpha iota (*ai*), British derivatives retain the diphthong in its Latin form, *ae*: **anaesthesia**.

Exercises

A. Analyze the italicized words in the sentences below.

1. Perhaps, he thought, the pleasant surroundings were intended to *anesthetize* us from the realities of the situation.

2. She said that the proposed renovation was *esthetically* unsatisfactory.

3. The speaker resorted to *hyperbole* to stress his point of view.

4. A *parley* with the government officials was set for the following week.

5. He was an admitted *agnostic*.

6. What is the *diagnosis*?

7. What is the *prognosis*?

8. These developments are thought of as taking place during the *Mesolithic* period.

9. The flying reptiles came into existence during the *Mesozoic* period.

10. Part of the treatment included *plastic* surgery.

11. The *prototype* of this device is made of wood.

12. The doctor has suggested *rhinoplasty* for me.

13. *Rhinoscopy* revealed the presence of an abnormal growth.

14. The mayor's *apostasy* was a severe blow to his political supporters.

15. Flavius Claudius Julianus, the Roman emperor of the mid-fourth century A.D., came to be known as Julian the *Apostate*.

16. Please regulate the *thermostat*.

17. The population of this town has remained *static* for three decades.

18. His views were *antithetical* to those of the ruling order.

19. She is the *antithesis* of her sister.

20. These students are *atypical*.

21. The scientists fear that we may be faced with an *epizootic*.

22. The specialty of this professor is *protozoology*.

23. The X rays revealed *hyperplasia* of the heart muscle.

24. Reluctance to venture out of the house at night is part of the fear *syndrome* in our big cities.

25. Treatment for the Stokes-Adams *syndrome* includes intracardiac epinephrine.

26. Such views as these were *anathema* to him.

27. When we saw her, she was *ecstatic* over the news.

28. The assassination of this popular hero was the *catalyst* for the revolution which ultimately toppled the government.

29. Isn't there a *metathesis* in melonade?

30. Her prompt response to our request was *typical*.

B. Answer each of the following questions. Consult the Index of Stems and/or the dictionary where necessary.

1. What is the characteristic that defines an *esthete*?

2. What is a *palindrome*? Give an example.

3. What took place in ancient Rome in the *hippodrome*?

4. What is meant by a *palindromic* disease? Give an example.

5. What is the meaning and what is the etymology of *palimpsest*?

6. What is meant by the procedure of *dialysis,* often used on those with renal dysfunction?

7. What does a *hemolysin* do?

8. Give the etymological meaning of the two nouns *synthesis* and *analysis.*

9. What is a *parable,* and from what Greek verb is this word derived?

10. What is the name of the country that today occupies part of the land of ancient *Mesopotamia*? What is meant by this Greek name?

11. What is blood *plasma*?

12. What is meant by a *stereotype*? What is the meaning of the stem *stere-*? What is *stereophonic* sound?

13. What is a *hypothetical* situation?

14. What is the etymological relationship between the two words *symbol* and *devil*?

15. What is an *embolus*?

16. What is meant by a *diabolic* plan?

17. What is meant by the *parlance* of diplomacy?

18. How are the words *parole, parlor,* and *parliament* related etymologically?

19. Anabolism and catabolism are names of two opposing processes within the body. What is the name given to the sum of these two processes?

20. What is *ballistics*?

21. What is meant by a *zoophyte*? Give an example.

22. What is meant by a *neoplasm*? Give an example.

23. What is meant by the *plastic* arts?

24. The creature called the dromedary takes its name from the Late Latin word *dromedarius*, from the Greek adjective *dromas, dromados*, related to the noun *dromos*. What is a *dromedary*, and why was it so named?

C. Consult the Index of Stems and determine the etymology of each of the words below.

1. pachyderm_____

2. dinosaur_____

3. rhinoceros _____

4. hippopotamus_____

D. Give the etymology and the meaning of the two words below.

1. brontosaurus _____

2. pterodactyl_____

E. Each of the Greek words below has yielded but a single or very few English derivatives. Learn the meaning of these Greek words and define their italicized derivatives in the sentences following.

Greek Word	Stem	Meaning
χαριζεσθαι *charizesthai*	**charis-**	show favor *or* kindness
διδασκειν *didaskein*	**didact-**	teach
ἀλκυων *halkyon n.*	**halcyon**	a bird, the kingfisher, which the ancient Greeks thought built its nest on the sea, an act which had a calming effect on the wind and waves.
πολεμος *polemos n.*	**polem-**	war

1. She was a *charismatic* person.

2. He considered himself an *autodidact*.

3. Those were *halcyon* days.

4. The speaker's address soon turned into a *polemic*.

F.   Each of the Greek words below has been borrowed into English, either in its original form, or with the ending dropped from the stem or changed to agree with English morphology. Give each of these English words. (These Greek words will not be listed in any of the Indices of this book.)

1. πυραμις, πυραμιδος "a geometrical figure" _____

2. ῥυθμος "measured motion or time" _____

3. χαρακτηρ "mark, impression"_____

4. ισθμος "narrow neck of land" _____

5. χορος "band of singers and dancers" _____

Lesson 12

Δός μοι ποῦ στῶ καὶ κινῶ τὴν γῆν.

Give me a place to stand and I'll move the earth. [Archimedes]

Greek Numerals

These numerals are adjectives, but are frequently used as nouns.

Greek Numeral	Stem	English Numeral
ἑν *hen*	hen-	one
δυο *dyo*	dy-	two
τρεις *treis*	tri-, tris-	three
τετταρες *tettares*	tetr-	four
πεντε *pente*	pent-	five
ἑξ *hex*	hex-	six
ἑπτα *hepta*	hept-, hebd-	seven
οκτω *oktō*	oct-	eight
εννεα *ennea*	enne-	nine
δεκα *deka*	dec-, dek-	ten
ἑνδεκα *hendeka*	hendec-	eleven
δωδεκα *dōdeka*	dodec-	twelve
ἑκατον *hekaton*	hect-	one hundred
χιλιοι *chilioi*	kil-	one thousand

Note that the dictionary form of some of the numerals is used as a stem, and that -a- is used as a combining vowel for others: **dekagram**, **tetrameter**. The form **kil-** for the numeral *chilioi*, "one thousand," was adopted when the metric system of measurement was established in France at the end of the eighteenth century.

Vocabulary

Greek Word	Stem(s)	Meaning
αγειν *agein*	**agog-**	lead
αγων, αγωνος *agōn, agōnos n.*	**agon-**	struggle, contest
αρχειν *archein*	**arch-**	begin, rule
αϑλον *athlon n.*	**athl-**	contest
γλυφειν *glyphein*	**glyph-**	carve
γωνια *gōnia n.*	**gon-**	angle
ἑδρα *hedra n.*	**hedr-**	seat, chair; surface
ἱερος *hieros adj.*	**hier-**	holy, sacred
ὁλος *holos adj.*	**hol-**	whole, entire
ιατρος *iatros n.*	**iatr-**	physician
λεγειν *legein*	**lex-, lec-**	choose; speak
παις, παιδος *pais, paidos n.*	**ped-**	child
πους, ποδος *pous, podos n.*	**-pus, pod-**	foot

Suffixes

Greek Suffix	English Suffix	Meaning
-ας, -αδος	**-ad** *n.*	a group
-ον	**-on** *n.*	(noun ending)

Notes

English words in **-agogue** are borrowed from French words that are derived from Latin nouns in *-agogus*, which, themselves, are borrowings from Greek nouns in *-agōgos*. The Greek forms are from the noun *agōgos*, "guide, leader," which is from the verb *agein*, "lead," a word that is cognate with the Latin verb *agere*, "do, drive." The word **pedagogue**, for example, was borrowed into Middle English from the Middle French word *pedagogue*, which is from Latin *paedagogus*, a borrowing from Greek *paidagōgos*, the name given to a slave who escorted children to and from school.

Not all English words in **-agogue** can be traced through Latin; some French words, like *démagogue*, are borrowed directly from Greek:

dēmagōgos, "a leader of the people." The word is not found in Latin literature.

Synagogue is from the French, borrrowed from Late Latin from Greek *synagōgē,* "a meeting," or, in the Scriptures, "a meeting place," from *agōgē,* "gathering, assembly."

There are recent coinages in the terminology of medicine in which words in **-agogue** refer to agents that expel something from the body or which promote the flow of liquid in or from the body: **lithagogue,** "an agent that expels stones"; **hemagogue,** "an agent that promotes the flow of blood" (Greek *haima, haimatos,* "blood").

English nouns ending in **-logue** are derived ultimately from Greek nouns in *-logos,* from *logos,* "word" (introduced in Lesson 8), related to the verb *legein,* "choose; speak." The **-ue** ending is a formation in French (either in the modern period or in Old or Middle French) of Latin words that have been borrowed from Greek. **Epilogue,** for example, is from French *épilogue,* borrowed from Latin *epilogus,* from Greek *epilogos,* "the concluding part of a speech," from *epi-,* "on, upon, after." Today, an epilogue is the final part of a drama, musical composition, or prose work. The same route of transmission can be traced for other words with this ending, such as **analogue** (Greek *ana-,* "up, back, again"), **dialogue** (Greek *dia-,* "across, between, through"), and **prologue** (Greek *pro-,* "before, in front of"). Some of these words are now spelled without the final **-ue: catalog, analog.**

The Greek verb *legein,* "choose; speak," is cognate with Latin *legere,* "choose; read," and it is often difficult to tell which language has supplied a word with the stem **leg-.** The adjective **eligible** is from Latin *e-,* "out," and *legere,* "choose," while the noun **elegy** is from Greek *elegos,* "song of mourning," from *legein.* The noun **election** is from the past participle, *lectus,* of Latin *legere,* while the adjective **eclectic** is from the stem **lec-** of Greek *legein,* plus the suffix **-tic** from Greek *-tikos.* Another form of the Greek verb has provided the stem **lex-** in such words as **lexicon, lexicography,** and **dyslexia.**

The words **athlete** and **athletic** are from Greek *athlētēs,* "contestant," and *athlētikos,* "for a contestant," both from *athlon,* "contest." These two words are sometimes mispronounced, with the insertion of an extra syllable, as in "ath-a-lete" and "ath-a-letic." The insertion of a syllable or a sound in a word in which it does not belong is called **epenthesis,** from Greek *epi-,* "on," + *en-,* "in," and *thesis,* "a placing." The extra "a" sound in these two words is called an epenthetic vowel.

When the terminology of the metric system of measurement was adopted in France at the end of the eighteenth century, it was decided that Greek numerals would indicate multiples and that Latin numerals would indicate fractions of units. Thus, the terms **dekameter,**

hectometer, and **kilometer** represent ten, a hundred, and a thousand meters, while **decimeter, centimeter,** and **millimeter** represent a tenth, a hundredth, and a thousandth of a meter. The same system is used for units of capacity and weight: **dekaliter/deciliter; dekagram/decigram,** and so forth. The form **-liter** was adapted from Medieval Latin *litra*, "measure of capacity," from Greek *litra*, "a weight, one pound." The forms **meter** and **liter** are used in the United States for British "metre" and "litre." The word **gram**, a metric unit of weight and mass, one thousandth of a kilogram, and the combining form **-gram**, are from Late Latin *gramma* from Greek *gramma*, "a small weight." The British form of this word is "gramme."

Exercises

A. Analyze each of the italicized words in the sentences below.

1. The program, as envisioned, did not seem *pedagogically* sound.

2. He was a *demagogue* of the worst sort.

3. She was an early *protagonist* of the Women's Rights Movement.

4. This new drug is an effective *antagonist* to the effects of morphine.

5. Cornwall remained independent of the Anglo-Saxon *heptarchy*.

6. He was under the superintendent in the *hierarchy* of school administrators.

7. The struggle for independence left the country in a state of *anarchy*.

8. The British House of Commons is the *archetype* for all representative assemblies.

9. The *monarchy* will not outlast this century.

10. They were both winners, she in the *pentathlon*, and he in the *decathlon*.

11. Shall we still cling to the superstition of *triskaidekaphobia*?

12. This long poem of the Roman poet Ovid was translated into English *hendecasyllabic* verse. (Greek *syllabē*, "syllable.")

13. Homer set the pattern for epic *hexameter* verse.

14. This author's *tetralogy* has been the inspiration for two motion pictures.

15. Each Sunday he had the same *hebdomadal* debate with himself over which newspaper to buy.

16. The building has the shape of a *pentagon*.

17. The house was built in the shape of a *hexagon*.

18. It was a piece of solid silver in the shape of a *tetrahedron*.

19. The walls of the tomb of Tutankhamen were covered with *hieroglyphics*.

20. The new credit card has a distinctive *hologram* on it.

21. The letter, a *holograph,* was of great worth.

22. My friend has *catholic* tastes.

23. He decided on a career in *pediatrics.*

24. She is a *podiatrist.*

25. I must visit an *orthopedic* surgeon.

26. My brother suffers from *dyslexia.*

27. The author was *eclectic* in his borrowings from the ancient writers.

28. While still in college he worked part-time for a *lexicographer.*

29. This is a *lexicon* of the Greek language.

30. Last year we journeyed to the *antipodes.*

31. His political orientation was *antipodal* to hers.

32. The political difficulties now experienced by our mayor are *analogous* to those of his predecessor.

33. The author drew an *analogy* between the present situation and one that existed in England at the beginning of the century.

34. The fins of a fish can be considered the *analogues* of the wings of a bird.

35. It is often mistakenly thought that a *dialogue* must be restricted to two persons.

36. The president of this tiny country ruled by *ex cathedra* pronouncements.

37. They decided to take their dog to a veterinarian who practiced *holistic* medicine.

B. Answer each of the following questions.

1. What characterizes a *tripod*?

2. What characterizes an *octopus*?

3. What characterizes a *myriapod*?

4. What is the etymology of the word *trigonometry*?

5. Consult the Index of Stems and determine the meaning of the stem **platy-** in the word *platypus*.

6. What is meant by the physical condition called *platypodia*?

7. What is the etymology of the word *hyphen*?

8. What is meant by an *ennead*?

9. What are *petroglyphs*?

10. Consult the Index of Stems and determine the meaning of the stem **-ptych** in the word *triptych*. What does this word mean?

11. In music, what is the meaning of a *dodecaphonic* scale?

12. What is a *dodecahedron*?

13. What is a *dodecagon*?

14. Consult the Index of Stems and determine the meaning of the stem **-tect** in the word *architect*.

15. What is a *polygon*?

C. Each of the four proper names below has yielded an English derivative. Define these italicized derivatives in the sentences following.

Ακαδημεια *Akadēmeia*, the Academy, a park on the outskirts of ancient Athens and the name of the school founded by Plato in the fourth century B.C., which survived until it was closed by the Roman emperor Justinian in the sixth century A.D. after a life of a thousand years. As the school developed, much work was done in mathematics and astronomy, but later, in the third and second centuries B.C., chief attention was paid to the study of philosophy.

Πυρρος *Pyrrhos*, Pyrrhus, a king of Epirus in Greece. In 280 B.C. he and his army of 25,000 sailed to southern Italy, hired as mercenaries by the people of Tarentum, a Greek city on the coast, to protect the Tarentines from attack by the Romans. In two battles, in 280 and 279 B.C., Pyrrhus defeated the Roman forces sent against him, but his losses in the second battle were so great that he said that another victory like that would be his ruin.

Σολοι *Soloi*, Soli, a Greek colony in what is now southern Turkey, whose inhabitants spoke Greek so badly that the Athenians coined a word, *soloikismos*, "solecism," for their misuse of the language.

Συβαρις Sybaris, a Greek city on the southern coast of Italy, founded in the eighth century B.C. The inhabitants of this city became so wealthy through trading with the Etruscans to the north and the Greeks of the mainland, that the name for a citizen of this city, *Sybaritēs*, "Sybarite," became synonymous with luxurious living.

1. Since the governor has abandoned support for this legislation, any questions as to its merit are now *academic*.

2. Although his client was acquitted of the charges, it was a *Pyrrhic* victory for the attorney, as he was later disbarred for bribing a juror in the case.

3. I am surprised at hearing such a *solecism* from you.

4. Now that he no longer had to go to the office every day, he began to lead a truly *sybaritic* life.

D. Analyze each of the following words. Consult the Index of Stems where necessary.

1. cosmopolitan _____

2. epitaph _____

3. cenotaph _____

4. iridescence _____

E. Each of the Greek words below has been borrowed into English, either in its original form, or with the ending dropped from the stem or changed to agree with English morphology. Give each of these English words. (These Greek words will not be listed in any of the Indices of this book.)

1. κριτικος "able to discern or decide"_____

2. οβελισκος "pointed instrument" _____

3. ορχηστρα "place in the theater for dancing"_____

4. οπιον "juice of the poppy" _____

5. λαβυρινθος "maze"_____

F. Answer each of the following questions.

1. The word *athlete* is often mispronounced in three syllables, as "ath-a-lete," by the insertion of an extra vowel in the word. What is this extra vowel called?

2. What is the difference between a *dekagram* and a *decigram*? Between a *centimeter* and a *hectometer*? A *milliliter* and a *kiloliter*?

Lesson 13

Τοὺς οὔτε νιφετός, οὐ ὄμβρος, οὐ καῦμα, οὐ νὺξ ἔργει μὴ οὐ
κατανύσαι τὸν προκείμενον αὐτῷ δρόμον τὴν ταχίστην.

Neither snow nor rain nor heat nor night prevents these men from completing
their appointed journey in the swiftest way.
[Herodotus, *The Histories*, discussing the Persian Pony Express]

Vocabulary

Greek Word	Stem(s)	Meaning
γενος, γενεος *genos, geneos n.*	**gen-, gene-**	birth, origin
ὁδος *hodos n.*	**hod-, od-**	road, way, journey
εικων *eikōn n.*	**icon-**	image, likeness
ιδιος *idios adj.*	**idi-**	one's own, private
μαινεσθαι *mainesthai*	**man-**	be mad
μνησις *mnēsis n.*	**mne-**	memory
μνημων *mnēmōn adj.*	**mnemon-**	remembering
μνηστις *mnēstis n.*	**mnest-**	remembrance
μωρος *mōros adj.*	**mor-**	dull, foolish, stupid
οξυς *oxys adj.*	**oxy-, ox-**	sharp, acid; oxygen
φαινειν *phainein*	**pha-, phan-**	show, cause to appear
φανταζειν *phantazein*	**phantas-**	make an appearance
τασσειν *tassein*	**tac-**	put in order, arrange
θανατος *thanatos n.*	**thanat-, thana-**	death

Suffixes

Greek Suffix	English Suffix	Meaning
-ιακος -*iakos n.*	-iac	person affected by
-ωμα, -ωματος -*ōma, -ōmatos n.*	-om, -oma, -omat-	state, condition
-ωτης -*ōtēs n.*	-ot	person concerned with
-της -*tēs n.*	-t	person concerned with

Notes

The Greek noun *genos, geneos,* "birth, origin," is derived from the verb *gignesthai,* "to be born," and is cognate with the Latin noun *genus, generis,* "race, kind, origin," as well as with the native English noun **kind**, from Old English *cynd,* and is related to English **kin**, from OE *cyn,* as well as to **king**, from OE *cyning.* Another related Greek noun, *genea,* "race, family, generation," has supplied the stem for **genealogy**, "an account of one's ancestry." The two words **gentile** and **gentle** are both from Latin *gentilis,* "of a clan or family," from *gens, gentis,* "race, clan, family," and **gentleman** originally meant "a man of noble birth." Other related words from Latin include **gentry, gender,** and **gentility**.

Genesis is the name given to the first book of the Old Testament by the Greek translators. The name was retained in the Vulgate, the Latin translation of the Scriptures, and is found in English literature as early as *c.* 1000, in the Old English of Aelfric, an English abbot. The Greek translation of the Hebrew Scriptures is called the **Septuagint**, abbreviated LXX, and was given that Latin name from *septuaginta,* the number 70, because it was thought that the translation from Hebrew into Greek had been made by seventy-two scholars in seventy-two days, under the orders of one of the early Ptolemaic kings of Egypt in the third century B.C., an attribution that is now held to be groundless. The Greek word *genesis* is from *gene-,* the stem of *genos, geneos,* and the suffix *-sis.*

In ancient Athens, the place where democracy, rule by the people, first became a reality, every citizen was expected to take part in public affairs. Anyone who kept to himself, one who never spoke up in the public assembly, was thought to be a little strange, and the word *idiōtēs,* "a private person," was applied to him. The word came to mean one who was ill-informed about public affairs and, thus, ignorant: an **idiot**.

The Greek words *mainesthai,* "be mad," *mania,* "madness," *mnēsis,* "memory," *mnēmōn,* "remembering," and *mnēstis,* "remembrance," are but five of a number of words in both Greek and Latin that contain the sounds of the letters *m* and *n* and all having to do with thought processes. The Latin words *mens, mentis*, "mind," *meminisse*, "remember," *mentio, mentionis*, "a calling to mind, mention," and *mentiri*, "lie, tell a falsehood," also show these two sounds, as does the native English noun **mind**, from Old English (*ge*)*mynd*.

The Greek word for prophet was *mantis*, and the most famous of all ancient prophets was Tiresias, the blind seer of Thebes, perhaps best known from Sophocles' tragedy *Oedipus the King*, in which he plays a prominent part. Tiresias had a daughter named Manto, also a prophet, and this was the name of a prophetic Italian nymph whose son was said to be the founder of the Italian town which he named after her, Mantua, in Lombardy, the birthplace of the Roman poet Vergil.

In Greek mythology, Mnemosyne, one of the twelve Titans, offspring of the primeval couple, Sky (Uranus) and Earth (Ge), was the goddess of Memory. Zeus, one of the six children of two other Titans, Cronus and Rhea, slept with Mnemosyne for nine consecutive nights, and, in due time, Mnemosyne bore nine children, all girls, the Muses (from Greek *Mousa*, Latin *Musa*, "Muse"), patron goddesses of the Arts: Calliope, Clio, Euterpe, Melpomene, Terpsichore, Erato, Polyhymnia, Urania, and Thalia. The birthplace of these nine goddesses was said to have been Pieria, a district on the slopes of Mt. Olympus, the home of the gods. This is the explanation of the reference in the following lines from Alexander Pope's *Essay on Criticism*:

> A little learning is a dang'rous thing:
> Drink deep, or taste not the Pierian spring.

A *Mouseion* in ancient Greece was any temple dedicated to the Muses, but the word came to be applied to educational institutions, as, for example, the *Mouseion* in the Academy of Plato in Athens. By far the most famous Museum, to give the word its Latin spelling, was the one in the Egyptian city of Alexandria. This great institution was established by Ptolemy I, the Macedonian general who took over the Egyptian part of Alexander's empire following his death in 323 B.C., and it became the model for all subsequent museums—places for the crafts inspired by the Muses.

The Greek adjective *oxys* had all of the meanings of the English words "sharp," "pointed," "keen (of sense)," "pungent (of odors)," "sour (of taste)," and so forth. Many words beginning in **oxy-** in the terminology of medicine have such meanings: **oxyacusia** (Greek *akouein*, "hear"), "abnormally acute hearing," **oxyesthesia**, "abnormal acuteness of sensation," **oxyopia** (*ōps, ōpos*, "eye"), "unusual acuteness of vision," **oxyosmia** (*osmē*, "odor"), "unusual keenness of the sense of smell," **oxycephalous** (*kephalē*, "head"), "having a high, pointed head," **oxyrhine**, "having a sharp, pointed nose."

The element **oxygen** was first isolated by the British chemist, Joseph Priestly (1733-1804), and was named *oxygène*, "acid-producing," by the French scientist, Antoine-Laurent Lavoisier. In many English words, the stem **ox-** means "oxygen": **hypoxia**, "deficiency of oxygen," **anoxia**, "extreme deficiency of oxygen," **hypoxemia** (Greek *haima, haimatos*, "blood"), "deficient oxygenation of the blood."

Exercises

A. Analyze the italicized words in the sentences below.

1. *Pathogenic* organisms have been found in this food.

2. The *genesis* of the revolution can be found in the meeting of these two men.

3. Subsequent investigation showed that her disorder was *iatrogenic*.

4. Marriage between first cousins was thought of as being *eugenically* unsound.

5. As these two species developed in widely-separated areas, *genetic* differences became evident.

6. What is the reading on the *odometer*?

7. The general had a collection of *icons* from each of his battles.

8. Her speech was full of *idiomatic* expressions from her own language—expressions which sounded strange when spoken in English.

9. It was an *idiotic* move on his part.

10. Rheumatism is an *idiopathic* disorder.

11. It was a *maniacal* act.

12. In his *manic* haste to leave the country, he abandoned his family.

13. It was apparent that she was an *amnesiac*.

14. I'll have to find an effective *mnemonic* for this.

15. In a list of their demands, *amnesty* came first.

16. Everyone agreed that this was a *sophomoric* action.

17. She was rushed to the hospital, suffering from *anoxia*.

18. The sudden and unexpected *epiphany* of this legendary hero, long thought dead, had a quieting effect upon the uprising.

19. In this painter's depiction of Venus and Cupid, the goddess is clothed in a *diaphanous* veil.

20. We read of this psychologist's work on *thanatology*.

21. The subject of *euthanasia* is now openly discussed.

22. This composition is full of *syntactic* errors.

B.   Answer each of the following questions. Stems in these words that have not been presented thus far in the vocabularies can be found in the Index of Stems.

1. What is a *tachometer*?

2. What does it mean if a person is said to be an *iconoclast*? What is the etymology of this word?

3. What is meant by *iconolatry*?

4. Define each of the following: *pyromaniac, dipsomaniac, kleptomaniac.*

5. What is the etymology of the word *oxymoron*? What does the term mean? Give an example.

6. What is the etymology of the noun *fancy*?

7. What is the etymology of the word *taxidermy* and what does it mean?

8. What is meant by the expression, "These two drugs act *synergistically*"? What is the etymology of this word? What do *ergonomists* do? What is meant by the expression, "The perfect office chair is an *ergonomic* ideal"?

9. What is the etymology of the word *idiosyncrasy*, and what does it mean?

10. The term "tropics" refers to the torrid zone, an area on the surface of the earth lying between the tropic of Cancer and the tropic of Capricorn, each roughly 23 1/2 degrees north and south, respectively, of the equator. The word "tropic" is from the Greek noun *tropē*, "turn, turning." What does a "turning" have to do with this? That is, what is it that turns? Consult your dictionary.

11. The Greek noun *tropē* in the preceding question has supplied the stem for the English word *tropism*. Consult your dictionary and determine the meaning of this word. What is *hydrotropism*? *phototropism*? What is the characteristic of any of the plants of the genus *Heliotropium*?

12. What is the etymology of each of the following? *Methodist, Episcopal, Presbyterian.*

13. The word *bishop* comes to us disguised from its original Greek by changes in Old English. What is the etymology of this word?

14. The word *parish*, meaning an area under the influence of or governed by one church or its pastor, is derived from the Latin noun *parochia*, with the same meaning. The Latin noun is derived from the Greek adjective *paroikos*, "living nearby," from *para-*, "alongside," and *oikos*, "house, household." The English adjective meaning "relating to a parish" is *parochial*. What today is meant by a *parochial* point of view?

15. What is meant by *hypoxemia*?

16. In Roman mythology, *Aurora* was a goddess, the equivalent of the Greek goddess *Eos*, and Latin *Boreas* was the equivalent of Greek *Boreas*, the North Wind. With what were the goddesses Aurora and Eos associated, and what is the *aurora borealis*? What is the *aurora australis*? Where are the *hyperborean* regions?

17. What is the meaning of the Greek word from which the English word *planet* is derived? What is the significance of this name?

18. Consult the Index of Stems and determine the meaning of the stem of the English word *periphrasis*. What does this word mean, and what is another English word derived from Latin elements that means the same thing?

19. The Greek noun *lykos* meant "wolf." What is the meaning of the word *lycanthropy*?

20. The Greek adjective *isos* meant "equal." What is an *isotherm*? An *isobar*? What is the meaning of the Greek noun *skelos* that has provided the stem for the word *isosceles*? The word "skeleton" comes from the Greek adjective *skeletos*. What did this Greek word mean?

21. The Greek word for "air" was *aēr, aeros*. What characterizes an *anaerobic* organism?

22. The Greek verb *temnein*, with a stem **tom-**, which will be introduced in the vocabulary of the next Lesson, meant "cut." What is the etymology and what is the meaning of the word *entomology*?

23. What is the etymological meaning of the word *atom*?

C. The four Greek words below have produced few commonly used English derivatives. Define the italicized derivatives of these words in the sentences following.

λαος *laos n.* , "the people"

λιτανεια *litaneia n.*, "prayer, entreaty"

φημη *phēmē n.*, "speech"

τριβειν *tribein*, "rub, pound, grind"

1. He was a gentle man, a *lay* preacher.

2. She began each day with a *litany* of her aches and pains.

3. These activities are *euphemistically* called "peacekeeping."

4. When asked to speak, he commenced a lengthy *diatribe*.

D. Answer each of the following questions.

1. What is meant by a person's *genealogy*?

2. What is a doublet of the word *gentile*?

3. What is the *Septuagint*? What does this name have to do with the Latin numeral *septuaginta*, "seventy"?

4. What is the etymological meaning of the word *museum*?

5. The Greek word *Genesis* has been retained in both the Latin and the English translations of the Scriptures for the first book of the Old Testament. What is the original meaning of this Greek word?

E. The following words are listed in medical dictionaries but do not appear in most English dictionaries. Consult the Index of Stems where necessary and give the meaning of each of these words.

1. oxyacusia _____

2. oxyosmia _____

3. oxyopia _____

4. oxycephalous _____

5. oxyrhine _____

F. Each of the Greek words below has been borrowed into English, either in its original form, or with the ending dropped from the stem or changed to agree with English morphology. Give each of these English words. (These Greek words will not be listed in any of the Indices of this book.)

1. ϑρονος "chair for royalty" _____

2. τραυμα "wound" _____

3. χασμα "open space" _____

4. ειδωλον "image" _____

5. μυϑος "story" _____

Lesson 14

Τὸ ψυχρὸν πολέμιον ὀστέοισιν, ὀδοῦσι, νεύροισιν, ἐγκεφάλῳ, νωτιαίῳ μυελῷ, τὸ δὲ θερμὸν ὠφέλιμον.

Cold is harmful to the bones, the teeth, the sinews, the brain, and the marrow of the spine, but heat is beneficial. [Hippocrates, *Aphorisms*]

Greek Words in Medical Terminology

The terminology of the medical sciences is comprised mainly of words derived from Greek, with a considerable admixture of Latin-derived terms. The overwhelming influence of Greek is due to the fact that much of this terminology comes down to us in the form established by Hippocrates, the Greek physician of the fifth century B.C. The Hippocratic corpus consists of a large number of writings under his name, some taking the form of essays, such as, "Concerning Airs, Waters, and Places," dealing with the effect of environment on health, and others of observations on the course of various diseases on individual patients—day-to-day accounts of the progress of the patient from the onset of the disease up to either recovery or death. Many of the seventy-two works attributed to him are now thought to be by his pupils, but the true scientific spirit runs through the entire corpus, and Hippocrates deserves the honorific title, "The Father of Medicine."

Vocabulary

Greek Word	Stem(s)	Meaning
αλγος, αλγεος *algos, algeos n.*	alg-, alge-	pain
καρδια *kardia n.*	cardi-	heart
κεφαλη *kephalē n.*	cephal-	head
εγκεφαλος *enkephalos n.*	encephal-	brain
εντερον *enteron n.*	enter-	intestine
γαστηρ, γαστρος *gastēr, gastros n.*	gastr-	stomach
αἱμα, αἱματος *haima, haimatos n.*	hem, -em-, hemat-	blood
ἡπαρ, ἡπατος *hēpar, hēpatos n.*	hepat-	liver
λιπος *lipos n.*	lip-	fat
μεγας, μεγαλου *megas, megalou adj.*	mega-, megal-	large
μυς, μυος *mys, myos n.*	my-	muscle
νεφρος *nephros n.*	nephr-	kidney
νευρον *neuron n.*	neur-	nerve
οδυνη *odynē n.*	odyn-	pain
τεμνειν *temnein*	tom-	cut
τρεφειν *trephein*	troph-	nourish

Prefixes

The prefixes used in the terminology of medicine are the same as those already presented in this book. Three of them, however, are used with specialized meanings.

Prefix	Meaning
dys-	unhealthy, abnormal, difficult, painful
eu-	healthy, normal
peri-	surrounding (often used to refer to the tissues surrounding an organ or part of the body)

Suffixes

Greek Suffix	English Suffix	Meaning
-α -a n.	-a	state, condition
-ια -ia n.	-ia	state, condition
-ιασις -iasis n.	-iasis	state, condition
-ιον -ion n.	-ium	membrane, tissue
-ιτις -itis n.	-itis	inflammation
-ωμα, -ωματος -ōma, -ōmatos n.	-oma, -omat-	swelling, tumor, cancer
-ωσις -ōsis n.	-osis	non-inflammatory abnormal condition

Combining Forms

Greek Word	Combining Forms	Meaning
temnein, "cut"	-ectomy	surgical excision
	-tome	surgical knife
	-tomy	surgical incision

Notes

The Greek suffix -itis has a plural, -itides, and we can speak of the various forms of arthritis (arthron, "joint") as the **arthritides**. The suffix indicates that the part of the body concerned is inflamed. Inflammation of a part is conveniently defined by the four "-or" words, Latin nouns ending in these letters: calor, "heat," rubor, "redness," tumor, "swelling," and dolor, "pain." The suffix -osis indicates any abnormal condition of the body or of a part of it but without inflammation. The suffix -iasis (pronounced "eye-a-sis," with the accent on the first syllable) usually indicates the presence of something in the body, as in **lithiasis**, "the presence of calculi (small stones) in the body."

Our word **carcinoma**, "cancer," was known to Hippocrates, and, to him, meant an ulcer, or sore, named from the fact that such an affliction usually spread out like the claws of a crab (karkinos). The English word **cancer** is from the Latin word cancer, "crab, malignant tumor." Today, the suffix -**oma** means any tumor, whether malignant, that is, cancerous, or not. **Melanoma**, a dark-pigmented tumor of the skin (Greek melas, melanos, "dark, black"), for example, is a malignancy, while a **lipoma**, a tumor comprised of fatty tissue (Greek lipos, "fat"), is benign, non-cancerous. The suffix -**oma** indicates one of two things about the tumor depending upon the word element that precedes it: it indicates either the material which comprises the tumor, such as **lipoma**, or it indicates the location of the tumor, such as **nephroma**, "a tumor of the kidney" (Greek *nephros*, "kidney").

The Greek suffix *-ion* was used in its Latin form *-ium* in the formation of English words without regard for its original meaning, which was that of a diminutive, as in *podion*, "a small foot" (*pous, podos*, "foot"), English **podium**. The British scientist Sir Humphrey Davy used this suffix to give names to various new metals, as their existence was realized: sodium, potassium, magnesium, for example. In medical terminology the suffix **-ium** usually means a membrane or tissue, such as the **pericardium**, the membrane surrounding the heart, or the **perinephrium**, the tissue surrounding the kidney (*nephros*). Sometimes, however, this suffix indicates an area of the body, as the **epigastrium**, the region over the pit of the stomach (*gastēr, gastros*).

Although the form -**pathy** in many English words indicates no more than "feeling, " as in **sympathy** and **empathy**, in medical terminology it invariably means "a diseased condition," as in **cardiopathy**, "any disease of the heart (*kardia*)."

While the terminology of the medical sciences is usually precise, some words do not mean exactly what they seem to designate. For example, the word "anemia" would seem to mean "a state of no blood," but the negative prefix **a-** in this word indicates a lessened amount, and the -**em**-stem does not refer to whole blood, but only to erythrocytes, red blood cells; thus, **anemia** means "a condition in which there is a deficiency in the number of red blood cells in the circulating blood." Often a word can have one or more specialized meanings, as in **hyperemia**, from **hyper-**, "over" + -**em**-, "blood" and -**ia**, "state, condition." The medical dictionary tells us that the term can mean: 1. A congestion of blood in a part of the body. 2. Red spots on the skin. 3. A localized redness of an area of skin due to an increase in the flow of blood to that part. However, the essential meaning of the word, "an excess of blood," is present in each of these conditions.

The verb *trephein*, with a stem **troph-**, meant "nourish, feed," and, thus, the noun **atrophy** should mean, "a state of no nourishment" or "lack of nourishment." Its meaning as a medical term, however, takes that state one step further; the word means "a wasting away, a decrease in the size of a part of the body." This condition is usually caused by malnutrition or by an interference in the flow of blood to a part. The word is used also as a verb, and we can say that a certain part has atrophied.

Exercises

A. Define each of the words below. Many of these can be found only in a medical dictionary, but a knowledge of the meaning of the words in the vocabulary of this and of previous Lessons, and of the prefixes and suffixes given in this book, should enable you to see the meaning of each of these words.

1. endocardium _____

2. endocarditis _____

3. pericardium _____

4. pericarditis _____

5. cardiomegaly _____

6. cardiotomy _____

7. cardiogram _____

8. cephalalgia _____

9. megalocephaly _____

10. cephalometry _____

11. cephalotome _____

12. encephalitis _____

13. periencephalitis _____

14. encephalogram _____

15. encephalopathy _____

16. encephalolith _____

17. encephalography _____

18. enteritis _____

19. endoenteritis _____

20. perienteritis _____

21. gastroenteritis _____

22. gastroenterology _____

23. perigastritis _____

24. gastrolithiasis _____

25. gastromegaly _____

26. gastropathy _____

27. gastroplasty _____

28. gastroscopy _____

29. gastrectomy _____

30. gastrotomy _____

31. gastrotome _____

32. hyperemia_____

33. hemolysis _____

34. toxemia _____

35. hematoma_____

36. hematologist_____

37. hematopathology_____

38. hemopathy _____

39. hemophobia _____

40. hemotoxin_____

41. hepatalgia _____

42. hepatatrophia _____

43. hepatitis _____

44. hepatolith_____

45. hepatolithiasis_____

46. hepatolytic_____

47. hepatoma _____

48. hepatomegaly _____

49. hepatodynia_____

50. hepatopathy _____

51. lipemia _____

52. hyperlipemia_____

53. hyperliposis_____

54. lipolysis _____

55. lipoma _____

56. lipogenesis _____

57. lipogenic _____

58. megalopodia _____

59. megalocardia _____

60. megalogastria _____

61. megalencephaly _____

62. myatrophy _____

63. myocardium _____

64. myocarditis _____

65. myoma _____

66. myopathy _____

67. myalgia _____

68. myography _____

69. perinephrium _____

70. perinephritis _____

71. nephrosis _____

72. nephrotomy _____

73. nephrectomy _____

74. nephroma _____

75. nephromegaly _____

76. nephralgia _____

77. nephrolithiasis _____

78. nephrolithotomy _____

79. neuralgia _____

80. neuropathology _____

81. neuropathogenesis _____

82. neurotoxin _____

83. neurotoxic_____

84. neuronephric _____

85. myoneuralgia_____

86. dystrophy _____

87. myodystrophy _____

88. hypertrophy_____

89. atrophy _____

90. hypermyotrophy _____

91. dysphonia_____

92. euphonia_____

B.   Consult the Index of Stems and determine the meaning of any unfamiliar stems in the words below. Define each of these words.

1. tachypnea _____

2. dyspnea_____

3. eupnea_____

4. apnea _____

5. bradycardia _____

6. bradylexia _____

7. arthrodynia _____

8. arthropathy __ _____

9. dysarthrosis _____

10. arthrotome _____

11. arthrendoscopy _____

12. otoscope _____

13. otoscopy _____

14. otalgia _____

15. otitis _____

16. otology _____

17. otoplasty _____

18. otopathy _____

19. otoneurology _____

20. ostealgia _____

21. osteoma_____

22. osteopathology_____

23. osteodystrophy _____

24. osteoneuralgia _____

25. ophthalmalgia _____

26. endophthalmitis_____

27. ophthalmiatrics _____

28. ophthalmologist_____

29. ophthalmoscopy _____

30. ophthalmomyitis _____

31. ophthalmomyotomy _____

32. phlebitis _____

33. endophlebitis _____

34. phlebolith _____

35. phlebolithiasis _____

36. phlebotome _____

37. phlebotomy _____

38. phlebectomy _____

39. cardiosclerosis _____

40. hepatosclerosis _____

41. encephalosclerosis _____

42. nephrosclerosis _____

43. phlebosclerosis _____

44. arteriosclerosis _____

C. Answer each of the questions below. Consult the Index of Stems and/or the dictionary where necessary.

1. What is a *hematozoon*?

2. What is an *enterozoon*?

3. What is *otorhinolaryngology*?

4. What is meant by the condition called *hydrocephalus*?

5. What is meant by the term *analgesia*?

6. What is the meaning of *anodyne*?

7. What are the manifestations of the disorder called *acromegaly*?

8. What is meant by the procedure of *lithotripsy*?

9. What is the meaning of the stem of the word *anorexia*, and what does this word mean?

10. What is the meaning of the stem of the word *aneurysm*, and what condition does this word designate?

11. What is the meaning of the stem of the word *thrombosis*, and what is the meaning of this condition?

12. What is the etymology of the word *symptom*, and what does this word mean?

13. What is meant by *cardiac myopathy*?

14. The Greek prefix *pro-* meant "before." What is meant by the *prodromal* symptoms of a disease?

   D. Using the combining forms below and stems from Greek words in these exercises, form English words answering to the definitions following.

Greek Word	Combining Form	Meaning
teinein, "stretch"	**-ectasia**	a stretching out, distention, dilation
rhēgnynai, "burst forth, gush"	**-rrhagia**	discharge of blood, hemorrhage

1. Distention of a vein _____

2. Discharge of blood from the ear _____

3. Dilation of the heart _____

4. Hemorrhage from the brain _____

5. The stretching of a nerve _____

6. Hemorrhage from the eye _____

7. Dilation of the intestine _____

8. Hemorrhage from the stomach_____

E. All of the words below are found in the works of Hippocrates. Give the English form of each of these and define each. Consult the dictionary if necessary. (These Greek words will not be listed in any of the Indices of this book.)

1. διαφορησις _____

2. επισταξις _____

3. διαρῥοια _____

4. παροξυσμος _____

5. δυσεντερια _____

6. επιληψια _____

7. ασϑμα _____

8. αποπληξια _____

9. ερυσιπελας _____

10. κρισις _____

Words in the Exercises

Exercise words are given here for each Lesson in the order in which they appear.

Lesson 1

aviary
corporal
brevity
fatuous
grave
gravity
levity
mundane
provincial
province
temporal
ursine
urban
ubane
vacuous
verbose
vulgar
Vulgate
avian
sanitarium
cordiality
mentality
vacuum
temporary
vocal
civil
civility
vulpine
taurine
aquiline

bovine
feline
canine
leonine
porcine
piscine
equine
feral
arcane
acerbity
penurious
hibernal
senile
probity
venal
uxorious
vital

Lesson 2

recession
decedent
concessions
unprecedented
cursive
incursion
cursory
concurrence
concurrent
deduction
induction
traduce
frangible

fractious
infringement
infraction
collusion
illusion
elusive
prelude
remote
commotion
emote
incontinent
pertinacious
pertinent
tenure
detention
sedentary
assiduous
insidious
obsession
supersede
assessment
subsidence
tangent
contingent
tactile
intangible
contiguous
introvert
inadvertent
perversely
subvert
obverse

221

subsidized
subsidiary
untenable
extrovert
sedimentary
residual
dissident
excursus
discourse
contingency
averse
exceed
refraction
allude
abstain
decease
recourse
session
contact
inversion
succor
extemporize
contemporaneous
extemporaneous
temporize
tempus fugit
consider
secant

Lesson 3

capsule
indignant
deign
aggregate
egregious
invidious
diligence
eloquent
elocution
interlocutory
circumlocution
loquacious

odious
odium
ennui
imprecations
deprecate
incorrigible
obsequious
undulant
undulate
undulating
redundancy
visionary
providential
improvidence
Providence
visualization
rectitude
purview
obsequies
regimen
provisional
pursue
annoy
maneuver
dainty
royal
maintain
loyal
lieutenant
envy
surround
survey
disdain
vis-à-vis
locum tenens
locus classicus
lector
rector
visor
segue
sequela
incorrect

collectible
executive
interlocutor
encapsulate
deregulation
desegregation
inoperative
inundation
precarious
inconsequential
unintelligible
infatuate
alleviate
evacuate
divulge
aviation
verbatim
defenestration
eradicate
defoliation
elaborate
reverberate
scintillate
eliminate
equivocate
subliminal
visage
prudence
imprudent
interregnum

Lesson 4

incipient
dormant
gradient
ingress
retrograde
Renaissance
renascent
naive
Nativity
ingenuous

disingenuous
genus
species
specious
generic
orient
abortive
orientation
expeditious
expedite
prescience
unconscionable
consciousness
impassive
impassioned
inception
nascent
auditor
audit
audition
auditorium
audience
contraception
ingredient
naturalization
dormitory
impedimenta
generalize
incompatible
patience
principality
participation
Noel
receive
deceit
naivité
morsel
muscle
gladiolus
pupil
libel
opuscule

umbrella
corpuscle
calculus
particular
curriculum vitae
principal
principle
facetious
primus inter pares
erudite
piedmont

Lesson 5

candescent
candor
incarnation
carnal
florid
defoliant
intransitive
ambient
ambience
seditious
derelict
innocuous
ambivalence
efflorescence
noxious
evanescent
provenance
subvention
circumvent
adventitious
devious
venue
via
viable
obviate
contravention
obit
vain
voracious

facile
facility
fiat
pellucid
lucid
translucent
voyage
issue
surfeit
nuisance
chowder
vanish
convey
perish
chauffeur
carnage
unambitious
innocence
defection
reconvene
validation
eventuality
efficacious
elucidate
contrary
insufficiency
impervious
somnifacient
munificence
remuneration
immunity
convalescence
trivial
carnivorous
herbivorous
piscivorous
frugivorous
insectivorous
omnivorous
fervid
languid
morbid

sordid
torpid
turgid
vapid
pacific
prolific
soporific
sudorific
mortify
nullify
ossify
petrify
vilify

Lesson 6

actuary
ambiguous
exigent
exiguous
benefactor
beneficence
caveat
indictment
interdiction
circadian
diurnal
circumstantial
redemption
preemptive
preempted
intransigent
ineffable
nefarious
indifference
infer
maledictions
otiose
negotiable
resilient
salient
desultory
constituency

intractable
distractions
valedictorian
indict
peremptory
journey
redeem
dismal
adjourn
bounty
maltreat
portray
assailant
distrait
assault
deactivate
beneficiary
addictive
infantile
preference
malcontent
subsistence
insult
diary
dictator
subtrahend
referendum
agenda
corrigenda
legendary
relation
cf. (confer)
stationary
stationery
trace
essay
revisionist
verdict
litigious
caveat emptor
Q.E.D.
fatalist

infantry
stable (*adj.*)
stable (*n.*)
prodigal
ubiquitous
stet
caret
delirium
ebullient
inoculate
irascible
jocular
lapidary
obfuscate
profane
rugose
serrated
impeccable
reactor
fatal
result
translation

Lesson 7

deciduous
cadence
incidence
incisive
infanticide
cognoscenti
incognito
cognizance
confluence
effluents
effusive
infusion
inhospitable
magisterial
diminuendo
minuend
inexorable
oracular

oscillations
implication
imply
implicit
construe
superstructure
restructure
conspectus
circumspect
perspicacious
introspective
extradition
precipitous
precipitated
precipitation
minor
minuscule
minority
chance
reconnoiter
chef
menu
destroy
despise
traitor
decay
cadenza
hostel
influenza
mister
treason
connoisseur
minuet
terra incognita
maître d'hôtel
capitol
Occident
affluent
disinter
terrarium
extraterrestrial
companion

infrastructure
cadaver
accident
conifer
peninsula
enervating
querulous
supercilious
ineluctable
vitiate
vicissitude
exhume
funicular
fervent
refulgent
latent
mordant
diffident

Lesson 8

aristocracy
microbiology
microbe
democratic
geometry
sophistic
telescopic
psychic
chronometer
chronic
philosophic
microcosm
cosmic
cosmetic
cosmos
Philadelphia
philodendron
plutocrat
sophomore
xenophobe
zone
Bible

cynic
strategy
arctic
Xerox
agoraphobia
ailourophobia
arachnophobia
claustrophobia
heliophobia
hypnophobia
necrophobia
ornithophobia
panphobia
ponophobia
thanatophobia
zoophobia
hydrophobia
cybernetics
governor
sophistry
Phi Beta Kappa
cosmologist
cosmetologist
dendrologist
dermatologist
enologist
ethnologist
gerontologist
herpetologist
ichthyologist
ornithologist
petrologist
seismologist
speleologist
trichologist

Lesson 9

autobiography
autocratic
androgynous
gynecologist's
philanthropist

anthropoid
cryptographer
cryptic
polygamy
epigrammatic
helicoid
eponymous
anonymity
antonym
synonymous
eulogy
apathetic
pathos
psychopath
telepathy
aphonia
phonology
symphony
euphonious
phosphorescence
photophobia
theocratic
monotheistic
pantheon
Pantheon
toxophilite
antitoxin
toxicologist
symbiotic
symbiosis
antibiotic
Apocrypha
apocryphal
polygraph
double helix
onomatopoeia
euphoria
epidemiologist
pandemic
Christopher
metaphor
apotheosis

graphologist
android
toxicosis
acronym
acrophobia
acropolis
pseudonym
homonym
paleoanthropology
misogynist
orthography
stenography
calligraphy
polychromatic
helicopter
autochthonous
semaphore
monochrome
angiogram
cardiography
cardiopathy
pathetic
apathy
empathy
antipathy
sympathy
pathology
polyandry
polygyny
polytheism
pantheism
monogyny
monogamy
monogram
monograph
monocracy
dysphoria
Pan-American
theologian
cacophony
homeopathy
encrypt

decrypt
cryptogram
crypt
radiologist
radiography
virologist
audiologist
audiophile

Lesson 10

archaic
archaeological
archaisms
asteroid
archaeoastronomy
anachronism
synchronous
orthodox
paradoxically
Neolithic
Paleolithic
monolithic
monoliths
anthropomorphic
amorphous
autonomy
periodontist
orthodontia
thermography
hypothermia
thermals
diathermy
topography
toponyms
topically
lithograph
morphology
disaster
astronomy
astrology
neologism
endodontics

paleographer
neonatology
metamorphosis
asterisk
endoscope
neolith
agronomy
economics
Eolithic
heterodox
neophyte
Paleozoic
taxonomy
thermolabile
lithosphere
astronaut
hedonist
ephemeral
miasma
myriad
pelagic

Lesson 11

anesthetize
esthetically
hyperbole
parley
agnostic
diagnosis
prognosis
Mesolithic
Mesozoic
plastic
prototype
rhinoplasty
rhinoscopy
apostasy
Apostate
thermostat
static
antithetical
antithesis

atypical
epizootic
protozoology
hyperplasia
syndrome
anathema
ecstatic
catalyst
metathesis
typical
esthete
palindrome
hippodrome
palindromic
palimpsest
dialysis
hemolysin
synthesis
analysis
parable
Mesopotamia
plasma
stereotype
stereophonic
hypothetical
symbol
devil
embolus
diabolic
parlance
parole
parlor
parliament
ballistics
zoophyte
neoplasm
plastic (arts)
dromedary
pachyderm
dinosaur
rhinoceros
hippopotamus

brontosaurus
pterodactyl
charismatic
autodidact
halcyon
polemic

Lesson 12

pedagogically
demagogue
protagonist
antagonist
heptarchy
hierarchy
anarchy
archetype
monarchy
pentathlon
decathlon
triskaidekaphobia
hendecasyllabic
hexameter
tetralogy
hebdomadal
pentagon
hexagon
tetrahedron
hieroglyphics
hologram
holograph
catholic
pediatrics
podiatrist
orthopedic
dyslexia
eclectic
lexicographer
lexicon
antipodes
antipodal
analogous
analogy

analogues
dialogue
ex cathedra
holistic
tripod
octopus
myriapod
trigonometry
platypus
platypodia
hyphen
ennead
petroglyphs
triptych
dodecaphonic
dodecahedron
dodecagon
architect
polygon
academic
Pyrrhic
solecism
sybaritic
cosmopolitan
epitaph
cenotaph
iridescence
dekagram
decigram
centimeter
hectometer
milliliter
kiloliter

Lesson 13

pathogenic
genesis
iatrogenic
eugenically
genetic
odometer
icons

idiomatic
idiotic
idiopathic
maniacal
manic
amnesiac
mnemonic
amnesty
sophomoric
anoxia
epiphany
diaphanous
thanatology
euthanasia
syntactic
tachometer
iconoclast
iconolatry
pyromaniac
dipsomaniac
kleptomaniac
oxymoron
fancy
taxidermy
synergistically
ergonomists
ergonomic
idiosyncrasy
tropics
tropism
hydrotropism
phototropism
Heliotropium
Methodist
Episcopal
Presbyterian
bishop
parochial
hypoxemia
aurora borealis
aurora australis
hyperborean

planet
periphrasis
lycanthropy
isotherm
isobar
isosceles
skeleton
anaerobic
entomology
atom
lay
litany
euphemistically
diatribe
genealogy
gentile
Septuagint
museum
Genesis
oxyacusia
oxyosmia
oxyopia
oxycephalous
oxyrhine

Lesson 14

endocardium
endocarditis
pericardium
pericarditis
cardiomegaly
cardiotomy
cardiogram
cephalalgia
megalocephaly
cephalometry
cephalotome
encephalitis
periencephalitis
encephalogram
encephalopathy
encephalolith

encephalography
enteritis
endoenteritis
perienteritis
gastroenteritis
gastroenterology
perigastritis
gastrolithiasis
gastromegaly
gastropathy
gastroplasty
gastroscopy
gastrectomy
gastrotomy
gastrotome
hyperemia
hemolysis
toxemia
hematoma
hematologist
hematopathology
hemopathy
hemophobia
hemotoxin
hepatalgia
hepatatrophia
hepatitis
hepatolith
hepatolithiasis
hepatolytic
hepatoma
hepatomegaly
hepatodynia
hepatopathy
lipemia
hyperlipemia
hyperliposis
lipolysis
lipoma
lipogenesis
lipogenic
megalopodia

megalocardia
megalogastria
megalencephaly
myatrophy
myocardium
myocarditis
myoma
myopathy
myalgia
myography
perinephrium
perinephritis
nephrosis
nephrotomy
nephrectomy
nephroma
nephromegaly
nephralgia
nephrolithiasis
nephrolithotomy
neuralgia
neuropathology
neuropathogenesis
neurotoxin
neurotoxic
neuronephric
myoneuralgia
dystrophy
myodystrophy
hypertrophy
atrophy
hypermyotrophy
dysphonia
euphonia
tachypnea
dyspnea
eupnea
apnea
bradycardia
bradylexia
arthrodynia
arthropathy

dysarthrosis
arthrotome
arthrendoscopy
otoscope
otoscopy
otalgia
otitis
otology
otoplasty
otopathy
otoneurology
ostealgia
osteoma
osteopathology
osteodystrophy
osteoneuralgia
ophthalmalgia
endophthalmitis
ophthalmiatrics
ophthalmologist
ophthalmoscopy
ophthalmomyitis
opthalmomyotomy
phlebitis
endophlebitis
phlebolith
phlebolithiasis
phlebotome
phlebotomy
phlebectomy
cardiosclerosis
hepatosclerosis
encephalosclerosis
nephrosclerosis
phlebosclerosis
arteriosclerosis
hematozoon
enterozoon
otorhinolaryngology
hydrocephalus
analgesia
anodyne

acromegaly
lithotripsy
anorexia
aneurysm
thrombosis
symptom
cardiac myopathy
prodromal

Appendix

Additional Words for Study
Latin Numerals
Notes
Latin Phrases in English
Latin Abbreviations
Special Index of Stems

Additional Words for Study

Analyze each of the italicized words in the sentences below. With few exceptions, stems of these words have not been used in the words in the preceding Lessons. Stems for the words here will be found in the Special Index of Stems at the end of this Appendix.

1. This action *abrogated* the compact.

2. Her *acrimony* was ill-concealed.

3. He showed an amazing *acumen* in this transaction.

4. The prime minister is *adamant* on this point.

5. Let me give you a friendly *admonition*.

6. How can this *ameliorate* the situation?

7. The *apparition* unnerved all of us.

8. When questioned on the matter, the witness was *articulate*.

9. He had the manner of a true *ascetic*.

10. Our *avaricious* landlord has had a setback.

11. My *bibulous* companion is late.

12. It was a *cataclysmic* event.

13. Please do not *cavil*.

14. She often consulted the *chiromancer*.

15. He was a *choleric* individual.

16. The writer of this article is a *colossus* of the business world.

17. Independence had its *concomitant* problems for this tiny nation.

18. Do you *condone* this action?

19. The election results *confuted* the experts.

20. The look that the defendant gave the attorney was full of *contumely*.

21. What is the *criterion* for this evaluation?

22. Do you think that I am a *Croesus*?

23. It appears that the president is guilty of *defalcation*.

24. It will not have a *deleterious* effect.

25. Is this a *desideratum* in our venture?

26. *Detritus* from the excavation clogged the water supply.

27. There is a *dichotomy* of thought concerning the influence of this composer.

28. I suspect that this person is *dissimulating*.

29. *Empirical* evidence is lacking for this theory.

30. We listened to the *encomium* with divided thoughts.

31. It was an *enigmatic* reply to the question.

32. This group met each week for *esoteric* pursuits.

33. The house stood on a hill near the *estuary*.

34. The *fecundity* of the area was apparent.

35. It was an *infelicitous* suggestion.

36. We entered the *fetid* room.

37. The reply showed *flagrant* disregard for the rights of the group.

38. The red clay bank of the river was *fissured* from the tropical sun.

39. The chairman *fulminated* at this suggestion from the floor.

40. My *garrulous* friend has deserted us.

41. Are these matters *germane*?

42. "Nine a.m. in the morning" is a *pleonasm*!

43. Coming from a member of this prestigious group, it was nothing short of *heresy*.

44. One could almost hear the rain *impinge* upon the distant mountain.

45. Each day they went about their *inscrutable* business.

46. As an *irenic*, the speech was a dismal failure.

47. If you maintain this *Jovian* attitude, I cannot help you.

48. High tariffs on imports, rigid product inspection, and a *labyrinthine* distribution system all act to hinder the free flow of trade to this country.

49. My friend is a *lepidopterist*.

50. *Licentiousness* was fiercely denounced from the pulpit.

51. We listened carefully to the *lurid* details of the event.

52. She went about her *matutinal* duties without complaint.

53. The stream, rising in the mountain, *meanders* through the fields.

54. A *minatory* notice was posted on the fence.

55. My friend is a confirmed *mycophile*.

56. Undertaking that arduous task proved to be his *nemesis*.

57. It was an obvious example of *nepotism*.

58. A faint *nimbus* hung above the tree tops.

59. The leader of the opposition made some *nugatory* comments and quickly sat down.

60. Some of these machines appear to have *obsolescence* built into them.

61. The suitcase fell from the dock into the *oleaginous* water of the bay.

62. Her brother is an *oncologist*.

63. There was a *palpable* feeling of apprehension among those gathered there.

64. The candidate opened his speech with the full *panoply* of his resources.

65. Our landlord was *parsimonious* with the heat on cold days.

66. The candidate finished his speech with a few *pejorative* remarks about his opponent.

67. The hostess greeted us with a *perfunctory* smile.

68. The effects of this legislation were *pervasive*.

69. *Plangent* sounds came from the forest.

70. The *plebiscite* will be held next month.

71. Following these events, the evaluation of the property *plummeted*.

72. I live in a *polyglot* neighborhood.

73. Aristotle is considered to have been a *polymath*.

74. *Ponderous* footsteps were heard in the hallway.

75. He was disliked for his use of *procrustean* methods in his business dealings.

76. The *profundity* of her remarks did not escape us.

77. The speaker was tall, lean, and had a *prognathous* face.

78. Her *protean* features convulsed in laughter.

79. My friend is a student of *psephology*.

80. We were disappointed to find that we did not have *riparian* rights.

81. They were all *recalcitrant* students.

82. A *schism* developed in the movement during his tenure.

83. The candidate waged a *scurrilous* campaign.

84. It was decided that the choice would be made by *sortition*.

85. Your friend is a *rara avis*.

86. At that *stentorian* call, we all paused in our rush to get out of the room.

87. A colleague of the expedition leader joined us as a *supernumerary*.

88. We were surprised to find him there at the *symposium*.

89. This is a *tautological* statement.

90. Have you ever seen a genuine example of *telekinesis*?

91. The review of the book was long and emphatically *tendentious*.

92. We walked slowly into the *tenebrous* forest.

93. This easy resolution of the problem seemed to be an act of *thaumaturgy*.

94. The book contained a *thesaurus* of information on the subject.

95. The stranger approached *timorously*.

96. The manager of the bank had an *unctuous* manner.

97. The bottle contained a pale, *viscous* fluid.

98. The sea swirled past the ship in a *vitreous* rush.

99. Many reptiles are *viviparous*.

100. These creatures are *xylophagous*.

101. The *peripatetic* candidate has been hospitalized.

102. You need not *proselytize*; I intend to vote for your candidate.

103. I didn't know what to say to the *importunate* fellow.

104. A strange *concatenation* of events had led to this disaster.

105. The crowd grew restless as the speaker *expatiated*.

106. The food here is *execrable*.

107. Let us discuss these matters *seriatim*.

108. A *sinuous* path led to the house.

109. This is a *precocious* child.

110. As a reward for his efforts, he was given this *sinecure*.

111. She said that she had no longing for the *bucolic* life.

112. I have become quite familiar with this area through my *vicarious* travels there in these books.

113. Who is there who can supply a *panacea*?

114. At the doorway stood this *lugubrious* person.

115. It was a magnificent *panegyric*.

116. There are no *compensatory* rewards for this.

117. Here we have a *compendium* of all of the errors committed during his tenure.

118. She said that *draconian* measures were not necessary.

119. Reference to these events can be found on the first page of chapter 5 and *passim*.

120. The Greek word *kynosoura* was a name given to the constellation Ursa Minor, the Little Bear. The name was borrowed into Latin as *cynosura*, and into English as **Cynosure**. This constellation served as a guide for early mariners, as the North Star was part of it. The Greek word is a combination of the two nouns *kynos* and *oura*. What do these two Greek words mean, and what is the meaning of the expression, "The president of this country is now the *cynosure* of all of the small nations of the world."

Latin Numerals

Cardinal Numbers

unus "one"
duo "two"
tres, tri- "three"
quattuor, quadri- "four"
quinque "five"
sex "six"
septem "seven"
octo "eight"
novem "nine"
decem "ten"
centum "one hundred"
mille "one thousand"

Ordinal Numbers

primus "first"
secundus "second"
tertius "third"
quartus "fourth"
quintus "fifth"
sextus "sixth"
septimus "seventh"
octavus "eighth"
nonus "ninth"
decimus "tenth"

Distributive Numerals

singuli "one each"
bini "two each"
terni "three each"
quaterni "four each"
quini "five each"
seni "six each"
septeni "seven each"
octoni "eight each"

noveni "nine each"
deni "ten each"
quinquageni "fifty each"
sexageni "sixty each"
septuageni "seventy each"
octogeni "eighty each"
nonageni "ninety each"
centeni "one hundred each"

Numeric Adverbs

sesqui "one and a half times"
bis, bi- "two times"
ter "three times"

Notes

The Roman year originally had ten months, beginning with March (*Martius*) and continuing through December. Thus, September, October, November, and December were truly the seventh, eighth, ninth, and tenth months. Eventually the calendar year was so out of step with the solar year that two months, January and February, were added at the beginning of the year, before March. Later, following the death of Julius Caesar and of his adoptive son Caesar Augustus, the original fifth and sixth months, *Quinctilis* and *Sextilis*, were renamed *Julius* (July) and *Augustus* (August).

The Latin noun *annus*, "year," is frequently compounded with one of the cardinal or distributive numerals or a numeric adverb to form a word meaning an anniversary or the celebration of an anniversary. When this is the case, the stem of *annus* usually becomes **-enn-** and the suffix **-ial** is used: **biennial**, "occurring every two years," **centennial**, "a hundredth anniversary or the celebration of it," but **biannual**, "occurring twice a year."

When the distributive numerals are used, the suffix is **-ary** and *annus* is not part of the word: **centenary**, "a centennial celebration." The suffix **-arian**, from Latin *-arius + -anus*, means a person of so-many years: **octogenarian**, "a person in his or her eighties."

In the metric system, Latin numerals are used to indicate fractions of length, volume, or weight: **decimeter**, "a tenth of a meter," **centiliter**, "a hundredth of a liter," **milligram**, "a thousandth of a gram." As seen in Lesson 12, Greek numerals indicate multiples of these measurements: **dekameter**, "ten meters," **hectoliter**, "one hundred liters," **kilogram**, "one thousand grams."

Latin Phrases in English

These Latin phrases are now part of the vocabulary of English. The abbreviation *adj.* following any one of them indicates that the expression is used an an adjective in English, *n.* indicates that it is used as a noun, and *adv.* indicates adverb. The literal meaning of each phrase follows this abbreviation, and below this is an example of the use of the phrase in an English sentence.

ad hoc, *adj.*: "for this thing," for a particular purpose

An *ad hoc* committee was appointed to investigate the charges.

ad lib, ad libitum, *adv.*: "according to (one's) desire"

The detective conducted the investigation *ad lib,* disregarding his orders.

ad valorem, *adj.*: "according to the value"

A 25% *ad valorem* tax was imposed on certain imports.

alter ego, *n.*: "another I," a second self

At times and, especially, under stress, his *alter ego* would surface.

casus belli, *n.*: "cause for war"

The appropriation of this territory seemed to be a *casus belli* to its citizens.

de facto, *adj.*: "derived from fact" (as opposed to resting on legal grounds)

The generalissimo established a *de facto* rule over the tiny nation.

de jure, *adj.*: "derived from law"

The Western powers gave *de jure* recognition to the exiled government.

ex officio, *adj.*: "from official privilege"

The Dean is an *ex officio* member of every committee.

ex post facto, *adj.*: "from after the fact"

Ex post facto judgments are easy to form.

ipso facto, *adv.*: "by the fact itself"

As president of the organization, he was *ipso facto* thought to be aware of its activities.

modus operandi, *n.*: "method of working"

The robbery shows the *modus operandi* of several known criminals.

modus vivendi, *n.*: "manner of living"

The exiles were forced to adopt a *modus vivendi* that was alien to them.

ne plus ultra, *n.*: "not more beyond," highest point

This painting was thought to be the *ne plus ultra* of renaissance art.

non sequitur, *n.*: "it does not follow," a statement that does not logically follow what precedes it

His absurd statement was a *non sequitur*.

per diem, *adj.* and *adv.*: "for the day"

The delegates were give a *per diem* allowance sufficient to cover expenses.

per se, *adv.*: "by itself"

Just because they were present at that time, it does not follow *per se* that they were aware of what happened.

prima facie, *adv.* and *adj.*: "at first appearance"

There is *prima facie* evidence for considering this person the culprit.

pro forma, *adj.*: "as a formality"

There are a few *pro forma* questions that you will be asked.

pro tem, pro tempore, *adv.*: "for the time (being)"

Following her brother's resignation, she was appointed president *pro tem*.

quid pro quo, *n.*: "something (received) for something (given)"

The congressman expected a *quid pro quo* for his vote on the resolution.

sine qua non, *n.*: "without which not," an absolute essential

Prior settlement of the boundary dispute was a *sine qua non* of the final treaty.

terminus ad quem, *n.*: "the limit to which," the goal of a course of action

For her, happiness was the *terminus ad quem*, not wealth.

Latin Abbreviations

Learn the Latin words from which the following abbreviations are taken and learn what these abbreviations mean in English.

a.m. *ante meridiem* (for *medium diem*): before mid-day

c., ca. *circa*: around (This abbreviation precedes a date.)

cf. *confer* (literally, "bring together"): compare

e.g. *exempli gratia*: for example

et al. *et alii*: and others

etc. *et cetera*: and other things (of the same kind)

fl. *floruit*: flourished (This abbreviation precedes the date around which someone produced his or her creative work or the approximate time in which the person lived.)

ibid. *ibidem*: in the same place

i.e. *id est*: that is

loc. cit. *loco citato*: in the place cited (referring to a previous literary citation)

op. cit. *opere citato*: in the work cited (referring to a previous literary citation)

p.m. *post meridiem*: after mid-day

Special Index of Stems

In this Index will be found stems for the words in *Additional Words for Study*. Entries in this Index are not listed in the Index of Stems at the end of this book, except for a few from that Index that are used here in multiple-stem words. Stems of Greek words will be identified by an asterisk (*) preceding each. Adjectives are identified by the abbreviation *adj.*, nouns by *n.*, adverbs by *adv.*, and prepositions by *prep.* Words not so identified are verbs.

*ace- (*akesthai*, from *akos*, cure, remedy), heal, cure, repair.

acr- (*acer, acris, adj.*), sharp.

acu- (*acuere, acutus*), sharpen.

*adamant- (*adamas, adamantos, adj.*), unyielding.

articul- (*articulus, n.*, diminutive of *artus*, joint), part, division.

*ascet- (*askētēs, n.*) one who practices an art.

avar- (*avarus, adj.*), greedy.

avis (*avis, n.*), bird.

bib- (*bibere, _____*), drink.

*bucol- (*boukolos, n.*), herdsman.

calcitr- (*calcitrare*, from *calx, calcis*, heel, foot), kick, resist.

caten- (*catena, n.*), chain.

cavil- (*cavillari, cavillatus*), criticize.

*chir- (*cheir, n.*), hand.

*chol- (*cholē, n.*), bile; anger.

*clys- (*klyzein*), wash over, break over.

*coloss- (*kolossos, n.*), huge statue, especially the Colossus of Apollo which stood over the harbor at Rhodes.

comit- (*comes, comitis, n.*), companion.

contumel- (*contumelia, n.*), abusive language.

*cri- (*krinein*), judge.

*Croesus (*Kroisos, n.*), an early king of Lydia, in Asia Minor, fabled for his great wealth.

cur- (*cura, n.*), care.

*cyn- (*kynos, n.*), dog.

deleter- (*deleterius, adj.*), harmful.

desiderat- (*desiderare, desideratus*), wish for.

*dich- (*dicha, adv.*), in two parts.

don- (*donare, donatus*), give.

*dracon- (*Drakōn, n.*), Draco (ca. 620 B.C.), said to be the first Athenian lawgiver, known for the severity of his legislation and the harshness of his penalties.

*egyr- (*ēgyris, n.*, dialectal form of Attic *agora*, market place), crowd, gathering of people.

*encomi- (*enkomion, n.*), song of praise.

*enigmat- (*ainigma, ainigmatos, n.*), riddle, puzzle.

*esoter- (*esōterō, adv.*, comparative of *esō*, within), inner.

estu- (*aestus, n.*), surge of the sea, tide.

execr- (*exsecrari, exsecratus*, from *ex-*, out, + *sacer*, holy, sacred), curse, hate, detest.

expati- (*exspatiari, exspatiatus*, from *ex-*, out, + *spatium*, space, distance), wander away.

falc- (*falx, falcis, n.*), sickle, curved knife for pruning vines.

fecund- (*fecundus, adj.*), fruitful, fertile.

felic- (*felix, felicis, adj.*), bringing good fortune, favorable.

fet- (*fetēre, _____*), have a bad smell, stink.

fiss- (*findere, fissus*), split.

flagr- (*flagrare, _____*), be on fire, blaze.

fulmin- (*fulmen, fulminis, n.*), lightning flash, thunderbolt.

funct- (*fungi, functus*), busy oneself, be engaged.

fund- (*fundus, n.*), bottom, lowest part.

-fut- (*-futare, -futatus*), repress, check.

garr- (*garrire, _____*), chatter, talk idly.

german- (*germanus, adj. and n.*), one's own brother.

*geront- (*gerōn, gerontos, n.*), old man.

*glot- (*glōtta, n.*), tongue, language.

*gnath- (*gnathos, n.*), jaw.

*here- (*hairein*), take, choose.

importun- (*importunus, adj.*), troublesome, rude.

*iren- (*eirēnē, n.*), peace.

Jovi- (*Juppiter, Jovis, n.*), Jove, another name for Jupiter, king of the Roman gods.

*kine- (*kinein*), move.

*labyrinth- (*labyrinthos, n.*), a place built in the form of a maze. The original labyrinth was constructed in Crete by the craftsman Daedalus to house the monster Minotaur, half human and half bull, later slain by the Athenian hero Theseus.

*lepid- (*lepis, lepidos, n.*), scale, flake.

licent- (*licentia, n.*, from *licēre, licitus*, be permitted), freedom of action.

lugubri- (*lugubris, adj.*, from *lugēre*, mourn, lament), mourning.

lurid- (*luridus, adj.*), pale yellow, ghastly.

*mant- (*manteia, n.*), prophecying.

*math- (*manthanein*), learn, understand.

matut- (*Matuta, n.*), Matuta, Roman goddess of early morning.

*meander (*Maiandros, n.*), the Meander river in Asia Minor, noted for its many twists and turns.

melior- (*melior, adj.*, comparative of *bonus*, good), better.

minat- (*minari, minatus*), threaten, menace.

monit- (*monēre, monitus*), warn.

*myc- (*mykēs, mykētos, n.*), mushroom, fungus.

*nemesis (*Nemesis, n.*, Greek goddess of retribution, who punishes the arrogant and proud), retribution.

nepot- (*nepos, nepotis, n.*), grandson, nephew.

nimb- (*nimbus, n.*), raincloud.

nugat- (*nugari, nugatus*, from *nugae*, trifles), jest, talk idly.

numer- (*numerus, n.*), number.

obsolesc- (*obsolescere, obsoletus*), wear out, grow old, decay.

oleagin- (*oleaginus, adj.*, from *olea*, Greek *elaia*, olive), of the olive tree, oily.

*onc- (*onkos, n.*), bulk, mass.

*opl- (*hopla, n.*), arms, armor.

palp- (*palpari, palpatus*), touch lightly.

*pan- (*pas, pantos, adj.*), all, every.

par- (*parere, partus*), give birth.

parit- (*parēre, paritus*), appear.

parsimoni- (*parsimonia, n.*, from *parcere, parsus*, be sparing), frugality.

passim (*passim, adv.*, from *pandere, passus*, spread out, extend), scattered here and there.

*pate- (*patein*), walk.

pejor- (*pejor, adj.*, comparative of *malus*, bad), worse.

pend- (*pendere, pensus*), weigh, pay.

pens- (*pendere, pensus*), weigh, pay.

*phag- (*phagein*), eat.

-ping- (*pangere, pactus*), fasten.

*pir- (*peiran*), try, attempt.

plang- (*plangere, planctus*), strike one's breast), lament.

pleb- (*plebs, plebis, n.*), the common people.

*pleonasm- (*pleonasmos, n.*, from *pleiōn, adj.*, more), excess.

plum- (OF *plom-*, from L *plumbum, n.*), lead.

*poly- (*polys, adj.*), many.

ponder- (*ponderosus, adj.*, from *pondus, n.*, weight), weighty, heavy.

-posium (-posion*, from *posis*, drink), drinking.

precoci- (*praecox, praecocis, adj.*, from *prae-*, before, + *coquere, coctus*, cook), ripe before its time.

*procrust- (*Prokroustēs, n.*), Procrustes, a mythological innkeeper who lengthened or shortened his guests in order to fit them into his one bed. He was killed by the Athenian hero Theseus.

*proselyt- (*prosēlytos, n.*, from *pros-*, near, + *ēlytos*, arrival, from *erchesthai*, come, return), a convert (to Judaism).

*prote- (*Prōteus, n.*), Proteus, a sea-divinity who was able to change himself into various forms. His encounter with Menelaus, the Spartan king and husband of Helen, is described by Homer in the *Odyssey*.

*pseph- (*psēphos, n.*), small stone used for voting in ancient Athens; the vote itself.

*pter- (*pteron, n.*), wing.

rara (feminine form of *rarus*, *adj.*), rare, uncommon.

rip- (*ripa, n.*), bank of a river, shore of the sea.

rogat- (*rogare, rogatus*), ask.

*schis- (*schizein*), split.

scit- (*scitum, n.*), ordinance, decree.

scrut- (*scrutari, scrutatus*), search carefully, examine.

scurr- (*scurrus, n.*), clown.

seriatim (ML *adv.*, from L *series*, succession), one at a time, in a series.

simulat- (*simulare, simulatus*), pretend, copy.

sine (*prep.*), without.

sinu- (*sinus, -u-, n.*), curve.

sortit- (*sortiri, sortitus*, from *sors, sortis*, lot, chance), cast lots.

*spele- (*spēlaion, n.*), cave.

*stentor- (*Stentōr, n.*), Stentor, a herald in Homer's *Iliad*, known for his loud voice.

*taut- (*ta auta, n.*), the same things.

*tele- (*tēle, adv.*), far away.

tend- (*tendere, tensus*), stretch, be inclined.

tenebr- (*tenebrae, n.*), darkness, gloom.

-terion (-tērion*, noun-forming suffix), means, instrument.

*thaumat- (*thauma, thaumatos, n.*), wonder, marvel, miracle.

*thesaurus (*thēsauros, n.*), treasure, treasury.

timor- (*timor, n.*), fear, dread.

trit- (*terere, tritus*), wear away.

unctu- (*unctus, n.*, from *ungere, unctus*, smear with oil or fat), anointing.

*ur- (*oura, n.*), tail.

-urg- (-ourgos, n.*, from *ergon*, work), working.

vas- (*vadere, vasus*), go, proceed.

vicari- (*vicarius, adj.*, from *vicus*, change), substituted.

visc- (*viscum, n.*), mistletoe, from whose berries the Romans prepared a sticky substance with which to catch small birds.

vitre- (*vitreus, adj.*, from *vitrum*, glass), of glass, glassy.

viv- (*vivus, adj.*), living, alive.

*xyl- (*xylon, n.*), wood.

Complete List of Exercise Words

Following is an alphabetized list of all the words in the exercises of Lessons 1-14. Letters following the number of the Lesson indicate the part of the exercises in which the word is found. Words for additional study, found in the Appendix, are not listed here.

A

abortive 4a
abstain 2b
academic 12c
accident 7d
acerbity 1b
acromegaly 14c
acronym 9b
acrophobia 9b
acropolis 9b
actuary 6a
addictive 6c
adjourn 6b
adventitious 5a
affluent 7d
agenda 6c
aggregate 3a
agnostic 11a
agoraphobia 8e
agronomy 10c
ailourophobia 8e
alleviate 3f
allude 2b
ambience 5a
ambient 5a
ambiguous 6a
ambivalence 5a

amnesiac 13a
amnesty 13a
amorphous 10a
anachronism 10a
anaerobic 13b
analgesia 14c
analogous 12a
analogues 12a
analogy 12a
analysis 11b
anarchy 12a
anathema 11a
androgynous 9a
android 9b
anesthetize 11a
aneurysm 14c
angiogram 9c
annoy 3b
anodyne 14c
anonymity 9a
anorexia 14c
anoxia 13a
antagonist 12a
anthropoid 9a
anthropomorphic 10a
antibiotic 9a
antipathy 9d

antipodal 12a
antipodes 12a
antithesis 11a
antithetical 11a
antitoxin 9a
antonym 9a
apathetic 9a
apathy 9d
aphonia 9a
apnea 14b
Apocrypha 9b
apocryphal 9b
apostasy 11a
Apostate 11a
apotheosis 9b
aquiline 1b
arachnophobia 8e
arcane 1b
archaeoastronomy 10a
archaeological 10a
archaic 10a
archaisms 10a
archetype 12a
architect 12b
arctic 8d
aristocracy 8b

arteriosclerosis 14b

arthrendoscopy 14b

arthrodynia 14b

arthropathy 14b

arthrotome 14b

assailant 6b

assault 6b

assessment 2a

assiduous 2a

asterisk 10b

asteroid 10a

astrology 10b

astronaut 10c

astronomy 10b

atom 13b

atrophy 14a

atypical 11a

audience 4b

audiologist 9f

audiophile 9f

audit 4a

audition 4a

auditor 4a

auditorium 4b

aurora australis 13b

aurora borealis 13b

autobiography 9a

autochthonous 9c

autocratic 9a

autodidact 11e

autonomy 10a

averse 2a

avian 1a

aviary 1a

aviation 3f

B

ballistics 11b

benefactor 6a

beneficence 6a

beneficiary 6c

Bible 8d

bishop 13b

bounty 6b

bovine 1b

bradycardia 14b

bradylexia 14b

brevity 1a

brontosaurus 11d

C

cacophony 9e

cadaver 7d

cadence 7a

cadenza 7c

calculus 4d

calligraphy 9c

candescent 5a

candor 5a

canine 1b

capitol 7d

capsule 3a

cardiac myopathy
   14c

cardiectasia 14d

cardiogram 14a

cardiography 9c

cardiomegaly 14a

cardiopathy 9c

cardiosclerosis 14b

cardiotomy 14a

caret 6d

carnage 5b

carnal 5a

carnivorous 5d

catalyst 11a

catholic 12a

caveat 6a

caveat emptor 6d

cenotaph 12d

centimeter 12f

cephalalgia 14a

cephalometry 14a

cephalotome 14a

chance 7b

charismatic 11e

chauffeur 5b

chef 7b

chowder 5b

Christopher 9b

chronic 8b

chronometer 8b

circadian 6a

circumlocution 3a

circumspect 7a

circumstantial 6a

circumvent 5a

civil 1a

civility 1a

claustrophobia 8e

cognizance 7a

cognoscenti 7a

collectible 3d

collusion 2a

commotion 2a

companion 7e

concessions 2a

concurrence 2a

concurrent 2a

confer 6d

confluence 7a

conifer 7d

connoisseur 7d

consciousness 4a

consider 2d

conspectus 7a

constituency 6a

construe 7a

contact 2b

contemporaneous 2c

contiguous 2a

contingency 2a

contingent 2a

contraception 4b

contrary 5c

contravention 5a

convalescence 5c

convey 5b

cordiality 1a

corporal 1a

corpuscle 4d

corrigenda 6c

cosmetic 8b

cosmetologist 8f

cosmic 8b

cosmologist 8f

cosmopolitan 12d

cosmos 8b

crypt 9e

cryptic 9a

cryptogram 9e

cryptographer 9a

curriculum vitae 4e

cursive 2a

cursory 2a

cybernetics 8f

cynic 8d

D

dainty 3b

deactivate 6c

decathlon 12a

decay 7b

decease 2b

decedent 2a

deceit 4c

deciduous 7a

decigram 12f

decrypt 9e

deduction 2a

defection 5c

defenestration 3g

defoliant 5a

defoliation 3g

deign 3a

dekagram 12f

delirium 6e

demagogue 12a

democratic 8b

dendrologist 8g

deprecate 3a

deregulation 3e

derelict 5a

dermatologist 8g

desegregation 3e

despise 7b

destroy 7b

desultory 6a

detention 2a

devil 11b

devious 5a

diabolic 11b

diagnosis 11a

dialogue 12a

dialysis 11b

diaphanous 13a

diary 6c

diathermy 10a

diatribe 13c

dictator 6c

diffident 7f

diligence 3a

diminuendo 7a

dinosaur 11c

dipsomaniac 13b

disaster 10b

discourse 2a

disdain 3b

disingenuous 4a

disinter 7d

dismal 6b

dissident 2a

distractions 6a

distrait 6b

diurnal 6a

divulge 3f

dodecagon 12b

dodecahedron 12b

dodecaphonic 12b

dormant 4a

dormitory 4b

double helix 9b

dromedary 11b

dysarthrosis 14b

dyslexia 12a

dysphonia 14a

dysphoria 9d

dyspnea 14b

dystrophy 14a

E

ebullient 6e
eclectic 12a
economics 10c
ecstatic 11a
efficacious 5c
efflorescence 5a
effluents 7a
effusive 7a
egregious 3a
elaborate 3g
eliminate 3g
elocution 3a
eloquent 3a
elucidate 5c
elusive 2a
embolus 11b
emote 2a
empathy 9d
encapsulate 3e
encephalitis 14a
encephalogram 14a
encephalography 14a
encephalolith 14a
encephalopathy 14a
encephalorrhagia 14d
encephalosclerosis
  14b
encrypt 9e
endocarditis 14a
endocardium 14a
endodontics 10b
endoenteritis 14a
endophlebitis 14b
endophthalmitis 14b
endoscope 10b
enervating 7e

ennead 12b
ennui 3a
enologist 8g
enterectasia 14d
enteritis 14a
enterozoon 14c
entomology 13b
envy 3b
Eolithic 10c
ephemeral 10d
epidemiologist 9b
epigrammatic 9a
epiphany 13a
Episcopal 13b
epitaph 12d
epizootic 11a
eponymous 9a
equine 1b
equivocate 3g
eradicate 3g
ergonomic 13b
ergonomists 13b
erudite 4e
essay 6d
esthete 11b
esthetically 11a
ethnologist 8g
eugenically 13a
eulogy 9a
euphemistically 13c
euphonia 14a
euphonious 9a
euphoria 9b
eupnea 14b
euthanasia 13a
evacuate 3f
evanescent 5a

eventuality 5c
ex cathedra 12a
exceed 2b
excursus 2a
executive 3d
exhume 7e
exigent 6a
exiguous 6a
expedite 4a
expeditious 4a
extemporaneous 2c
extemporize 2c
extradition 7a
extraterrestrial 7d
extrovert 2a

F

facetious 4e
facile 5a
facility 5a
fancy 13b
fatal 6f
fatalist 6d
fatuous 1a
feline 1b
feral 1b
fervent 7f
fervid 5e
fiat 5a
florid 5a
fractious 2a
frangible 2a
frugivorous 5d
funicular 7e

G

gastrectomy 14a
gastroenteritis 14a

gastroenterology 14a
gastrolithiasis 14a
gastromegaly 14a
gastropathy 14a
gastroplasty 14a
gastrorrhagia 14d
gastroscopy 14a
gastrotome 14a
gastrotomy 14a
genealogy 13d
generalize 4b
generic 4a
genesis 13a
Genesis 13d
genetic 13a
gentile 13d
genus 4a
geometry 8b
gerontologist 8g
gladiolus 4d
governor 8f
gradient 4a
graphologist 9b
grave 1a
gravity 1a
gynecologist 9a

H

halcyon 11e
hebdomadal 12a
hectometer 12f
hedonist 10d
helicoid 9a
helicopter 9c
heliophobia 8e
Heliotropium 13b
hematologist 14a

hematoma 14a
hematopathology 14a
hematozoon 14c
hemolysin 11b
hemolysis 14a
hemopathy 14a
hemophobia 14a
hemotoxin 14a
hendecasyllabic 12a
hepatalgia 14a
hepatatrophia 14a
hepatitis 14a
hepatodynia 14a
hepatolith 14a
hepatolithiasis 14a
hepatolytic 14a
hepatoma 14a
hepatomegaly 14a
hepatopathy 14a
hepatosclerosis 14b
heptarchy 12a
herbivorous 5d
herpetologist 8g
heterodox 10c
hexagon 12a
hexameter 12a
hibernal 1b
hierarchy 12a
hieroglyphics 12a
hippodrome 11b
hippopotamus 11c
holistic 12a
hologram 12a
holograph 12a
homeopathy 9e
homonym 9c
hostel 7c

hydrocephalus 14c
hydrophobia 8f
hydrotropism 13b
hyperbole 11a
hyperborean 13b
hyperemia 14a
hyperlipemia 14a
hyperliposis 14a
hypermyotrophy 14a
hyperplasia 11a
hypertrophy 14a
hyphen 12b
hypnophobia 8e
hypothermia 10a
hypothetical 11b
hypoxemia 13b

I

iatrogenic 13a
ichthyologist 8g
iconoclast 13b
iconolatry 13b
icons 13a
idiomatic 13a
idiopathic 13a
idiosyncrasy 13b
idiotic 13a
illusion 2a
immunity 5c
impassioned 4a
impassive 4a
impeccable 6e
impedimenta 4b
impervious 5c
implication 7a
implicit 7a
imply 7a

imprecations 3a

improvidence 3a

imprudent 3i

inadvertent 2a

incarnation 5a

inception 4a

incidence 7a

incipient 4a

incisive 7a

incognito 7a

incompatible 4b

inconsequential 3e

incontinent 2a

incorrect 3d

incorrigible 3a

incursion 2a

indict 6a

indictment 6a

indifference 6a

indignant 3a

induction 2a

ineffable 6a

ineluctable 7e

inexorable 7a

infanticide 7a

infantile 6c

infantry 6d

infatuate 3f

infer 6a

influenza 7c

infraction 2a

infrastructure 7d

infringement 2a

infusion 7a

ingenuous 4a

ingredient 4b

ingress 4a

inhospitable 7a

innocence 5c

innocuous 5a

inoculate 6e

inoperative 3e

insectivorous 5d

insidious 2a

insufficiency 5c

insult 6c

intangible 2a

interdiction 6a

interlocutor 3d

interlocutory 3a

interregnum 3i

intractable 6a

intransigent 6a

intransitive 5a

introspective 7a

introvert 2a

inundation 3e

inversion 2b

invidious 3a

irascible 6e

iridescence 12d

isobar 13b

isosceles 13b

isotherm 13b

issue 5b

J

jocular 6e

journey 6b

K

kiloliter 12f

kleptomaniac 13b

L

languid 5e

lapidary 6e

latent 7f

lay 13c

lector 3c

legendary 6c

leonine 1b

levity 1a

lexicographer 12a

lexicon 12a

libel 4d

lieutenant 3b

lipemia 14a

lipogenesis 14a

lipogenic 14a

lipolysis 14a

lipoma 14a

litany 13c

lithograph 10b

lithosphere 10c

lithotripsy 14c

litigious 6d

locum tenens 3c

locus classicus 3c

loquacious 3a

loyal 3b

lucid 5a

lycanthropy 13b

M

magisterial 7a

maintain 3b

maître d'hôtel 7d

malcontent 6c

maledictions 6a

maltreat 6b

maneuver 3b

maniacal 13a

manic 13a

megalencephaly 14a

megalocardia 14a

megalocephaly 14a

megalogastria 14a

megalopodia 14a

mentality 1a

menu 7b

Mesolithic 11a

Mesopotamia 11b

Mesozoic 11a

metamorphosis 10b

metaphor 9b

metathesis 11a

Methodist 13b

miasma 10d

microbe 8b

microbiology 8b

microcosm 8b

milliliter 12f

minor 7a

minority 7a

minuend 7a

minuet 7d

minuscule 7a

misogynist 9c

mister 7c

mnemonic 13a

monarchy 12a

monochrome 9c

monocracy 9d

monogamy 9d

monogram 9d

monograph 9d

monogyny 9d

monolithic 10a

monoliths 10a

monotheistic 9a

morbid 5e

mordant 7f

morphology 10b

morsel 4d

mortify 5e

mundane 1a

munificence 5c

muscle 4d

museum 13d

myalgia 14a

myatrophy 14a

myocarditis 14a

myocardium 14a

myodystrophy 14a

myography 14a

myoma 14a

myoneuralgia 14a

myopathy 14a

myriad 10d

myriapod 12b

N

naive 4a

naivité 4c

nascent 4a

Nativity 4a

naturalization 4b

necrophobia 8e

nefarious 6a

negotiable 6a

neolith 10b

Neolithic 10a

neologism 10b

neonatology 10b

neophyte 10c

neoplasm 11b

nephralgia 14a

nephrectomy 14a

nephrolithiasis 14a

nephrolithotomy 14a

nephroma 14a

nephromegaly 14a

nephrosclerosis 14b

nephrosis 14a

nephrotomy 14a

neuralgia 14a

neurectasia 14d

neuronephric 14a

neuropathogenesis 14a

neuropathology 14a

neurotoxic 14a

neurotoxin 14a

Noel 4c

noxious 5a

nuisance 5b

nullify 5e

O

obfuscate 6e

obit 5a

obsequies 3a

obsequious 3a

obsession 2a

obverse 2a

obviate 5a

Occident 7d

octopus 12b

odious 3a

odium 3a

odometer 13a

omnivorous 5d

onomatopoeia 9b

ophthalmalgia 14b

ophthalmiatrics 14b
ophthalmologist 14b
ophthalmomyitis 14b
ophthalmomyotomy 14b
ophthalmorrhagia 14d
ophthalmoscopy 14b
opuscule 4d
oracular 7a
orient 4a
orientation 4a
ornithologist 8g
ornithophobia 8e
orthodontia 10a
orthodox 10a
orthography 9c
orthopedic 12a
oscillations 7a
ossify 5e
ostealgia 14b
osteodystrophy 14b
osteoma 14b
osteoneuralgia 14b
osteopathology 14b
otalgia 14b
otiose 6a
otitis 14b
otology 14b
otoneurology 14b
otopathy 14b
otoplasty 14b
otorhinolaryngology 14c
otorrhagia 14d
otoscope 14b
otoscopy 14b

oxyacusia 13e
oxycephalous 13e
oxymoron 13b
oxyopia 13e
oxyosmia 13e
oxyrhine 13e

P

pachyderm 11c
pacific 5e
paleoanthropology 9c
paleographer 10b
Paleolithic 10a
Paleozoic 10c
palimpsest 11b
palindrome 11b
palindromic 11b
Pan-American 9d
pandemic 9b
panphobia 8e
pantheism 9d
pantheon 9a
Pantheon 9a
parable 11b
paradoxically 10a
parish 13b
parlance 11b
parley 11a
parliament 11b
parlor 11b
parochial 13b
parole 11b
participation 4b
particular 4d
pathetic 9d
pathogenic 13a
pathology 9d

pathos 9a
patience 4b
pedagogically 12a
pediatrics 12a
pelagic 10d
pellucid 5a
peninsula 7e
pentagon 12a
pentathlon 12a
penurious 1b
peremptory 6a
pericarditis 14a
pericardium 14a
periencephalitis 14a
perienteritis 14a
perigastritis 14a
perinephritis 14a
perinephrium 14a
periodontist 10a
periphrasis 13b
perish 5b
perspicacious 7a
pertinacious 2a
pertinent 2a
perversely 2a
petrify 5e
petroglyphs 12b
petrologist 8g
Phi Beta Kappa 8f
Philadelphia 8c
philanthropist 9a
philodendron 8c
philosophic 8b
phlebectasia 14d
phlebectomy 14b
phlebitis 14b
phlebolith 14b

phlebolithiasis 14b

phlebosclerosis 14b

phlebotome 14b

phlebotomy 14b

phonology 9a

phosphorescence 9a

photophobia 9a

phototropism 13b

piedmont 4e

piscine 1b

piscivorous 5d

planet 13b

plasma 11b

plastic 11a

plastic (arts) 11b

platypodia 12b

platypus 12b

plutocrat 8c

podiatrist 12a

polemic 11e

polyandry 9d

polychromatic 9c

polygamy 9a

polygon 12b

polygraph 9b

polygyny 9d

polytheism 9d

ponophobia 8e

porcine 1b

portray 6b

precarious 3e

precipitated 7a

precipitation 7a

precipitous 7a

preempted 6a

preemptive 6a

preference 6c

prelude 2a

Presbyterian 13b

prescience 4a

primus inter pares 4e

principal 4e

principality 4b

principle 4e

probity 1b

prodigal 6d

prodromal 14c

profane 6e

prognosis 11a

prolific 5e

protagonist 12a

prototype 11a

protozoology 11a

provenance 5a

Providence 3a

providential 3a

province 1a

provincial 1a

provisional 3a

prudence 3i

pseudonym 9c

psychic 8b

psychopath 9a

pterodactyl 11d

pupil 4d

pursue 3b

purview 3a

pyromaniac 13b

Pyrrhic 12c

Q

Q.E.D. 6d

querulous 7e

R

radiography 9f

radiologist 9f

reactor 6f

receive 4c

recession 2a

reconnoiter 7b

reconvene 5c

recourse 2b

rectitude 3a

rector 3c

redeem 6b

redemption 6a

redundancy 3a

referendum 6c

refraction 2b

refulgent 7f

regimen 3a

relation 6c

remote 2a

remuneration 5c

Renaissance 4a

renascent 4a

residual 2a

resilient 6a

restructure 7a

result 6f

retrograde 4a

reverberate 3g

revisionist 6d

rhinoceros 11c

rhinoplasty 11a

rhinoscopy 11a

royal 3b

rugose 6e

S

salient 6a
sanitarium 1a
scintillate 3g
secant 2d
sedentary 2a
sedimentary 2a
seditious 5a
segue 3c
seismologist 8g
semaphore 9c
senile 1b
Septuagint 13d
sequela 3c
serrated 6e
session 2b
skeleton 13b
solecism 12c
somnifacient 5c
sophistic 8b
sophistry 8f
sophomore 8c
sophomoric 13a
soporific 5e
sordid 5e
species 4a
specious 4a
speleologist 8g
stable (*adj.*) 6d
stable (*n.*) 6d
static 11a
stationary 6d
stationery 6d
stenography 9c
stereophonic 11b
stereotype 11b

stet 6d
strategy 8d
subliminal 3h
subsidence 2a
subsidiary 2a
subsidized 2a
subsistence 6c
subtrahend 6c
subvention 5a
subvert 2a
succor 2b
sudorific 5e
supercilious 7e
supersede 2a
superstructure 7a
surfeit 5b
surround 3b
survey 3b
sybaritic 12c
symbiosis 9a
symbiotic 9a
symbol 11b
sympathy 9d
symphony 9a
symptom 14c
synchronous 10a
syndrome 11a
synergistically 13b
synonymous 9a
syntactic 13a
synthesis 11b

T

tachometer 13b
tachypnea 14b
tactile 2a
tangent 2a

taurine 1b
taxidermy 13b
taxonomy 10c
telepathy 9a
telescopic 8b
temporal 1a
temporary 1a
temporize 2c
tempus fugit 2c
tenure 2a
terra incognita 7d
terrarium 7d
tetrahedron 12a
tetralogy 12a
thanatology 13a
thanatophobia 8e
theocratic 9a
theologian 9d
thermals 10a
thermography 10a
thermolabile 10c
thermostat 11a
thrombosis 14c
topically 10a
topography 10a
toponyms 10a
torpid 5e
toxemia 14a
toxicologist 9a
toxicosis 9b
toxophilite 9a
trace 6d
traduce 2a
traitor 7b
translation 6f
translucent 5a

treason 7c

trichologist 8g

trigonometry 12b

tripod 12b

triptych 12b

triskaidekaphobia 12a

trivial 5c

tropics 13b

tropism 13b

turgid 5e

typical 11a

U

ubiquitous 6d

umbrella 4d

unambitious 5c

unconscionable 4a

undulant 3a

undulate 3a

undulating 3a

unintelligible 3e

unprecedented 2a

untenable 2a

urban 1a

urbane 1a

ursine 1a

uxorious 1b

V

vacuous 1a

vacuum 1a

vain 5a

valedictorian 6a

validation 5c

vanish 5b

vapid 5e

venal 1b

venue 5a

verbatim 3f

verbose 1a

verdict 6d

via 5a

viable 5a

vicissitude 7e

vilify 5e

virologist 9f

visage 3i

vis-à-vis 3c

visionary 3a

visor 3c

visualization 3a

vital 1b

vitiate 7e

vocal 1a

voracious 5a

voyage 5b

vulgar 1a

Vulgate 1a

vulpine 1b

X

xenophobe 8c

Xerox 8d

Z

zone 8d

zoophobia 8e

zoophyte 11b

Index of Prefixes

Assimilated forms of prefixes follow the entry form. Greek prefixes are identified by an asterisk (*). The number of the Lesson in which the prefix was introduced follows the definition.

*a-, an-, not, without 9

ab-, abs-, a-, away from 2

ad-, ab-, ac-, af-, ag-, al-, an-, ap-, ar-, as-, at-, to, toward 2

ambi-, around 5

*ana-, up, back 10

*anti-, against, opposite 9

*apo-, away from 9

*cata-, down, according to 11

circum-, around 3

con-, co-, col-, com-, cor-, together, with; thoroughly 2

contra-, against 5

de-, down, from 2

*dia-, through, across 10

dis-, di-, dif-, apart 3

*dys-, bad, disordered 9; unhealthy, abnormal, difficult, painful 14

*ec-, out, out of 11

en-, in, into 3

*en-, em-, in, into 9

*epi-, on, upon, after 9

*eu-, good, well, pleasant 9; normal, healthy 14

ex-, e-, ef-, out of 2

extra-, extro-, outside, outward 2

*hyper-, over, excessive 11

*hypo-, under 10

in-, il-, im-, ir- (*only with adjectives*), not 2

in-, il-, im-, ir-, in, into 2

inter-, intel-, between 3

intro-, within 2

*meta-, after, change 10

nec-, neg-, not 6

ob-, o-, obs-, oc-, of-, op-, against 2

*para-, alongside, contrary to 10

per-, pel-, through; thoroughly, very 2

*peri-, around 10; surrounding 14

pre-, before 2

pro-, in front 3

pur-, in front 3

re-, back, again 2

retro-, back, backward 4

se-, apart, away 2

sub-, suc-, suf-, sug-, sup-, sur-, sus-, under 2

super-, over 2

sur-, over 3

*syn-, sym-, syl-, sys-, with 9

trans-, tra-, across, beyond 2

un-, not 2

Index of Suffixes

Suffixes that form nouns are indicated by the abbreviation *n.* following the entry, and those that form adjectives by *adj.* Definitions are given here only as a guide, and a proper definition must often be made up to fit the word. The numbers indicate the Lesson in which the suffix was introduced. Greek suffixes are identified by an asterisk (*).

*-a *n.*, state, condition 14

-able *adj.*, capable of being 2

-acious *adj.*, characterized by 2

-acity *n.*, state, quality 2

*-ad *n.*, a group 12

-al *adj.*, characterized by 1

-an, -ane *adj.*, characterized by 1

-ar *adj.*, characterized by 1

-arium *n.*, place for 1

-ary *n.*, place for 1

-ary *n.*, person concerned with 6

-ary *adj.*, characterized by 1

-ate *adj.*, characteristic of 6

-ation *n.*, state, quality, action 2

-bile *adj.*, characteristic of 6

-ble *adj.*, characteristic of 6

-ble *n.*, place for 6

-culus, -cle, -cule, -culum *n.*, little 4

-ellus, -el, -ella *n.*, little 4

-er *n.*, person who 10

*-etic *adj.*, characterized by 9

-ety *n.*, state, condition 1

*-ia *n.*, process, condition 8

*-ia *n.*, state, condition 14

*-iac *n.*, person affected by 13

*-iasis *n.*, state, condition 14

-ible *adj.*, capable of being 2

-ic *adj.*, characteristic of 6

*-ic *adj.*, characteristic of 8

*-ics *n.*, the science of 10

-id *adj.*, having the quality of 5

-il, -ile *adj.*, characterized by 1

-il *n.*, little 4

-ine *adj.*, having the quality of 1

*-in, -ine *n.*, a substance 9

-ion *n.*, state, quality, action 2

*-isk *n.*, little 10

*-ism *n.*, belief in 6, 9

*-ist *n.*, *adj.*, person concerned with; characteristic of 6, 8

*-itis *n.*, inflammation 14

-itude *n.*, state, condition 3

-ity *n.*, state, condition 1

*-ium *n.*, membrane, tissue 14

-ive *adj.*, characterized by 2

*-ize, -iz- (*forms verbs from nouns and adjectives*) 2, 9

*-ma, -mat- *n.*, state, condition, procedure 11

265

-men *n.*, state, condition, action 3

-ment *n.*, state, quality, action 2

*-oid *adj.*, having the form *or* appearance of 9

-ole *n.*, little 4

*-om, -oma, -omat- *n.*, state, condition 13; swelling, tumor, cancer 14

*-on *n.*, (*noun ending*) 12

-or *n.*, someone, something 3

-or *n.*, the quality of 5

-orium *n.*, place for 4

-ory *n.*, place for 4

-ory *adj.*, characterized by 2

-ose *adj.*, full of 1

*-osis *n.*, state, process 9

*-osis *n.*, non-inflammatory, abnormal condition 14

*-ot *n.*, person concerned with 13

-ous *adj.*, full of 1

*-sia *n.*, state, condition, procedure 11

*-sis *n.*, state, condition, procedure 11

*-t *n.*, person concerned with 13

*-tic *adj.*, characterized by 9

-u- (stem of *-uus* before another suffix) 2

-ulus, -ula, -ule *n.*, little 3, 4

-ure *n.*, state, quality, action 2

-us *n.*, state, condition 14

-y *n.*, state, quality, action 2

*-y *n.*, process, condition 8

Index of Stems

All of the Latin and Greek words used in the formation of English words in the fourteen exercises of this book are found here listed alphabetically by their stem(s). The full form of the Latin or Greek word follows the entry in parentheses, with an indication of whether it is a noun (*n.*), adjective (*adj.*), or adverb (*adv.*); without such a designation, the word is a verb. Numbers and letters following the definition of the word indicate the number of the Lesson and the part of the exercise in which the word is found. The letter v. following the number shows that the word is in the vocabulary of that Lesson. Examples of the word in the exercises of that Lesson will not be noted. Greek words are identified by an asterisk (*).

A

*academ- (*Akadēmia, n.*), the Academy, a school in Athens 12c.

acerb- (*acerbus, adj.*), harsh, bitter 1b.

*acr- (*akros, adj.*), outermost, topmost 9b, 14c.

act- (*agere, actus*), do, drive 6v.

actu- (*actus, -u-, n.*), impulse, drive 6v.

*acu- (*akouein*), hear 13e.

*adelph- (*adelphos, n.*), brother 8c.

*aer- (*aēr, n.*) air 13b.

*aesthe- (*aisthēsis, n.*), feeling, perception 11v.

ag- (*agere, actus*), do, drive 6v.

*agog- (*agein*), lead 12v.

*agon- (*agōn n.*), struggle, contest 12v.

*agora- (*agora, n.*), market place 8e.

*agr- (*agros, n.*), field, land 10c.

*ailour- (*ailouros, n.*), cat 8e.

*alg(e)- (*algos, algeos, n.*), pain 14v.

*andr- (*anēr, andros, n.*) man, a male 9v.

*angi- (*angeion, n.*), blood vessel 9c.

ann- (*annus, n.*), year (Appendix).

*anthrop- (*anthrōpos, n.*), human being 9v, 10a, 13b.

aquil- (*aquila, n.*), eagle 1b.

*arachn- (*arachnē n.*), spider 8e.

arcan- (*arcanus, adj.*), secret 1b.

*arch- (*archein*), begin, rule 12v.

*archa(e)- (*archaios, adj.*), old, ancient 10v.

*arct- (*arktos, n.*), bear 8d.

*arist- (*aristos, adj.*), best 8v.

*arteri- (*artēria, n.*), artery 14b.

*arthr- (*arthron, n.*), joint 14b.

*aster- (*astēr, n.*), star 10v.

*astr- (*astron, n.*), star 10v.

*athl- (*athlon, n.*), contest 12v.

aud(i)- (*audire, auditus*), hear 4v, 9f.

audit- (*audire, auditus*), hear 4v.

auror- (*aurora, n.*), dawn 13b.

austr- (*auster, n.*), the South 13b.

*aut- (*autos, adj.*), self 9v, 10a, 11e.

av(i)- (*avis, n.*), bird 1v, 3f.

B

*ball- (*ballein*), throw 11v.

*bar- (*baros, n.*), weight 13b.

ben(e)- (*bene, adv.*), well 6v.

*bi- (*bios, n.*), life 8v, 9a, 13b.

*bibl- (*biblion, n.*), book 8d.

*bol- (*bolē, n.*), a throwing 11v.

bon- (*bonus, adj.*) good 6v.

bore- (*boreas, n.*), the North 13b.

bov- (*bos, bovis, n.*), cow 1b.

*brady- (*bradys, adj.*), slow 14b.

brev(i)- (*brevis, adj.*), short 1v.

*bront- (*brontē, n.*), thunder 11d.

bull- (*bullire, _____*), boil 6e.

C

*cac- (*kakos, adj.*), bad, unpleasant 9e.

cad- (*cadere, casus*), fall 7v.

cal- (*calēre, _____*), be warm 5v.

calc- (*calx, calcis, n.*), stone 4d.

*calli- (*kallos, n.*), beauty 9c.

can- (*canis, n.*), dog 1b.

cand- (*candēre, _____*), glow, shine 5v.

capit- (*caput, capitis, n.*), head 7v.

caps- (*capsa, n.*), box 3v.

capt- (*capere, captus*), take, seize 4v.

car- (*carēre, _____*), be without, lack 6d.

*cardi- (*kardia, n.*), heart 9c, 14v.

carn- (*caro, carnis, n.*), flesh 5v.

cas- (*cadere, casus*), fall 7v.

casu- (*casus, -u-, n.*), chance 7v.

cav- (*cavēre, cautus*), be on one's guard 6v.

ced- (*cedere, cessus*), go, yield 2v.

*cen- (*kenos, adj.*), empty 12d.

cent- (*centum, adj.*), one hundred 12f.

*cephal- (*kephalē, n.*), head 13e, 14v.

-cept- (*capere, captus*), take, seize 4v.

*cer- (*keras, keratos, n.*), horn 11c.

cess- (*cedere, cessus*), go, yield 2v.

*charis- (*charizesthai*), show favor *or* kindness 11e.

*christ- (*christos, adj.*), annointed 9b.

*chrom- (*chrōma, chrōmatos, n.*), color 9c.

*chromat- (*chrōma, chrōmatos, n.*), color 9c.

*chron- (*chronos, n.*) time 8v, 10a.

*chthon- (*chthōn, n.*), earth, land 9c.

-cid- (*cadere, casus*), fall 7v.

-cid- (*caedere, caesus*), cut, kill 7v.

cili- (*cilium, n.*), eyelid 7e.

-cip- (*capere, captus*), take, seize 4v.

-cipit- (*caput, capitis, n.*), head 7a.

circa- (*circa, adv.*), around 6v.

-cis- (*caedere, caesus*), cut, kill 7v.

civ- (*civis, n.*), citizen 1v.

*clas- (*klan*), break 13b.

claus- (*claudere, clausus*), shut 5f.

claustr- (*claustrum, n.*), enclosed place 8e.

clin- (*clinare, clinatus*), lean 4f.

clinat- (*clinare, clinatus*), lean 4f.

-clud- (*claudere, clausus*), shut 5f.

-clus- (*claudere, clausus*), shut 5f.

cognit- (*cognoscere, cognitus*), learn, understand 7v.

cognosc- (*cognoscere, cognitus*), learn, understand 7v.

con- (*conus, n.*), cone 7d.

cord(i)- (*cor, cordis, n.*), heart 1v.

corpor- (*corpus, corporis, n.*), body 1v.

corpus- (*corpus, corporis, n.*), body 4d.

*cosm- (*kosmos, n.*), order; the universe 8v.

*cosmet- (*kosmētos, adj.*), well-adorned 8f.

*cras- (*krasis, n.*), a mixing 13b.

*crat- (*kratos, n.*), power, rule 8v, 9a, 9d.

*cryph- (*kryptein*), hide (something) 9v.

*crypt- (*kryptein*), hide (something) 9v.

cur(r)- (*currere, cursus*), run 2v, 4e.

curs- (*currere, cursus*), run 2v.

*cybernet- (*kybernētēs, n.*), helmsman 8f.

*cyn- (*kynos, n.*), dog 8d.

D

*dactyl- (*daktylos, n.*), finger, toe 11d.

dec- (*decem, adj.*), ten 12f.

*dec- (*deka, adj.*), ten 12v.

*dek- (*deka, adj.*), ten 12v.

*dem- (*dēmos, n.*), the people 8v, 9b.

*dendr- (*dendron, n.*), tree 8c, 8g.

*derm- (*derma, dermatos, n.*), skin, hide 11c, 13b.

*dermat- (*derma, dermatos, n.*), skin 8g.

di- (*dies, n.*), day 6v.

dic- (*dicere, dictus*), speak 6v.

dict- (*dicere, dictus*), speak 6v.

*didact- (*didaskein*), teach 11e.

dign- (*dignus, adj.*) worthy 3v.

*din- (*deinos, adj.*), terrible, fearful 11c.

*dips- (*dipsa, n.*), thirst 13b.

diurn- (*diurnus, adj.*), by day 6v.

*dodec- (*dōdeka, adj.*), twelve 12v.

dorm- (*dormire, dormitus*), sleep 4v.

dormit- (*dormire, dormitus*), sleep 4v.

*dox- (*doxa, n.*), opinion 10v.

*drom- (*dromos, n.*) a running, race 11v, 14c.

duc- (*ducere, ductus*), lead 2v.

duct- (*ducere, ductus*), lead 2v.

*dy- (*dyo, adj.*), two 12v.

E

*ec- (*oikos, n.*), house, household 10c, 13b.

*-em- (*haima, haimatos, n.*), blood 13b, 14v.

empt- (*emere, emptus*), buy 6v.

*en- (*oinos, n.*), wine 8g.

*encephal- (*enkephalos, n.*), brain 14v.

*end- (*endon, adv.*), within 10v, 14a, 14b.

-enn- (*annus, n.*), year (Appendix).

*enne- (*ennea, adj.*), nine 12v.

*enter- (*enteron, n.*), intestine 14v.

*eo- (*ēōs, n.*), dawn 10c.

equ- (*aequus, adj.*), equal 3g.

equ- (*equus, n.*), horse 1b.

*erg- (*ergon, n.*), work 13b.

erudit- (*erudire, eruditus*), educate, teach 4e.

*esthe- (*aisthēsis, n.*), feeling, perception 11v.

*ethn- (*ethnos, n.*), race, people, nation 8g.

*eury- (*eurys, adj.*), wide 14c.

F

f- (*fari, fatus*), speak 6v.

fac- (*facere, factus*), make 5v.

faceti- (*facetiae, n.*), witty sayings 4e.

fact- (*facere, factus*), make 5v.

fan- (*fanum, n.*), temple, sacred place 6e.

-fant- (*fari, fatus*), speak 6v.

fat- (*fari, fatus*), speak 6v.

fatu- (*fatuus, adj.*), foolish 1v, 3f.

-fect- (*facere, factus*), make 5v.

fel- (*feles, felis, n.*), cat 1b.

fenestr- (*fenestra, n.*), window 3g.

fer- (*ferre, latus*), carry 6v.

fer- (*ferus, adj.*), wild 1b.

ferv- (*fervēre, _____*), be hot, boil 5e, 7f.

-fic- (*facere, factus*), make 5v.

fid- (*fidere, fisus*), trust, have confidence in 7f.

flect- (*flectere, flexus*), bend 6g.

flex- (*flectere, flexus*), bend 6g.

flor- (*florēre, _____*), blossom 5v.

flu- (*fluere, fluxus*), flow 7v.

flux- (*fluere, fluxus*), flow 7v.

foli- (*folium, n.*), leaf 3g, 5v.

fract- (*frangere, fractus*), break 2v.

frang- (*frangere, fractus*), break 2v.

-fring- (*frangere, fractus*), break 2v.

frug- (*_____, frugis, n.*), fruit 5d.

fug- (*fugere, fugitus*), flee 2c.

fulg- (*fulgēre, _____*), shine, glitter 7f.

fund- (*fundere, fusus*), pour 7v.

funi- (*funis, n.*), rope 7e.

fus- (*fundere, fusus*), pour 7v.

fusc- (*fuscus, adj.*), dark 6e.

G

*gam- (*gamos, n.*), marriage 9v.

*gastr- (*gastēr, gastros, n.*), stomach 10c, 14v.

*ge- (*gē, n.*), the earth 8v.

*gen(e)- (*genos, geneos, n.*), birth, origin 13v, 14a.

*genea- (*genea, n.*), race, family 13d.

gener- (*genus, generis, n.*), race, kind, origin 4v.

gent- (*gens, gentis, n.*), race, clan, family 13d.

genus (*genus, generis, n.*), race, kind, origin 4v.

geront- (*gerōn, gerontos, n.*), old man 8g.

gladi- (*gladius, n.*), sword 4d.

glyph- (*glyphein*), carve 12v.

gno- (*gnōsis, n.*), knowledge 11v.

gnost- (*gnōstos, adj.*), known 11v.

gon- (*gōnia, n.*), angle 12v.

grad- (*gradi, gressus*), step, walk 4v.

gram- (*gramma, grammatos, n.*), something written 9v, 12a, 14a; small weight 12f.

grammat- (*gramma, grammatos, n.*), something written 9v.

graph- (*graphein*), write, record 9v, 10a, 10b, 12a, 14a.

grav- (*gravis, adj.*), heavy 1v.

-gred- (*gradi, gressus*), step, walk 4v.

greg(i)- (*grex, gregis, n.*), herd, flock 3v.

gress- (*gradi, gressus*), step, walk 4v.

gubernator- (*gubernator, n.*), helmsman 8f.

gyn- (*gynē, gynaikos, n.*), woman 9v.

gynec- (*gynē, gynaikos, n.*), woman 9v.

H

halcyon (*halkyōn, n.*), a bird, the kingfisher 11e.

hebd- (*hepta, adj.*), seven 12v.

hect- (*hekaton, adj.*), one hundred 12v.

hedon- (*hēdonē, n.*), pleasure 10d.

hedr- (*hedra, n.*), seat, chair; surface 12v.

heli- (*helios, n.*), the sun 8e, 13b.

helic- (*helix, helikos, n.*), spiral 9v.

helix (*helix, helikos, n.*), spiral 9v.

hem- (*haima, haimatos, n.*), blood 11b, 12b, 14v.

hemat- (*haima, haimatos, n.*), blood 14v.

hemer- (*hēmera, n.*), day 10d.

hen- (*hen, adj.*), one 12v.

hendec- (*hendeka, adj.*), eleven 12v.

hepat- (*hēpar, hēpatos, n.*), liver 14v.

hept- (*hepta, adj.*), seven 12v.

-her- (*haerēre, haesus*), stick 5f.

herb- (*herba, n.*), grass 5d.

herpet- (*herpeton, n.*), reptile 8g.

-hes- (*haerēre, haesus*), stick 5f.

heter- (*heteros, adj.*), other 10c.

hex- (*hex, adj.*), six 12v.

hibern- (*hibernus, adj.*), of or for winter 1b.

hier- (*hieros, adj.*), holy, sacred 12v.

hipp- (*hippos, n.*), horse 11b, 11c.

hod- (*hodos, n.*), road, way, journey 13v.

hol- (*holos, adj.*), whole, entire 12v.

hom- (*homos, adj.*), same 9c.

home- (*homoios, adj.*), like, resembling 9e.

hospit- (*hospes, hospitis, n.*), host, guest 7v.

hum- (*humus, n.*), ground, soil 7e.

*hydr- (*hydōr, hydatos, n.*), water 8f, 13b, 14c.

*hypn- (*hypnos, n.*), sleep 8e.

I

*iatr- (*iatros, n.*), physician 12v, 13a.

*ichthy- (*ichthys, n.*), fish 8g.

*icon- (*eikōn, n.*), image, likeness 13v.

*idi- (*idios, adj.*), one's own, private 13v.

-ient- (*ire, itus*), go 5v.

-ig- (*agere, actus*), do, drive 6v.

-im- (*emere, emptus*), buy 6v.

infra- (*infra, adv.*), below, beneath 7d.

ingenu- (*ingenuus, adj.*), frank, candid 4v.

insul- (*insula, n.*), island 7e.

invidi- (*invidia, n.*), ill will 3v.

ir- (*ira, n.*), anger 6e.

*irid- (*iris, iridos, n.*), rainbow 12d.

*is- (*isos, adj.*), equal 13b.

it- (*ire, itus*), go 5v.

J

joc- (*jocus, n.*), joke 6e.

K

*kai (*kai, conjunction*), and 12a.

*kil- (*chilioi, adj.*) one thousand 12v.

*klept- (*kleptein*), steal 13b.

L

*la- (*laos, n.*), the people 13c.

labil- (*labilis, adj.*), unsteady 10c.

labor- (*labor, n.*), work 3g.

langu- (*languēre,_____*), be weary, be faint 5e.

lapid- (*lapis, lapidis, n.*), stone, precious stone 6e.

*laryng- (*larynx, laryngos, n.*), larynx 14c.

lat- (*ferre, latus*), carry 6v.

lat- (*latēre, _____*), lie hidden 7f.

*latr- (*latreia, n.*), worship 13b.

*lec- (*legein*), choose; speak 12v.

lect- (*legere, lectus*), choose; read 3v.

leg- (*legere, lectus*), choose; read 3v.

leg- (*lex, legis, n.*), law 3v.

leon- (*leo, leonis, n.*), lion 1b.

lev(i)- (*levis, adj.*), light 1v, 3f.

*lex- (*legein*), choose; speak 12v, 14b.

libel- (*libellus, n.*, diminutive of *liber, n.*, book), written accusation 4d.

-lict- (-*linquere, -lictus*), leave 5v.

-lig- (*legere, lectus*), choose; read 3v.

limin- (*limen, liminis, n.*), threshold 3g, 3h.

-linqu- (-*linquere, -lictus*), leave 5v.

*lip- (*lipos, n.*), fat 14v.

lir- (*lira, n.*), furrow 6e.

lit- (*lis, litis, n.*), lawsuit 6d.

*litan- (*litaneia, n.*), prayer, entreaty 13c.

-liter (ML *litra, n.*, from Greek *litra, n.*, a weight, one pound), metric unit of capacity 12f.

*lith- (*lithos, n.*), stone 10v, 11a, 14a, 14b, 14c.

loc- (*locus, n.*), place 3v.

locut- (*loqui, locutus*), talk 3v.

*log- (*logos, n.*), word 8v, 9a, 9b, 9c, 9d, 9f, 10a, 10b, 12a, 13a, 13b, 13d, 14a, 14b, 14c.

loqu- (*loqui, locutus*), talk 3v.

luc- (*lucēre, _____*), be clear 5v.

luct- (*luctari, luctatus*), struggle 7e.

lud- (*ludere, lusus*), play 2v.

lus- (*ludere, lusus*), play 2v.

*ly- (*lyein*), loosen, break down 11v, 14a.

*lyc- (*lykos, n.*), wolf 13b.

M

magistr- (*magister, n.*), teacher, master 7v.

mal- (*malus, adj.*), bad, evil 6v.

male- (*male, adv.*), badly 6v.

*man- (*mainesthai*), be mad 13v.

manu- (*manus, -u-, n.*), hand 3v.

*mega- (*megas, megalou, adj.*), large 14v.

*megal- (*megas, megalou, adj.*), large 14v.

ment- (*mens, mentis, n.*), mind 1v.

*mes- (*mesos, adj.*), middle 11v.

-meter (L *metrum, n.*, from Greek *metron, n.*, measure), metric unit of length; instrument for measuring 8b, 12a, 12f, 13a, 13b.

*metr- (*metron, n.*), measure 8v, 12b, 14a.

*miasm- (*miasma, n.*), pollution 10d.

*micr- (*mikros, adj.*), small 8v.

mill- (*mille, adj.*), one thousand 12f.

minor- (*minor, minus, adj.*), less, smaller 7v.

minu- (*minuere, minutus*), lessen 7v.

minus- (*minor, minus, adj.*), less, smaller 7v.

minut- (*minuere, minutus*), lessen 7v.

*mis- (*misein*), hate 9c.

miss- (*mittere, missus*), send 7g.

mit(t)- (*mittere, missus*), send 7g.

*mne- (*mnēsis, n.*), memory 13v.

*mnemon- (*mnēmōn, adj.*), remembering 13v.

*mnest- (*mnēstis, n.*), remembrance 13v.

*mon- (*monos, adj.*), single, one 9v, 10a, 12a.

mont- (*mons, montis, n.*), mountain 4e.

*mor- (*mōros, adj.*), dull, foolish, stupid 8c, 13v.

morb- (*morbus, n.*), disease 5e.

mord- (*mordēre, morsus*), bite 7f.

*morph- (*morphē, n.*), form, shape 10v.

mors- (*morsus, n.*), bite 4d.

mort- (*mors, mortis, n.*), death 5e.

mot- (*movēre, motus*), move 2v.

mov- (*movēre, motus*), move 2v.

mun- (*munus, muneris, n.*), gift; service, duty 5c.

mund- (*mundus, n.*), world 1v.

muner- (*munus, muneris, n.*), gift; service, duty 5c.

mur- (*mus, muris, n.*), mouse 4d.

mus- (*mus, muris, n.*), mouse 4d.

*mus- (*Mousa, n.*), a Muse, one of the nine patron goddesses of the arts 13d.

mut- (*mutare, mutatus*), change 4f.

mutat- (*mutare, mutatus*),
change 4f.

*my- (*mys, myos, n.*), muscle 14v.

*myriad- (*myrias, myriados, n.*), ten
thousand 10d.

N

nasc- (*nasci, natus*), be born 4v.

nat- (*nasci, natus*), be born
4v, 10b.

*naut- (*nautēs, n.*), sailor 10c.

*ne- (*neos, adj.*), new, recent 10v,
11b.

*necr- (*nekros, n.*), dead body 8e.

nefari- (*nefarius, adj.*),
unspeakably evil 6v.

*nephr- (*nephros, n.*), kidney 14v.

nerv- (*nervus, n.*), sinew,
tendon 7e.

*neur- (*neuron, n.*), nerve 14v.

noc- (*nocēre, nocitus*), harm 5v.

*nom- (*nomos, n.*), law, rule
10v, 13b.

noxi- (*noxius, adj.*), harmful 5v.

null- (*nullus, adj.*), none 5e.

O

*oct- (*oktō, adj.*), eight 12v.

ocul- (*oculus, n.*), eye 6e.

*od- (*hodos, n.*), road, way, journey
13v.

odi- (*odium, n.*), hatred 3v.

*odont- (*odous, odontos, n.*), tooth
10v.

*odyn- (*odynē, n.*), pain 14v.

omni- (*omnis, adj.*), all 5d.

*onym- (*onyma, onymatos, n.*),
name 9v, 10a.

*onymat- (*onyma, onymatos, n.*),
name 9v.

*op- (*ōps, ōpos, n.*), eye 13e.

oper- (*opus, operis, n.*), work 3v.

*ophthalm- (*ophthalmos, n.*),
eye 14b.

opus- (*opus, operis, n.*), work
3v, 4d.

or- (*oriri, ortus*), rise 4v.

or- (*os, oris, n.*), mouth 7v.

*orec- (*orexis, n.*), desire 14c.

*ornith- (*ornithos, n.*), bird 8e, 8g.

ort- (*oriri, ortus*), rise 4v.

*orth- (*orthos, adj.*), straight,
correct 9c, 10v, 12a.

*osm- (*osmē, n.*), odor, scent 13e.

oss- (*os, ossis, n.*), bone 5e.

*oste- (*osteon, n.*), bone 14b.

*ot- (*ous, otos, n.*), ear 14b, 14c.

oti- (*otium, n.*), leisure 6v.

*ox- (*oxys, adj.*), oxygen 13v.

*oxy- (*oxys, adj.*), sharp, acid 13v.

P

pac- (*pax, pacis, n.*), peace 5e.

*pachy- (*pachys, adj.*), thick 11c.

*pale- (*palaios, adj.*), ancient
9c, 10v.

*palin-, palim- (*palin, adv.*), back,
backwards, again 11v.

pan- (*panis, n.*), bread 7e.

*pan- (*pas, pantos, adj.*), all, every
8e, 9v.

*pant- (*pas, pantos, adj.*), all, every
9v.

par- (*par, paris, adj.*), equal 4e.

part- (*pars, partis, n.*), part 4b, 4d.

pass- (*pati, passus*), suffer, endure
4v.

pat- (*pati, passus*), suffer, endure 4v.

*path- (*pathos, n.*), suffering; disease 9v, 13a, 14a, 14b, 14c.

pecc- (*peccare, peccatus*), commit a fault, sin 6e.

ped- (*pes, pedis, n.*), foot 4v.

*ped- (*pais, paidos, n.*), child 12v.

pel(l)- (*pellere, pulsus*), strike 5f.

*pelag- (*pelagos, n.*), the sea 10d.

pen- (*paene, adv.*), almost 7e.

*pent- (*pente, adj.*), five 12v.

penuri- (*penuria, n.*), want, need 1b.

pet- (*petere, petitus*), seek 7g.

petit- (*petere, petitus*), seek 7g.

*petr- (*petra, n.*), rock, stone 5e, 8g, 12b.

*pha- (*phainein*), show, cause to appear 13v.

*phan- (*phainein*), show, cause to appear 13v.

*phantas- (*phantazein*), make an appearance 13v.

*phem- (*phēmē, n.*), speech 13c.

*pher- (*pherein*), carry, bear 9v.

*phil- (*philos, adj.*), loving 8v, 9a, 9f.

*phleb- (*phleps, phlebos, n.*), vein 14b.

*phob- (*phobos, n.*), fear 8v, 9a, 9b, 12a, 14a.

phon- (*phōnē, n.*), sound, voice 9v, 11b, 12b, 14a.

*phor- (*pherein*), carry, bear 9v, 14c.

*phos- (*phōs, phōtos, n.*), light 9v.

*phot- (*phōs, phōtos, n.*), light 9v, 13b.

*phra- (*phrazein*), tell, relate 13b.

*phyt- (*phyton, n.*), plant 10c, 11b.

pisc- (*piscis, n.*), fish 1b, 5d.

*planet- (*planēs, planētos, n.*), wanderer 13b.

*plas- (*plassein*), form, shape 11v, 14a, 14b.

*platy- (*platys, adj.*), flat 12b.

plic- (*plicare, plicatus*), fold 7v.

plicat- (*plicare, plicatus*), fold 7v.

plicit- (*plicare, plicitus*), fold 7v.

*plut- (*ploutos, n.*), wealth 8c.

*pne- (*pnein*), breathe 14b.

*pod- (*pous, podos, n.*), foot 12v, 14a.

*poe- (*poiein*), make 9b.

*polem- (*polemos, n.*), war 11e.

*poli- (*polis, n.*), city 9b.

*polit- (*politēs, n.*), citizen 12d.

*poly- (*polys, adj.*), many 9v, 12b.

*pon- (*ponos, n.*), hard work 8e.

porc- (*porcus, n.*), pig 1b.

*potam- (*potamos, n.*), river 11b, 11c.

prec- (*prex, precis, n.*), prayer 3v.

precipit- (*praeceps, praecipitis, adj.*), headfirst, headlong, in haste 7a.

*presbyter- (*presbyteros, n.*), elder, an elder 13b.

prim- (*primus, adj.*), first 4b, 4e.

princip- (*princeps, principis, adj.*), first in order, foremost 4b, 4e.

prob- (*probus, adj.*), honest 1b.

prol- (*proles, prolis, n.*), offspring 5e.

*prot- (*prōtos, adj.*), first 11v, 12a.

provinci- (*provincia*, *n.*), province 1v.

prudent- (*prudentia*, *n.*), caution, good judgment 3i.

*psest- (*psēstos*, *adj.*), scraped away, rubbed off 11b.

*pseud- (*pseudēs*, *adj.*), false 9c.

*psych- (*psychē*, *n.*), the mind 8v, 9a.

*pt- (*piptein*), fall 14c.

*pter- (*pteron*, *n.*), wing 9c, 11d.

*ptych- (*ptychē*, *n.*), a folding tablet 12b.

puls- (*pellere*, *pulsus*), strike 5f.

pup- (*pupa*, *n.*), doll 4d.

*-pus (*pous*, *podos*, *n.*), foot 12v.

*pyr- (*pyr*, *n.*), fire 13b.

*pyrrh- (*Pyrrhus*, *n.*) a Greek king, 12c.

Q

quer- (*queri*, *questus*), complain 7e.

R

radi- (*radius*, *n.*), ray, beam 9f.

radic- (*radix*, *radicis*, *n.*), root 3g.

rect- (*regere*, *rectus*), straighten; rule 3v.

reg- (*regere*, *rectus*), straighten; rule 3v.

reg- (*rex*, *regis*, *n.*), king 3v.

regn- (*regnum*, *n.*), kingship, rule 3i.

*rhag- (*rhēgnynai*), burst forth, gush 14d.

*rhin- (*rhis*, *rhinos*, *n.*), nose 11v 13e, 14c.

-rig- (*regere*, *rectus*), straighten; rule 3v.

rod- (*rodere*, *rosus*), gnaw, eat away 7g.

ros- (*rodere*, *rosus*), gnaw, eat away 7g.

rud- (*rudis*, *adj.*), unformed, rough, ignorant 4e.

rug- (*ruga*, *n.*), wrinkle 6e.

S

sal- (*salire*, *saltus*), jump 6v.

san- (*sanus*, *adj.*), sound, healthy 1v.

*saur- (*sauros*, *n.*), lizard 11c.

sc- (*scire*, *scitus*), know 4v.

*scel- (*skelos*, *n.*), leg 13b.

scintill- (*scintilla*, *n.*), spark 3g.

*scler- (*sklēros*, *adj.*), hard 14b.

*scop- (*skopos*, *n.*), observer 8v, 10b, 11a, 13b, 14a, 14b.

scrib- (*scribere*, *scriptus*), write 6g.

script- (*scribere*, *scriptus*), write 6g.

sec- (*secare*, *sectus*), cut 2d.

sect- (*secare*, *sectus*), cut 5d, 13b.

secut- (*sequi*, *secutus*), follow 3v.

sed- (*sedēre*, *sessus*), sit 2v.

*seism- (*seismos*, *n.*), earthquake 8g.

*sema- (*sēma*, *sēmatos*, *n.*), sign, signal 9c.

sen- (*senex*, *senis*, *adj.*), old, aged 1b.

septuagint- (*septuaginta*, *adj.*), seventy 13d.

sequ- (*sequi*, *secutus*), follow 3v.

serr- (*serra*, *n.*), saw 6e.

sess- (*sedēre*, *sessus*), sit 2v.

-sid- (*sedēre*, *sessus*), sit 2v.

sider- (*sidus*, *sideris*, *n.*), star, heavenly body 2d.

-sil- (*salire, saltus*), jump 6v.

sist- (*sistere, status*), cause to
stand 6v.

*skelet- (*skeletos, adj.*), dried up,
withered 13b.

*solecism- (*soloikismos, n.*),
incorrect use of language 12c.

somn- (*somnus, n.*), sleep 5c.

*soph- (*sophos, adj.*), wise 8v, 13a.

sopor- (*sopor, n.*), sleep 5e.

sord- (*sordēre, _____*), be dirty 5e.

spec- (*specere, spectus*), look 7v.

speci- (*species, n.*), appearance 4v.

spect- (*specere, spectus*), look 7v.

*spele- (*spēlaion, n.*), cave 8g.

*spher- (*sphaira, n.*), globe,
sphere 10c.

-spic- (*specere, spectus*), look 7v.

spir- (*spirare, spiratus*), breathe 5f.

spirat- (*spirare, spiratus*), breathe
5f.

*sta- (*stasis, n.*), standing, position
11v.

sta- (*stare, status*), stand, be
standing 6v.

stat- (*stare, status*), stand, be
standing 6v.

stat- (*sistere, status*), cause to
stand 6v.

statu- (*statuere, statutus*), stand,
place 6v.

statut- (*statuere, statutus*), stand,
place 6v.

*sten- (*stenos, adj.*), narrow 9c.

*stere- (*stereos, adj.*), solid 11b.

-stitu- (*statuere, statutus*), stand,
place 6v.

-stitut- (*statuere, statutus*), stand,
place 6v.

*strateg- (*stratēgos, n.*), general 8d.

strict- (*stringere, strictus*),
tighten 6g.

string- (*stringere, strictus*),
tighten 6g.

stru- (*struere, structus*), build 7v.

struct- (*struere, structus*), build 7v.

sudor- (*sudor, n.*), sweat 5e.

-sult- (*salire, saltus*), jump 6v.

sum- (*sumere, sumptus*), take 4f.

sumpt- (*sumere, sumptus*), take 4f.

*sybar- (*Sybaris, n.*), a Greek city
in Italy 12c.

T

*ta- (*teinein*), stretch 14d.

*tac- (*tassein*), put in order,
arrange 13v.

*tach- (*tachos, n.*), speed 13b.

*tachy- (*tachys, adj.*), rapid 14b.

tact- (*tangere, tactus*), touch 2v.

tang- (*tangere, tactus*), touch 2v.

*taph- (*taphos, n.*), grave, burial
place 12d.

taur- (*taurus, n.*), bull 1b.

*tax- (*taxis, n.*), arrangement
10c, 13b.

*tect- (*tektōn, n.*), craftsman,
builder 12b.

*tele- (*tēle, adv.*), far away 8v, 9a.

tempor- (*tempus, temporis, n.*),
time 1v.

tempus (*tempus, temporis, n.*),
time 1v, 2c.

ten- (*tenēre, tentus*), hold 2v.

tent- (*tenēre, tentus*), hold 2v.

ter(r)- (*terra, n.*), earth, the earth 7v.

*tetr- (*tettares, adj.*), four 12v.

*thana(t)- (*thanatos, n.*), death 8e, 13v.

*the- (*theos, n.*), a god 9v.

*the- (*thesis, n.*), setting, placing 11v.

*therm- (*thermos, adj.*), hot 10v, 11a.

*therm- (*thermē, n.*), heat 13b.

*thromb- (*thrombos, n.*), blood clot 14c.

-tin- (*tenēre, tentus*), hold 2v.

-ting- (*tangere, tactus*), touch 2v.

*tom- (*temnein*), cut 13b, 14v.

*top- (*topos, n.*), place 10v.

torp- (*torpēre,_____*), be inactive 5e.

*tox- (*toxon, n.*), bow (in archery); poison 9v, 14a.

tract- (*trahere, tractus*), drag, draw 6v.

tradit- (*tradere, traditus*), hand over, deliver 7v.

trah- (*trahere, tractus*), drag, draw 6v.

tri- (*tres, tria, adj.*), three 5c.

*tri- (*treis, adj.*), three 12v.

*trib- (*tribein*), rub, grind, crush 13c.

*trich- (*thrix, trichos, n.*), hair 8g.

*trip- (*tribein*), rub, grind, crush 14c.

*tris- (*treis, adj.*), three 12v.

*trop- (*tropē, n.*), turn, turning 13b.

*troph- (*trephein*), nourish 14v.

trud- (*trudere, trusus*), push 4f.

trus- (*trudere, trusus*), push 4f.

turg- (*turgēre, _____*), be swollen 5e.

*typ- (*typos, n.*), impression, image, model 11v, 12a.

U

ubiqu- (*ubique, adv.*), everywhere 6d.

umbr- (*umbra, n.*), shade 4d.

und- (*unda, n.*), wave 3v.

urb- (*urbs, urbis, n.*), city 1v.

urs- (*ursus, n.*), bear 1v.

uxor- (*uxor, n.*), wife 1b.

V

vacu- (*vacuus, adj.*), empty 1v, 3f.

val- (*valēre,_____*), be strong 5v.

van- (*vanus, adj.*), empty 5v.

vapid- (*vapidus, adj.*), flat, tasteless 5e.

ven- (*venum, n.*), that which is for sale 1b.

ven- (*venire, ventus*), come 5v.

vent- (*venire, ventus*), come 5v.

ver- (*verus, adj.*), true 6d.

verb- (*verbum, n.*), word 1v, 3f.

verber- (*verber, n.*), whip 3g.

vers- (*vertere, versus*), turn 2v.

vert- (*vertere, versus*), turn 2v.

vi- (*via, n.*), road, way, journey 5v.

vic- (*vicis, n.*), change 7e.

vicissitud- (*vicissitudo, vicissitudinis, n.*), change, alternation 7e.

vict- (*vincere, victus*), conquer 7g.

vid- (*vidēre, visus*), see 3v.

vil- (*vilis, adj.*), cheap, worthless 5e.

vinc- (*vincere, victus*), conquer 7g.

vir- (*virus, n.*), poison, virus 9f.

vis- (*vidēre, visus*), see 3v.

visu- (*visus, -u-, n.*), sight 3v.

vit- (*vita, n.*), life 1b, 4e.

viti- (*vitium, n.*), defect, vice 7e.

voc- (*vox, vocis, n.*), voice 1v, 3g.

volut- (*volvere, volutus*), roll 6g.

volv- (*volvere, volutus*), roll 6g.

vor- (*vorare, voratus*), eat 5v.

vorat- (*vorare, voratus*), eat 5v.

vulg- (*vulgus, n.*), the crowd, ordinary people 1v, 3f.

vulp- (*vulpes, vulpis, n.*), fox 1b.

X

*xen- (*xenos, n.*), stranger, foreigner 8c.

*xer- (*xēros, adj.*), dry 8d.

Z

*zo- (*zōon, n.*), animal 8e, 10c, 11v, 14c.

*zon- (*zōnē, n.*), belt 8d.